Lecture Notes in Artificial Intelligence   1038

Subseries of Lecture Notes in Computer Science
Edited by J.G. Carbonell and J. Siekmann

Lecture Notes in Computer Science

Edited by G. Goos, J. Hartmanis and J. van Leeuwen

Springer
Berlin
Heidelberg
New York
Barcelona
Budapest
Hong Kong
London
Milan
Paris
Santa Clara
Singapore
Tokyo

Walter Van de Velde   John W. Perram (Eds.)

Agents Breaking Away

7th European Workshop on Modelling Autonomous
Agents in a Multi-Agent World, MAAMAW '96
Einhoven, The Netherlands, January 22-25, 1996
Proceedings

 Springer

Series Editors

Jaime G. Carbonell
School of Computer Science
Carnegie Mellon Universtiy
Pittsburgh, PA 15213-3891, USA

Jörg Siekmann
University of Saarland
German Research Center for Artificial Intelligence (DFKI)
Stuhlsatzenhausweg 3, D-66123 Germany

Volume Editors

Walter Van de Velde
Artificial Intelligende Laboratory, Vrije Universiteit Brussel
Pleinlaan 2, 1050 Brussel, Belgium

John W. Perram
Lindo Center for Applied Mathematics, Odense University
Forskerparken 10, 5230 Odense M, Denmark

Cataloging-in-Publication data applied for

Die Deutsche Bibliothek - CIP-Einheitsaufnahme

Agents breaking away : proceedings / 7th EuropeanWorkshop on Modelling Autonomous
Agents in a Multi-Agent World, MAAMAW '96, Eindhoven, The Netherlands, January
22 - 25, 1996. Walter VanDeVelde ; John W. Perram (ed.). - Berlin ; Heidelberg ; New
York ; Barcelona ; Budapest ; Hong Kong ; London ; Milan ; Paris ; Santa Clara ; Singa-
pore ; Tokyo : Springer, 1996
  (Lecture notes in computer science ; Vol. 1038 : Lecture notes in artificial intelligence)
  ISBN 3-540-60852-4

NE: VanDeVelde, Walter [Hrsg.]; European Workshop on Modelling Autonomous Agents in a Multi-Agent
  World <7. 1996. Eindhoven>; GT

CR Subject Classification (1991): I.2, D.2, C.2.4

ISBN 3-540-60852-4 Springer-Verlag Berlin Heidelberg New York

Typesetting: Camera-ready by author
SPIN 10512538   06/3142 – 5 4 3 2 1 0   Printed on acid-free paper

MAAMAW'96
7th European Workshop on Modelling Autonomous Agents in a Multi-Agent World

Preface

Walter Van de Velde[1] and John Perram[2]

[1] Artificial Intelligence Laboratory
Vrije Universiteit Brussel
walter@arti.vub.ac.be

[2] Lindo Center for Applied Mathematics
Odense University
jperram@imada.ou.dk

The MAAMAW workshops are the European forum for discussing progress on multi-agent systems. Multi-agent systems are, typically, distributed systems that are designed as a collection of interacting autonomous agents, each having their own capacities and goals that are related to a common environment. The notion of agent encompasses physical as well as software agents. The discipline, which emerged at the crossroads of distributed computing, artificial intelligence, and embedded systems now borrows actively from a diversity of disciplines including biology, ecology, and economics. Moreover, work on multi-agent systems is laying the foundations for new models of computing and interaction, tailored to the emerging large-scale infrastructure of open distributed information and communication platforms like the World-Wide Web (WWW).

Perhaps the biggest mistake in the history of the MAAMAW workshops has been the choice of its name. Back in 1987 we used to talk about MAGMA, as the acronym for an EEC funded project on "Modelling an Autonomous Agent in a Multiple-Agent World". In MAGMA the MAAMAW series of events has its historical roots. So this year's MAAMAW might as well be the 7th MAGMA workshop. At least it is easier to pronounce.

The writing of this preface was a good opportunity to look back at the original MAGMA proposal. Those were early days for agent research. Just about all of AI was still breaking its teeth on the problems of representation, reasoning, planning. Second Generation Expert Systems were a hot topic, and the symbolic knowledge-based approach was in its heyday with innovations in truth-maintenance systems, machine learning, meta-level reasoning, and reflection. The agent concept had been around, for instance as a computational model in Hewitt's work on actors. But for mainstream AI it rather played the role of setting a paradigmatic and ultimate goal of research. It was also the justification for most concrete work: an agent obviously needs planning, representation, image recognition, and so on, doesn't it? But the first unifying theories of intelligence that were aimed at piecing the puzzle together were only just appearing. They were all single-agent. A research project on modelling an autonomous agent in a multi-agent world, like MAGMA, was clearly a long shot at the time and considered very, very basic research.

The main goal of the MAGMA project was "to develop methods (software architecture, reasoning models, knowledge representation language) in order to enable an autonomous agent to coexist and cooperate with other agents". This immediately set it apart from distributed AI to become what today would be called research on multi-agent systems (MAS). In a sense MAGMA was a conservative and careful proposal - it probably had to be to get it funded in the first place. A simulated 2D environment with three (!) mobile robots was proposed as a testbed for studying cohabitation, cooperation, and collaboration. Robots were assumed to be benevolent, too. A number of pressing research issues were identified: representation of incomplete knowledge, intentions and knowledge about knowledge and about other agents; goal interaction; cooperation and collaboration; communication and knowledge acquisition about other agents; problems of reasoning about time and space; modelling and discovering social laws.

Most of these issues are still high on the agenda of MAS researchers, but some have become de-emphasized. For instance the commitment to using agents in a real or realistically simulated world, an essential one in MAGMA, has not become a hallmark of the field. Spatial reasoning has been largely replaced by reasoning about agent interaction. Also it is now taken for granted that agents may inhabit the electronic world of computers and computer networks, inducing different models of space-time. Notably absent at the time was the issue of learning and adaptation and indeed, still today, multi-agent learning is a largely unexplored area. More issues have appeared recently: open societies, non-cooperative behavior, emotion. Whether because of the maturity of the field or because of the boldness of its researchers, these are not simple problems!

But there may be another explanation of why precisely such issues are becoming prominent. It hinges on the technological evolution in computing in general. World-wide computer networks like the Internet are a reality, and the technological problems of setting up realistic multi-agent experiments are less of an obstacle than they used to be. For a growing group of researchers, the paradigmatic goal and justification used to be the intelligent robot, but this is being taken over by the image (?) of software agents living in Cyberspace. The characteristics of this medium emphasize exactly such issues as openness, multiple unrelated or conflicting goals, real agent relations based on trust, believability, and so on. In order for MAS work to be useful and relevant in this increasingly important context it needs to deal with these problems in a practical way.

Not that we should all be working on World-Wide Web technology, far from it. But this picture highlights how, since the MAS community took off, the technological context has dramatically changed. For example, in the original MAGMA proposal there was no mention of networking at all. In addition, and this is a potential threat to the field, agents are being re-invented in different communities: telecommunications, object-orientation, artificial life. All of these, and others, claim the agent concept in one form or another. What is at stake is, of course, not the honor. But chances are that these communities, some of which are heavily funded, will independently evolve these concepts in directions with much greater impact than we have ever envisaged, or even in directions that we may find useless, even counterproductive. For instance, the agent concept as implemented in Artificial Life is definitely a weaker one than what is typical in MAS. Or, as another example, hot developments in programming technology, like JAVA, are likely to shape the next couple of years in computing practice, yet they are not essentially agent-oriented. Indeed, from a MAS perspective most of the software agents that live on WWW are hardly worth the name. Yet these developments are there, visible and strong.

It seems we could indulge in our own wealth of ideas. This is not true. Not only will the confrontation with different views on agents result in a true advance in MAS work. More importantly, the global computer networks provide an infrastructure for multi-agent work that we could not dream of before. We should use it. It is a challenge to anyone taking the agent concept seriously to demonstrate it on this open infrastructure that is a reality now. This, more than a Nobel prize-winning idea, will improve the visibility and impact of the field.

Looking at the hype that WWW is generating, any sensible researcher will think twice before diving into it. But from a MAS perspective, there is plenty of space for innovation. After all, WWW remains an information-oriented endeavor, the concept of agent being used mainly in direct relation to the information: search agent, filtering agent, and so on. The MAS field has focused much more on goal-satisfying behavior in an open multi-agent context. Although this goal-satisfying view is a perfect fit with the actual use of Internet, this aspect is not actively supported by present-day networks. This is at least one point where MAS research can contribute a lot. Software reuse and the dynamic configuration of services is another case in point. Although JAVA-like technology may provide an element of a solution, a more radical agent-oriented view will prove to be necessary to realize 'Reuse in Cyberspace'.

The papers

The papers in this volume, 17 in total, have been selected out of 51 submissions. An additional 17 poster presentations have been retained. These are collected in a separate report.

Epistemological and Ontological Issues

What is an agent, and how can it be described? Beliefes, desires, and intentions (BDI) are the categories that are often used to characterize an agent. But formalization of this leads to a number of difficult problems. The most famous one is the logical omniscience problem. It is also a difficult one because it forces one to abandon classical logics for modelling the agent. As a consequence – or is this the definition of 'difficult'? – papers about this tend to be comprehensible for a small number of people only. The paper *Ideal and Real Belief about Belief* by Fausto and Enrico Giunchiglia is a notable exception. Real believers and reasoners are, so they argue, incomplete and incorrect. The formalization of this simple intuition turns into an interesting epistemological discussion.

What is an agent society, and how can it be described? Now this is a different problem altogether. It asks for the basic mechanism that underlies all interaction patterns between groups of agents. The paper by Michel Aubé and Alain Senteni, *Emotions as Commitments Operators : A Foundation for Control Structure in Multi-Agents Systems*, is an ontological analysis of control based on notions of resources and commitment. If successful, such an analysis may have profound technical impact on the MAS field, just like Newell and Simon's analysis of human problem solving determined – for better or for worse – the technical direction for 20 years of research on rule-based reasoning and weak problem solving methods.

Frameworks and Architectures

In practice there is still a gap between a theoretical analysis of a multi-agent system and its actual implementation. As in computer science there are many solutions to this. One is to have formal descriptions that are also operational. In *A Logical and Operational Model of Scalable Knowledge- and Perception-Based Agents*, Gerd Wagner describes such a logical model of single- and multi-agent systems, based on extending a knowledge base with action and reaction rules.

Another solution, call it reuse, is to take basically an architecture and to design a language that can be used to specify a specific instantiation of that architecture. This approach was followed by Anand S. Rao who, in *AgentSpeak(L): BDI Agents Speak Out in a Logical Computable Language*, reports on what is essentially a reverse engineering effort: starting from an implemented multi-agent architecture, a formal agent language is defined to reflect its essential properties. In this way, a practically useful combination of formal description and implementation framework is achieved.

To turn multi-agent research results into an engineering discipline a connection with established software engineering is needed. To this end, David Kinny, Michael Georgeff and Anand Rao extend existing object-oriented models into *A Methodology and Modelling Technique for Systems of BDI Agents*. In a somewhat similar direction, Mark d'Inverno and Michael Luck apply the specification language Z, known from software engineering, for *Formalising the Contract Net as a Goal-Directed System*. Although the details of such a formalization are always debatable, the paper provides a handle from outside the MAS field on hard problems of analysis, specification, and design.

Interaction and Coordination

Whereas planning used to be the central theme for a single-agent setting, coordination is the equivalent for multi-agent work. The paper *A Coordination Algorithm for Multi-Agent Planning* by Amal El Fallah-Seghrouchni and Serge

Haddad extends classical planning work to account for an agent jumping into an already coordinated group of agents. They describe an algorithm to augment but not re-plan ongoing plans, so that positive interactions are promoted and negative ones cancelled out.

Omar Belakhdar and Jacqueline Ayel work on a *Modelling Approach and Tool for Designing Protocols for Automated Cooperation in Multi-agent Systems.* The essential contribution of this paper is a language for describing conversation- and argumentation-based cooperation behaviors.

The work by Cheng Gu and Toru Ishida on *Analyzing the Social Behavior of Contract Net Protocol* not only provides interesting results on the performance of a contract net under different conditions of scale and agent uniformity but also illustrates a methodological direction that will be needed as the field matures toward practical applications and the selection of a coordination protocol becomes a crucial design choice.

In a similar spirit Amedeo Cesta, Maria Miceli, and Paola Rizzo study the *Effects of Different Interaction Attitudes on Multi-Agent System Performance.* What are the characteristics of a social system that results from a heterogeneous collection of agents that are either social, parasites, selfish, or solitary? Their analysis takes a snapshot of a social system, fixing the agent behaviors, and studies how such a society would evolve in time.

Emergence

There is no magic. If something emerges as a result of many simple asynchronous interactions, chances are that these interactions have been carefully chosen. For the time being there is no methodology of emergence, so any result that demonstrates an emerging phenomenon of, for instance, an evolutionary trend, a control scheme, a social structure, or some transformation of the environment is worthwhile.

Bacterial Evolution Algorithm for Rapid Adaptation by Chisato Numaoka is an input from artificial life research. A simple evolutionary mechanism is shown to be effective in a changing world with many interacting agents. Although limitations are clearly identified, the power and simplicity of this approach justifies the question to what extent similar ideas could be applied in a MAS setting.

The paper *Distributed Interaction with Computon* (Toru Ohira, Ryusuke Sawatari, and Mario Tokoro) proposes a fundamental model of interaction based on the exchange of a basic particle called a computon. The model is promising as a shared medium for interaction in a large and open collection of agents, and robust to scaling.

The paper by Christof Baeijs, Yves Demazeau, and Luis Alvares, *SIGMA: Application of Multi-Agent Systems to Cartographic Generalization,* can be read as an application in a challenging domain (i.e., cartography), but its true value is in showing how generalization can be made to be emergent from the interaction of a large collection of simple reactive agents. Although the results to date may not be convincing to all of us, its direction and the methodological issues it raises are definitely worth attention.

Task-Specific Analysis

Some would call this the category of applications, but the lessons learned go beyond the single instance or specific systems being built. Indeed, architectural solutions that are specific for a class of tasks are likely to be more useful, more usable, and more re-usable than general solutions. Paradigmatic systems of agents are for MAS what is becoming established as so-called 'frameworks' in software engineering.

The paper *A Decision-Theoretic Model for Cooperative Transportation Scheduling* by Klaus Fischer and Jörg Müller presents, besides an interesting application, the conceptual lessons learned from the exercise. For instance, it distinguishes between cooperative and competitive tasks and discusses the theoretical and practical differences.

Z. Guessoum and M. Dojat describe *A Real-Time Agent Model in an Asynchronous-Object Environment* in the context of and oriented toward an application in patient monitoring. The architecture brings together a number of ideas into an integrated whole.

Matthias Klusch and Onn Shehory discuss *Coalition Formation Among Rational Information Agents*. The scenario is one of multiple distributed and heterogeneous databases, guarded by information agents. The authors discuss how coalitions are formed and construct a local terminological information model capturing the dependencies between local schemata.

Giordano Lanzola, Sabina Falasconi, and Mario Stefanelli describe the early stages of a real application in *Cooperating Agents Implementing Distributed Patient Management*. One merit of this paper is that it provides a detailed discussion of the many practical problems and issues that arise when applying agent-ideas to such a real task in a realistic context.

Conclusion

Research on multi-agent systems, as exemplified by the present paper selection, will become increasingly relevant to the wider field of computing. Truly distributed and open demonstration and application platforms are no longer an issue: they exist and we should use them. This requires us to deal with new and challenging issues. It is the ambition of this MAAMAW to trigger a stronger trend in this direction. Three invited speakers were chosen with that purpose in mind: Henry Lieberman (MIT) on software agents on WWW, Joseph Bates (CMU) on believable agents, and Jacques Ferber (LAFORIA) on social behavior.

MAS agents are breaking away.

Brussels, December 1995   Walter Van de Velde

Acknowledgment

The chairs would like to thank Rudy Van Hoe, Judith Masthoff (IPO), and Carla Schreurs-van Hooijdonk (Eindhoven University of Technology) for getting MAA-MAW'96 practically organized, not only as a scientific but also as a social event. We also thank Brigitte Hönig (VUB AI-Lab) for maintaining the MAAMAW server, for exerting kind pressure on chairs and reviewers, and for getting the proceedings out in time. Our special gratitude also goes to the main sponsor, Philips. We also thank the members of the program committee for their time in reviewing and shaping the workshop program:

Magnus Boman	(Stockholm University and R.I.T., Sweden)
John Campbell	(University College, London, UK)
Christiano Castelfranchi	(University of Siena, Italy)
Helder Coelho	(INESC, Technical U. Lisbon, Portugal)
Yves Demazeau	(LIFIA/IMAG, Grenoble, France)
Aldo Dragoni	(University of Ancona, Italy)
Jean Erceau	(ONERA/GIA, Chatillon, France)
Jacques Ferber	(LAFORIA, Paris, France)
Francisco Garijo	(Telefonica, Madrid, Spain)
Nick Jennings	(Queen Mary and Westfield College, London, UK)
Wouter Joosen	(KU Leuven, Belgium)
George Kiss	(Open University, UK)
Paul Levi	(University of Stuttgart, Germany)
Judith Masthoff	(Institute for Perception Research, Eindhoven, NL)
Jean-Pierre Muller	(IIIA, Neuchatel, Switzerland)
Eugenio Oliveira	(Universidade do Porto, Portugal)
Jeffrey Rosenschein	(Hebrew University, Jerusalem, Israel)
Donald Steiner	(Siemens/DFKI, Germany)
Kurt Sundermeyer	(Daimler Benz AG, Germany)
Peter Wavish	(Philips Research Lab, Redhill, UK)

Assisting reviewers were Luis Antunes, Christof Baeijs, Joo Balsa, Pierre Bessiere, Amedeo Cesta, Rosaria Conte, Alessandro Cucchiarelli, Mark d'Inverno, Jerome Euzenat, Nils Ferrand, Thomas Gordon, Zhisheng Huang, Benedita Malheiro, Bernard Manderick, Maria Miceli, Michel Occello, Sylvie Pesty, Ana Paula Rocha, Marcos Shmeil, Paulo Jorge Cunha Vaz Dias Urbano, Salvatore Valenti, Francis van Aeken, Dirk Vermeir, Caroline Wintergerst, and Michael Wooldridge.

Table of Contents

Epistemological and Ontological Issues

Frameworks and Architectures

Interaction and Coordination

Emergence

Task-Specific Analysis

Ideal and Real Belief about Belief: Some Intuitions

Fausto Giunchiglia[1,2] Enrico Giunchiglia[3]
Mechanized Reasoning Group

[1] IRST, Povo, 38100 Trento, Italy
[2] DISA - University of Trento, Trento, Italy
[3] DIST - University of Genoa, Genoa, Italy
fausto@irst.itc.it
enrico@dist.unige.it

Abstract. It is widely recognized that intelligent and autonomous agents operating in a distributed environment must be able to reason about their own and other agents' beliefs. Standard possible world semantics, usually used for such an endeavor, lead to formalization in which agents suffer the "logical omniscience problem" — they believe all valid formulas and all the logical consequences of their own beliefs. As far as we know, no taxonomic analysis exists which describes all the possible ways in which this phenomenon can or can not arise. The goal of this paper is to fill this gap. Our approach is based on the idea of first providing a set-theoretic specification of agents' beliefs, and then to define constructors for such sets. This allows us first to provide a set of constructors modeling ideal believers, and then to analyze how such constructors can be modified to generate real believers. The constructors defined turn out to be inference rules inside a multicontext system.

1 Introduction

It is widely recognized that intelligent and autonomous agents operating in a distributed environment must be able to reason about their own and other agents' beliefs. Unfortunately, even the "simple" problem of formalizing agents' beliefs turned to be quite difficult (see for example [1, 2, 3, 4]). Standard possible world semantics, usually used for such an endeavor, lead to formalization in which agents suffer the "logical omniscience problem" (first pointed out by Hintikka [5]) — they believe all valid formulas and all the logical consequences of their own beliefs. Several proposals have been made to avoid such a problem. However, as far as we know, no taxonomic analysis exists which describes all the possible ways in which this phenomenon can or can not arise. The goal of this paper is to fill this gap.

Agents' beliefs, or agents' views of other agents' beliefs are modeled as abstract formal entities, called *reasoners*. We start considering the basic situation in which one reasoner R_0 has beliefs about another reasoner R_1 (we also say that R_0 is a *believer*). This situation is modeled introducing *belief systems*. Our approach is based on the idea of first providing a set-theoretic specification of belief systems, and then to define constructors for belief systems (we do this in Section 2). This allows us first to provide a set of constructors modeling ideal reasoners and/or ideal believers (Section 3), and then to analyze how such constructors can be modified to generate real reasoners and/or real believers (Section 4). The constructors defined turn out to be inference rules inside a multicontext system. Finally, we consider arbitrary configurations of reasoners, each possibly having beliefs about other reasoners (Section 5).

2 Reasoners and Believers

We start from the intuitive notion of *reasoner*: by reasoner we mean anything which is capable of having *beliefs*, *i.e.* facts that he is willing to accept as true. Some examples of reasoners are agents (as discussed in, *e.g.*, [6]), views about agents (as discussed in, *e.g.*, [4]), and frames of mind (as discussed in, *e.g.*, [2]). Formally, we represent a reasoner R as a pair $\langle L, T \rangle$, where L is a set of first order sentences and $T \subseteq L$. L is the *language* and T is the set of *beliefs* or *theorems* of R. (Notationally, in the following, R_i stands for the pair $\langle L_i, T_i \rangle$.)

Reasoners may have beliefs about the world or other reasoners' beliefs. By *belief about* (a reasoner's) *belief* we mean a belief which states that a reasoner has a certain belief; by *believer*, a reasoner which is capable of having beliefs about beliefs. In a reasoner's language, we represent beliefs about beliefs with sentences of the form B("*A*"). We call such sentences *belief sentences*, and A in B("*A*") is the *argument* of B.

The basic configuration of two reasoners in which one is having beliefs about the other, is described with *belief systems* defined as pairs $\langle R_0, R_1 \rangle_{\mathrm{B}}$: R_0 and R_1 are reasoners, and B is a unary predicate symbol, called the *belief predicate* of $\langle R_0, R_1 \rangle_{\mathrm{B}}$.

The components of a belief system can be extensionally characterized as sets of formulas satisfying certain conditions (this can be done along the same lines standard logics are presented). We can also "generate" the reasoners of a belief system, by representing

- their *reasoning capabilities* —*i.e.* their ability of deriving facts from what they already believe, and
- their *interaction capabilities* —*i.e.* their ability of deriving facts from what the other reasoner believes.

We do this by using a special kind of formal systems, called *multicontext systems* (*MC systems*). An MC system is a pair $\langle \{C_i\}_{i \in I}, BR \rangle$, where $\{C_i\}_{i \in I}$ is a family of *contexts* and BR is a set of *bridge rules*. A context C is a triple $\langle L, \Omega, \Delta \rangle$, where L is the language, Ω the set of axioms, and Δ the set of inference rules of C. The context C can be intuitively thought as an axiomatic formal system "interacting" via bridge rules with other contexts. (Notationally, in the following, a context C_i is implicitly intended to be defined as $\langle L_i, \Omega_i, \Delta_i \rangle$.) Bridge rules are inference rules with premises and conclusion in different contexts. Thus for instance, the bridge rule

$$\frac{\langle A_1,\ C_1\rangle}{\langle A_2,\ C_2\rangle}$$

allows to derive the formula A_2 in a context C_2 just because the formula A_1 has been derived in another context C_1. (Notationally, we write $\langle A,\ C_i\rangle$ to mean A and that $A \in L_i$.) Derivability in a MC system MS, in symbols $\vdash_{MS}$, is defined in [7] and [8]; roughly speaking, it is a generalization of Prawitz' notion of deduction inside a natural deduction system.

The class of MC systems which presents belief systems is called MR^- and is characterized as follows:

Definition 1 MR^-. An MC-system $\langle\{C_0, C_1\}, BR\rangle$ is an MR^- system if and only if BR is the following set of bridge rules:

$$\frac{\langle A,\ C_1\rangle}{\langle B(\text{``}A\text{''}),\ C_0\rangle}\ \mathcal{R}^{\text{B}}_{up.1} \qquad \frac{\langle B(\text{``}A\text{''}),\ C_0\rangle}{\langle A,\ C_1\rangle}\ \mathcal{R}^{\text{B}}_{dn.1}$$

and the restrictions for the applicability of the bridge rules include:
$\mathcal{R}^{\text{B}}_{up.1}$: $\langle A,\ C_1\rangle$ does not depend on any assumption in C_1.
$\mathcal{R}^{\text{B}}_{dn.1}$: $\langle B(\text{``}A\text{''}),\ C_0\rangle$ does not depend on any assumption in C_0.

The rule on the left is called reflection up, the one on the right, reflection down. The restrictions on these rules are such that the premise can be reflected up or reflected down only if it does not depend on any assumptions, *i.e.* if it is a theorem. Reflection up allows to prove $B(\text{``}A\text{''})$ in $C_0$ just because we have proved $A$ in $C_1$, while reflection down has the dual effect, *i.e.* it allows to prove $A$ in $C_1$ just because we have proved $B(\text{``}A\text{''})$ in C_0. The intuition is that the reasoner R_0 (whose reasoning capabilities are presented by C_0) believes $B(\text{``}A\text{''})$, *i.e.* it believes that the reasoner $R_1$ (whose reasoning capabilities are presented by $C_1$) believes $A$, if $R_1$ actually believes $A$ and the bridge rules allow $R_0$ to derive $B(\text{``}A\text{''})$.

To each MR^- system, there corresponds a belief system according to the following criteria. If $MS = \langle\{C_0, C_1\}, \{\mathcal{R}^{\text{B}}_{up.1}, \mathcal{R}^{\text{B}}_{dn.1}\}\rangle$ is an MR^- System, MS *presents* (we also say *generates*) the belief system $\langle R_0, R_1\rangle_{\text{B}}$ if and only if $T_i = \{A \mid \vdash_{MS} \langle A,\ C_i\rangle\}$ ($i \in \{0, 1\}$). (In practice, the beliefs of a reasoner R_i consist of all the theorems in L_i proved by the MR^- system MS.)

3 Ideal Reasoners and Believers

Reasoners and believers can be categorized depending on their capability of having beliefs and beliefs about beliefs, respectively.

Given a belief system $\langle R_0, R_1\rangle_{\text{B}}$, we say that:

- R_i ($i \in \{0, 1\}$) is an *Ideal Reasoner* if and only if
  (*i*) L_i is closed under the construction rules for propositional languages, and

(ii) T_i is closed under tautological consequence.

– R_0 is an *Ideal Believer* if and only if

(i) $L_1 = \{A \mid B(\text{``}A\text{''}) \in L_0\}$, and

(ii) $T_1 = \{A \mid B(\text{``}A\text{''}) \in T_0\}$.

Hence, R_0 and R_1 are ideal reasoners if they are able to believe all the (tautological) consequences of what they know. R_0 is an ideal believer, instead, if it is able to believe all and only those belief sentences whose argument is a belief of R_1. We thus judge a reasoner to be ideal not on the basis of its specific beliefs, but verifying whether its beliefs satisfy certain conditions. A similar perspective has been taken in [2], where it is observed that agents in Levesque' logic of implicit and explicit beliefs [9] are somehow ideal since perfect reasoners in relevance logic.

The conditions for ideality can be captured by posing appropriate restrictions on MR^- systems. Let us consider the following definition:

Definition 2. An MR^- system $\langle \{C_0, C_1\}, BR \rangle$ is an MBK^- system if and only if the following conditions are satisfied:

(i) L_0 and L_1 contain a given set P of propositional letters, the symbol for falsity $\bot$ and are closed under implication[4],

(ii) Δ_0 (Δ_1) is the set of inference rules

$$\frac{A_1, \ldots, A_k}{A} \ RPL_k$$

with the restriction that $(A_1 \wedge \ldots \wedge A_k) \supset A$ be a tautology and $k \in \{0, 2\}$[5],

(iii) $L_1 = \{A \mid B(\text{``}A\text{''}) \in L_0\}$,

(iv) the restrictions on the applicability of reflection up/down are only those listed in Definition 1.

If $\langle R_0, R_1 \rangle_B$ is a belief system generated by an MBK^- system, then:

(i) R_0 and R_1 are ideal reasoners, and

(ii) R_0 is an ideal believer.

The proof is straightforward. It is sufficient to observe that the first two conditions in Definition 2 ensure that each R_i is an ideal reasoner $(i \in \{0, 1\})$; while the last two ensure that R_0 is an ideal believer.

4 Real Reasoners and Believers

At first, one is tempted to define reality as not ideality. However we believe that this is not correct. Consider for instance a reasoner which is not aware

---

[4] We also use standard abbreviations from propositional logic, such as $\neg A$ for $A \supset \bot$, $A \vee B$ for $\neg A \supset B$, $A \wedge B$ for $\neg(\neg A \vee \neg B)$, $\top$ for $\bot \supset \bot$.

[5] We include the restriction that k shall belong to $\{0, 2\}$ to have systems in which any instance of an inference rule cannot be derived from the others. However such a restriction can be waved.

of a proposition or does not know an axiom, but which has construction and inference rules which are complete for propositional logic. This reasoner is an ideal reasoner, however we would like to say that it is also a real reasoner. Differently from what is the case for ideality, reality is intrinsically a relative notion which states the absence of certain properties with respect to a specific reference.

4.1 Realizing MR⁻ Systems

When talking of a real reasoner or a real believer one means that such a reasoner or believer believes too little or too much (*i.e.* it is incomplete or incorrect) with respect to the reasoner or believer taken as reference. This intuition is already informally articulated, even if limited to beliefs and reasoners, in [10]. In particular, in that paper a reasoner is defined real relatively to another reasoner, independently of (what we have called here) the belief system of which it is part. However, the formalization of these ideas is more complex than it might seem, and, as the technical development discussed below also shows, the notion of reality informally introduced in [10] is not quite right. The key observation is that two reasoners or believers cannot be compared independently of the belief system of which they are part.

The starting point is therefore to define when a belief system is (in)correct or (in)complete with respect to another (notationally, we write $\langle R_{A_0}, R_{A_1} \rangle_\text{B} \subseteq \langle R_{B_0}, R_{B_1} \rangle_\text{B}$ to mean $R_{A_0} \subseteq R_{B_0}$ and $R_{A_1} \subseteq R_{B_1}$):

Definition 3. A belief system $\langle R_{E_0}, R_{E_1} \rangle_\text{B}$ is *correct [complete]* with respect to a belief system $\langle R_{I_0}, R_{I_1} \rangle_\text{B}$ if $\langle R_{E_0}, R_{E_1} \rangle_\text{B} \subseteq \langle R_{I_0}, R_{I_1} \rangle_\text{B}$ $[\langle R_{I_0}, R_{I_1} \rangle_\text{B} \subseteq \langle R_{E_0}, R_{E_1} \rangle_\text{B}]$.

The idea is that, for instance, in a correct belief system, each reasoner maintains a subset of the beliefs of the corresponding reasoner in the reference belief system. If it is also the case that the beliefs of one reasoner (for example of R_{E_0}) are strictly contained in the beliefs of the corresponding reasoner (R_{I_0}) then the belief system is also incomplete. We say that a reasoner [believer] is an *incomplete reasoner [incomplete believer]* or an *incorrect reasoner [incorrect believer]* with the obvious meaning. We say that a belief system is *real*, to mean that it is incomplete or incorrect. *Real reasoners* and/or *real believers* are the components of a real belief system.

The next step is to "propagate" the notions of (in)correctness and (in)completeness from belief systems to MR⁻ systems. However things are complicated as a comparison between MR⁻ systems based simply on set inclusion of the components does not work. For instance it is easy to think of two different sets of axioms with the same proof-theoretic power. To solve this problem we introduce a new operation $\oplus$ such that, if $C = \langle L, \Omega, \Delta \rangle$ and $C' = \langle L', \Omega', \Delta' \rangle$ are two contexts, then $C \oplus C'$ is the context $\langle L \cup L', \Omega \cup \Omega', \Delta \cup \Delta' \rangle$. This allows us to give the following definition (notationally, in the following, $\text{MS}_E = \langle \{C_{E_0}, C_{E_1}\}, BR_E \rangle$ and $\text{MS}_I = \langle \{C_{I_0}, C_{I_1}\}, BR_I \rangle$ are MR⁻ systems generating $\langle R_{E_0}, R_{E_1} \rangle_\text{B}$ and $\langle R_{I_0}, R_{I_1} \rangle_\text{B}$, respectively):

Definition 4. We say that MS_E is a *correct [complete] realization* of MS_I, in formulas $MS_E \preceq MS_I$ [$MS_E \succeq MS_I$], if $\langle \{C_{E_0} \oplus C_{I_0}, C_{E_1} \oplus C_{I_1}\}, BR_E \cup BR_I \rangle$ and MS_I [MS_E] present the same belief system.

From the above definition, it trivially follows that MS_E is a correct realization of MS_I if and only if MS_I is a complete realization of MS_E. We also say that MS_E is *equivalent* to MS_I, in formulas $MS_E \asymp MS_I$, if it is correct and complete with respect to MS_I. $MS \prec MS'$ is defined as $MS_E \preceq MS_I$ and $MS_E \not\asymp MS_I$. We talk of *realization* to emphasize the process by which the constructors of a real belief system are defined starting from those of a reference belief system. Consider for instance the notion of correct realization. MS_E is a correct realization of MS_I if adding its proof-theoretic power to that of MS_I results into a system which still has the same proof-theoretic power as MS_I. As trivial examples, the "empty" system, *i.e.* the system with empty languages, is a correct realization of any reference system MS_I. The "absolutely contradictory" system, *i.e.* the system where the theorems of its two contexts are the same as their languages, is complete with respect to any reference system whose two languages stand in a subset relation with its languages. Two more complex examples in which MS_E is a correct but incomplete realization of MS_I are the following.

Example 1. Let MS_I be an MBK$^-$ system such that Ω_{I_0} and Ω_{I_1} are empty. Suppose MS_E is defined as MS_I except that Δ_{E_1} consists of the instances of RPL_2 (*i.e.* RPL_0 is not an instance of an inference rule in Δ_{E_1}). Such a system models a situation of an ideal reasoner R_{E_0} ideally interacting with a not ideal reasoner R_{E_1}.

Example 2. Let MS_I be an MBK$^-$ system such that Ω_{I_0} is empty. Suppose MS_E is defined as MS_I except that $\mathcal{R}^{\mathrm{B}}_{up.1}$ has the additional restriction that the premise belongs to a finite set Γ of formulas. This system models the situation of an ideal reasoner R_{E_0} whose interaction capabilities are restricted to a subset Γ of the ideal reasoner R_{E_1}'s beliefs.

To save space, from now on, we consider incompleteness only. With some provisos, all the results presented below can be replicated for incorrectness.

The link between MS_E being a correct, possibly incomplete, realization of MS_I and the correctness, with possible incompleteness, of $\langle R_{E_0}, R_{E_1} \rangle_\mathrm{B}$ with respect to $\langle R_{I_0}, R_{I_1} \rangle_\mathrm{B}$ can now be established.

If MS_E is a correct realization of MS_I then

(*i*) $\langle R_{E_0}, R_{E_1} \rangle_\mathrm{B}$ is correct with respect to $\langle R_{I_0}, R_{I_1} \rangle_\mathrm{B}$, and

(*ii*) $\langle R_{E_0}, R_{E_1} \rangle_\mathrm{B}$ is incomplete with respect to $\langle R_{I_0}, R_{I_1} \rangle_\mathrm{B}$ if and only if MS_E is an incomplete realization of MS_I.

These facts easily follow from the hypothesis that $\langle \{C_{E_0} \oplus C_{I_0}, C_{E_1} \oplus C_{I_1}\}, BR_E \cup BR_I \rangle$ and MS_I generate the same belief system. The second of the above items states that we have achieved what we wanted, *i.e.* that incompleteness between two MR$^-$ systems corresponds to incompleteness in the belief systems presented. Notice however that this result holds under the hypothesis that one MR$^-$ system is a correct realization of the other. This hypothesis is necessary in order to guarantee that $\langle R_{E_0}, R_{E_1} \rangle_B$ is correct with respect to $\langle R_{I_0}, R_{I_1} \rangle_B$. In fact, the viceversa of the first item does not hold. That is, MS_E can be an incorrect realization of MS_I and $\langle R_{E_0}, R_{E_1} \rangle_B$ be correct with respect to $\langle R_{I_0}, R_{I_1} \rangle_B$.

Example 3. Consider the system MS'_E obtained from MS_E in Example 1 by adding to Δ_{E_0} the inference rule

$$\frac{A \vee \neg A}{A} \rho$$

for any propositional letter $A \in L_{E_1}$. MS'_E is an incorrect realization of MS_I (as defined in Example 1) even though the belief systems generated by MS_E and MS'_E are the same. (In fact the premise of ρ is not a theorem in the original system, but it becomes so when "merged", via $\oplus$, into MS_I.)

Intuitively, Definition 4 says that we should not consider systems with rules which do not play any role in the original system, but which get activated when merged into MS_I.

4.2 Realizing Contexts and Bridge Rules

The next step is to find sufficient and necessary conditions for having realizations of MR^- systems.

Definition 5. Consider MS_E and MS_I. We say that

- C_{E_0} is an *incomplete* realization of C_{I_0} if and only if $MS_E \prec \langle \{C_{E_0} \oplus C_{I_0}, C_{E_1}\}, BR_E \rangle$;
- C_{E_1} is an *incomplete* realization of C_{I_1} if and only if $MS_E \prec \langle \{C_{E_0}, C_{E_1} \oplus C_{I_1}\}, BR_E \rangle$;
- BR_E is an *incomplete* realization of BR_I if and only if $MS_E \prec \langle \{C_{E_0}, C_{E_1}\} BR_E \cup BR_I \rangle$.

Example 4 (Continuation of Example 1). C_{E_0} is a complete realization of C_{I_0}, C_{E_1} is an incomplete realization of C_{I_1} and BR_E is a complete realization of BR_I.

Example 5 (Continuation of Example 2). C_{E_0} is a complete realization of C_{I_0}, C_{E_1} is a complete realization of C_{I_1} and BR_E is an incomplete realization of BR_I.

Notice that, according to our definition, in both of the above examples C_{E_0} turns out to be a complete realization of C_{I_0} even though R_{E_0} is a strict subset of R_{I_0}. This is what one would intuitively expect. The fact that R_{E_0} is a strict subset of R_{I_0} is not caused by an incompleteness of C_{E_0} if compared with C_{I_0}, but, rather, is caused by the incompleteness of other components of the MR^- system. In other words, we have identified the source of incompleteness.

We have the following result, which achieves the goal set up at the beginning of the Section.

MS_E is an incomplete realization of MS_I if and only if at least one of the following three conditions is satisfied:

- C_{E_0} is an incomplete realization of C_{I_0};
- C_{E_1} is an incomplete realization of C_{I_1};
- BR_E is an incomplete realization of BR_I.

Thus, the classification provided in by Definition 5 is exhaustive.

4.3 Realizing the Components of Contexts

Consider a context C of an MR$^-$ system MS. The next and last step is to analyze in which way the components (atomic formulas, construction rules, axioms and inference rules) of C can affect the reality of C and thus the reality of MS.

(Notationally, in the following, if C_i is a context, P_i and W_i are the set of atomic formulas and the set of construction rules for L_i, respectively. L_i is therefore defined as the smallest set generated from P_i and closed under W_i, in symbols $L_i = Cl(P_i, W_i)$.)

Definition 6. Consider MS$_E$ and MS$_I$. If $A \in \{P, W, \Omega, \Delta\}$, we say that A_{E_i} is an *incomplete realization of* A_{I_i} if MS$_E \prec \langle \{C_0, C_1\}, BR_E \rangle$, where[6]:

$$
C_j = \begin{cases}
\langle Cl(P_{E_j} \cup P_{I_j}, W_{E_j}), \Omega_{E_j}, \Delta_{E_j} \rangle & \text{if } j = i \text{ and } A = P \\
\langle Cl(P_{E_j}, W_{E_j} \cup W_{I_j}), \Omega_{E_j}, \Delta_{E_j} \rangle & \text{if } j = i \text{ and } A = W \\
\langle L_{E_j}, W_{E_j}, \Omega_{E_j} \cup \Omega_{I_j}, \Delta_{E_j} \rangle & \text{if } j = i \text{ and } A = \Omega \\
\langle L_{E_j}, W_{E_j}, \Omega_{E_j}, \Delta_{E_j} \cup \Delta_{I_j} \rangle & \text{if } j = i \text{ and } A = \Delta \\
C_{E_j} & \text{otherwise}
\end{cases}
$$

Example 6 (Continuation of Example 4). Δ_{E_1} is an incomplete realization of Δ_{I_1}.

The classification in Definition 6 fixes the intuitively correct but formally wrong classification provided in [10]. That paper discusses in detail the intuitions underlying this classification and provides various examples. As already discussed in [10], the various forms of incompleteness (in the atomic formulas, construction rules, axioms, inference rules) model very different situations. For instance, the incompleteness in the signature models the case in which a reasoner is not aware of some primitive propositions. This is the case, for example, of the Bantu tribesman in [2] who is not aware that personal computer prices are going down. A "more civilized" tribesman might be aware of computers and their prices, but he might not believe that their prices are decreasing. The latter situation is modeled with a reasoner incomplete in the axioms. Incompleteness in the construction rules and/or inference rules are best suited for modeling the limitation of resources that real reasoners have both in constructing sentences and in proving theorems.

In any case, incompleteness in the atomic formulas, or in the construction rules, or in the axioms, or in the inference rules affects the completeness of the context. In fact, C_{E_i} is an incomplete realization of C_{I_i} ($i \in \{0, 1\}$) if and only if at least one of the following four conditions is satisfied:

---

[6] Strictly speaking, $\langle L_{E_j}, W_{E_j}, \Omega_{E_j} \cup \Omega_{I_j}, \Delta_{E_j} \rangle$ is not assured to be a context unless $\Omega_{I_j} \subseteq L_{E_j}$. More carefully, we should write $\langle L_{E_j}, W_{E_j}, \Omega_{E_j} \cup (\Omega_{I_j} \cap L_{E_j}), \Delta_{E_j} \rangle$. Analogously for $\langle L_{E_j}, W_{E_j}, \Omega_{E_j}, \Delta_{E_j} \cup \Delta_{I_j} \rangle$.

- P_{E_i} is an incomplete realization of P_{I_i};
- W_{E_i} is an incomplete realization of W_{I_i};
- Ω_{E_i} is an incomplete realization of Ω_{I_i};
- Δ_{E_i} is an incomplete realization of Δ_{I_i}.

Notice that the classification provided by Definition 5 and Definition 6 is exhaustive in the sense that it considers all the constructors on MR⁻ systems. We have discussed how the reality of either one of the contexts or of the bridge rules of an MR⁻ system MS affects the reality of the whole MR⁻ system MS. We have also discussed how the reality either of the signature, or of the construction rules, or of the set of axioms, or of the set of inference rules of a context C affects the reality of C and thus of the MR⁻ system to which C belongs to. Thus, we have achieved the goal set up in Section 1, that is, we have provided an exhaustive classification of all the possible forms and sources of reality.

5 Multi-Agents and Nested Beliefs

A belief system $\langle R_0, R_1 \rangle_{\text{B}}$ allows for the representation of one reasoner (*i.e.* R_0) having beliefs about another reasoner (*i.e.* R_1) and expressing such beliefs with a belief predicate (*i.e* B). In the following, we will abbreviate such a case saying that R_0 *observes* R_1. In more complex configurations, we may have isolate reasoners (reasoners which neither observe nor are observed by other reasoners) as well as reasoners observing other reasoners which, in their own turn, are possibly observing other reasoners. Such arbitrary configurations of reasoners can be formally described with *complex belief systems*.

If I is a set of indices (each corresponding to a reasoner), a *complex belief system* is a pair $\langle \{R_i\}_{i \in I}, \mathbf{B} \rangle$ where $\{R_i\}_{i \in I}$ is a family of reasoners and $\mathbf{B}$ is an n-tuple of binary relations over I.

Intuitively, if $\langle i, j \rangle$ is an element of the k-th binary relation then R_i observes R_j and expresses its beliefs about R_j using the B^k predicate (we thus assume that to the k-th binary relation there corresponds a belief predicate B^k). It is easy to check that a basic belief system $\langle R_0, R_1 \rangle_{\text{B}}$ corresponds to the belief system $\langle \{R_0, R_1\}, \{\langle 0, 1 \rangle\} \rangle$. Notice that complex belief systems allow also for the representation of isolate reasoners.

As for belief systems, we present complex belief systems using MC systems. The following definition generalizes Definition 1.

Definition 7 MR$_I^{\text{B}}$⁻. Let I be a set of indexes and $\mathbf{B}$ a n-tuple of binary relations over I. An MC system $\langle \{C_i\}_{i \in I}, BR \rangle$ is an MR$_I^{\text{B}}$⁻ system if BR consists of the bridge rules

$$\frac{\langle A, C_j \rangle}{\langle \text{B}^k(\text{``}A\text{''}), C_i \rangle} \mathcal{R}_{up}^{\text{B}^k} \qquad \frac{\langle \text{B}^k(\text{``}A\text{''}), C_i \rangle}{\langle A, C_j \rangle} \mathcal{R}_{dn}^{\text{B}^k}$$

with $\langle i, j \rangle$ belonging to the k-th relation in $\mathbf{B}$ and the restrictions include:

$\mathcal{R}_{up}^{\text{B}^k}$: $\langle A, C_j \rangle$ does not depend on any assumption in C_j.

$\mathcal{R}_{dn}^{\text{B}^k}$: $\langle \text{B}^k(\text{``}A\text{''}), C_i \rangle$ does not depend on any assumption in C_i.

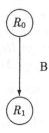

Fig. 1. A belief system.

We say that an $MR_I^B{}^-$ system MS *presents (generates)* the complex belief system $\langle\{R_i\}_{i\in I}, \mathbf{B}\rangle$ if $T_i = \{A \mid \vdash_{MS} \langle A, C_i\rangle\}$ $(i \in I)$.

It is possible to graphically represent the structure of a complex belief system as a directed graph, whose nodes are the reasoners and whose edges are the relations. Each edge is also labeled with the belief predicate corresponding to the relation. Thus, for example, the (complex) belief system $\langle\{R_0, R_1\}, \{\langle 0, 1\rangle\}\rangle$ corresponds to Figure 1.

The case in which the complex belief system is hierarchic, *i.e.* it corresponds to a tree of reasoners, (as the system in Figure 2) is particularly interesting.

In Figure 2 each reasoner $R_{i_1,\dots,i_k,i}$ $(k \geq 0)$ may be considered a model of an agent a_i as seen from agent $a_{i_1}, \dots, a_{i_k}$ perspective. Each agent a_i thus corresponds to countably many reasoners $R_{\alpha,i}$ (where α is a string over $\{1, \dots n\}$), each modeling a_i from different viewpoints. For example, with reference to Figure 2, the two reasoners R_{i12} and R_{in2} (representing a_2's beliefs but from two different perspectives) have in general different properties and/or relations with other reasoners. This is not possible (or at least not so simple to accomplish) in a "traditional" approach where one must characterize the beliefs of all the agents (from whatever perspective) in a single theory.

On the other hand, tree structures of reasoners are not always appropriate. For example, two reasoners may share the same view of a reasoner (the sharing of structures has obvious implementational advantages). Graphically, this amounts to have one node with two fathers. Yet another option is to have a reasoner R_i observing another reasoner R_j from more than one viewpoint. R_i may be an ideal observer of R_j from one viewpoint, but not from the other (see [11] for a presentation of an $MR_I^B{}^-$ system —provably equivalent to Fagin's and Halpern's logic of general awareness [2, 3]— in which this is indeed the case).

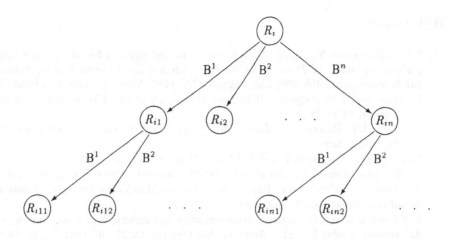

Fig. 2. A complex belief system.

6 Conclusion

In this paper we have provided a taxonomic analysis of ideal and real belief. As far as we know such an analysis has never been done before in any formalism for reasoning about belief. More important, such an analysis induces a classification on MR$^-$ systems which matches our intuitions.

Notice that all the previous work on the formalization of propositional attitudes makes use of a single theory. However, ideas similar to ours, which suggest the use of multiple distinct theories, have been exploited in much applied work in computational linguistics and AI (see for instance [6, 12, 13, 14]). This is indeed one of the main motivations underlying our work on contexts. In our view, context-based formalisms provide many implementational advantages, all deriving from the fact that reasoning becomes intrinsically localized [8, 10]. For instance, contexts allow for more "elaboration tolerant" representations: small variations of the input problem do not cause major revisions of the representation and of the solution strategy (see [15]). Another advantage seems to be computational efficiency: due to the modularization of the knowledge, the search space is divided in smaller search spaces (but no evidence of this fact has been provided yet).

Finally, our context-based approach for modeling knowledge in general and agents' beliefs in particular —besides having the above mentioned advantages— also allows for building particular hierarchical MC systems which are provably equivalent to various modal logics for beliefs presented in the literature (see for example [7, 10, 11]). As a last remark, MC systems have been implemented inside the **GETFOL** system [16], an extension of a re-implementation of the **FOL** system [17].

References

1. J.Y. Halpern and Y. Moses. A guide to the modal logics of knowledge and belief: preliminary draft. In *Proc. of the 9th International Joint Conference on Artificial Intelligence*, pages 480–490, Los Angeles, CA, 1985. Morgan Kaufmann Publ. Inc.

2. R. Fagin and J.Y. Halpern. Belief, awareness, and limited reasoning. *Artificial Intelligence*, 34:39–76, 1988.

3. R. Fagin, J.Y. Halpern, Y. Moses, and M. Y. Vardi. *Reasoning about knowledge*. Stanford Bookstore, 1992.

4. K. Konolige. *A deduction model of belief*. Pitnam, London, 1986.

5. J . Hintikka. *Knowledge and Belief*. Cornell University Press, Ithaca, NY, 1962.

6. A. Lansky. Localized Event-Based Reasoning for Multiagent Domains. *Computational Intelligence*, 4:319–339, 1988.

7. F. Giunchiglia and L. Serafini. Multilanguage hierarchical logics (or: how we can do without modal logics). *Artificial Intelligence*, 65:29–70, 1994. Also IRST-Technical Report 9110-07, IRST, Trento, Italy.

8. F. Giunchiglia. Contextual reasoning. *Epistemologia, special issue on I Linguaggi e le Macchine*, XVI:345–364, 1993. Short version in Proceedings IJCAI'93 Workshop on Using Knowledge in its Context, Chambery, France, 1993, pp. 39–49. Also IRST-Technical Report 9211-20, IRST, Trento, Italy.

9. H. Levesque. A logic of implicit and explicit belief. In *AAAI-84*, pages 198–202, 1984.

10. F. Giunchiglia, L. Serafini, E. Giunchiglia, and M. Frixione. Non-Omniscient Belief as Context-Based Reasoning. In *Proc. of the 13th International Joint Conference on Artificial Intelligence*, pages 548–554, Chambery, France, 1993. Also IRST-Technical Report 9206-03, IRST, Trento, Italy.

11. E. Giunchiglia, F. Giunchiglia, and L. Serafini. Agents as Resasoners, Observers or Believers. In *AI*IA 95, 4rd Congress of the Italian Association for Artificial Intelligence*, number 992 in LNAI, pages 414–425, Firenze, October 1995. Springer Verlag.

12. Y. Wilks and J. Biem. Speech acts and multiple environments. In *Proc. of the 6th International Joint Conference on Artificial Intelligence*, 1979.

13. F. Giunchiglia and R.W. Weyhrauch. A multi-context monotonic axiomatization of inessential non-monotonicity. In D. Nardi and P. Maes, editors, *Meta-level architectures and Reflection*, pages 271–285. North Holland, 1988. Also DIST Technical Report 9105-02, DIST, University of Genova, Italy.

14. J. McCarthy. Notes on Formalizing Context. In *Proc. of the 13th International Joint Conference on Artificial Intelligence*, pages 555–560, Chambery, France, 1993.

15. A. Cimatti and L. Serafini. Multi-Agent Reasoning with Belief Contexts II: Elaboration Tolerance. In *Proc. 1st Int. Conference on Multi-Agent Systems (ICMAS-95)*, pages 57–64, 1995. Also IRST-Technical Report 9412-09, IRST, Trento, Italy. To be presented at *Commonsense-96*, Third Symposium on Logical Formalizations of Commonsense Reasoning, Stanford University, 1996.

16. F. Giunchiglia. The GETFOL Manual - GETFOL version 1. Technical Report 92-0010, DIST - University of Genova, Genoa, Italy, 1992.

17. R.W. Weyhrauch. Prolegomena to a Theory of Mechanized Formal Reasoning. *Artificial Intelligence*, 13(1):133–176, 1980.

Emotions as Commitments Operators : A Foundation for Control Structure in Multi-Agents Systems

Michel Aubé

Université de Sherbrooke,
2500 Blvd Université,
Sherbrooke, Qc, CANADA, J1K 2R1
maube@granby.mtl.net

Alain Senteni

Université de Montréal,
C.P. 6128, succursale A,
Montréal, Qc, CANADA, H3C 3J7
senteni@iro.umontreal.ca

Abstract. Typically, multi-agent systems (MAS) relie on sociological theory and use centrally the concept of commitment. A definition as well as a tentative computational model of this concept, emerge from research in sociology and in computer science, leading naturally to the study of resource management. We claim that effective resource management in a distributed system requires powerful control structure yet to be founded. We then propose a model of control that stems from the psychology of human emotions as part of the fundamental definition of more autonomous, and adaptive multi-agent systems.

1 Introduction

In the beginning of their article, *Intention is Choice with Commitment*, [Cohen & Levesque 90a] introduce Willy, the household robot, who gets into trouble for not handling commitments properly. In the example, Willy is first asked to bring a beer, and intends to do so, but then decides to adopt some other goal. It is thus shipped back to the manufacturer for lack of commitment. Having been returned to its master, the robot is asked again for a beer. This time though, the master drops his request when he learns that the trade of the beverage is not of his prefered kind. Yet Willy sticks to the order, brings a beer, and ends being sent to the shop, for the reason of being overcommitted. After further tuning, the robot finally gets home, having been supposedly wired-in with the proper sense of commitment. Again, Willy is asked for a beer, actually the last one that is left in the fridge. Understanding correctly that its commitment will be over if it is impossible to fulfill, Willy deliberately smashes the bottle against the wall. In spite of its subtle reasoning capacities, the robot ends up being... dismantled!

The question we want to address here is how such a system as Willy could become capable of adjusting *from within* to the proper level of commitment, instead of having to be corrected and tuned up totally *from the outside*. In other words, what kind of mechanism should be designed inside of an agent so that it would handle variations of commitments by itself. This question will lead us to reconsider the relations between some of the basic concepts in distributed artificial intelligence [DAI] such as : autonomy, motivation and resource management.

Communities of cooperating autonomous agents as well as human societies use resources whose management is at the core of any organized activity. Resources are defined here more or less as energy is in physics : it basically amounts to the cost of work or actions. Within animals or animats, needs, such as hunger and thirst, appear to be the motivational processes that insure management and regulation of directly consumable resources, be it available food or water for animals or processing time for a computer. These are *first-order resources*. Besides, there exist *second-order resources*, which an agent gets only indirectly, through having other agents *committed* to provide them : for instance, newborns could have access to food only through having their parents get the feeding resources for them.

Commitments, essentially measured in terms of resource allocation and constraints upon resources, hence appear as one critical reason for the setting up of multi-agent societies. By regulating exchange, they enable using each other as a way to access additional resources otherwise unaccessible, or too costly to obtain. From their earliest definitions, multi-agent systems (MAS) rely on sociological theory [Gasser 91] and use centrally the concept of commitments [Fikes 82]. Building upon the seminal work of symbolic interactionists such as [Gerson 76], [Bond 90] and [Dongha 94] propose a definition and a computational model of the concept of commitment that leads naturally to the study of resource management. We think that effective resource management in a distributed system requires powerful control structures yet to be founded.

The main purpose of this paper is to sketch the design for such a model of control based upon resource management. The second section defines first-order and second-order resources, and revisit the concept of commitments in this context. The third section proposes a model of control that stems from the psychology of human emotions [Oatley 92]. It introduces emotions as powerful control structures that act so as to protect agents - and societies of agents - from running out of resources, typically second-order ones. The fourth section takes a closer look at the utilisation of speech acts as communication primitives between agents and introduces the new concept of *emotional acts*, as a way to resolve ambiguities inherent to the expressive and declarative illocutionary categories. We contend that emotion-like control structures should become part of the fundamental definition of more autonomous, and more adaptive multi-agent systems. The fifth section considers distributed meeting scheduling as a possible testbed for that kind of control structures and raises some implementation issues.

2 From Resources to Commitments

2.1 First-Order and Second-Order Resources

If agents are ever to get autonomous, it will only be through getting control over their motivations, by having ways of setting their own goals. The idea of providing agents with the capability to generate their own top level goals is not alien to the DAI community : it can be found in Maes' earlier work [Maes 91] while the concept of *motivated agency* is introduced by [Norman & Long 95]. Motivations essentially have to do with managing resources : this is what is most crucial and vital for the agents, and what becomes their ultimate goals. In the agent context, resources are defined more or less as energy is in physics : whatever enables - and is required for - producing work. It could be physical energy like heat or electricity or food, but also time, money, affiliation, power, knowledge... For instance, if a robot learns about a shorter route than usual to some target, this specific knowledge is clearly worth some economy in fuel. Basically, the concept of resource is tantamount to the cost of work or actions. However it is essential to refine it and distinguish at least two kinds of resources : first-order and second-order.

First-order resources. First-order resources are directly consumable ones that an agent already has at disposal (available food or water for animals, processing time or memory for computer). In animals, *needs* - such as hunger, thirst, fatigue, shelter, sex... - are the motivational processes [Toates 86] that insure management and regulation of first-order resources.

Second-order resources. Second-order resources are those that an agent gets only indirectly, through having other agents committed to give them to him : newborns could get access to food only through having their parents provide the resources for them. Money as well should be seen as a second-order resource : any piece of money always amounts to a commitment to exchange some goods for it. And as such, it is indeed also revocable, be it only through the variation of currency!

2.2 Commitments as second-order resources

Commitments are essentially measured in terms of allocation of resources and constraints upon resources [Gerson, 76] [Bond 90] [Dongha 94]. They thus appear as one critical reason for the setting up of multi-agent societies : by regulating exchange, they enable using each other as a way to access additional resources that would remain otherwise unaccessible, or would be too costly to obtain .

Typically, an agent A *commits* certain of its resources to another agent B (commits stands here for *does not give right away, but promises to give eventually*). As a consequence, B is *allocated* new resources, while A is *constrained* as to the usage of its own resources. For instance, A might be constrained not to consumate all of them and to take into account some amount that has to remain available to fulfill the commitment. On the other hand, such commitment could also involve for A setting the goal of acquiring for B some resources that A does not already possess.

One important corollary is that, by virtue of making resources available, *commitments themselves are to be counted as resources*. Within complex species that pursue multiple goals, and who absolutely require as such the cooperation of other agents, commitments might well become the most important of all resources! Hence, it is very likely that, in social species like ours, evolutionary forces would have favored and selected out precisely those organisms that would have become equipped with powerful mechanisms to insure control over commitments!

3 Emotions as a Metaphor for Control Structures

3.1 The Appraisal Structure of Emotions : Valence, Certainty, Agency

Valence : Positive and Negative Emotions. In higher (social, or at least nurturing) animals, *emotions* - such as anger, fear, joy, sadness, guilt... - are the motivational processes that insure management and regulation of second-order resources, namely commitments. Very much like needs, emotions are powerful control structures that act so as to protect agents - and societies of agents - from running out of resources. Hence they require being allocated a higher level of processing priority than most other mechanisms. These control processes are triggered by significant variations in the flow of resources available or required for an agent (or a community of agents). There indeed has to be regular variations in the daily consumption of resources, without these overpowerful processes intervening within the ongoing computation. Significant variations here means that the amount of increase or decrease of resources should exceed a certain predefined (although eventually ajustable) *threshold*.

There obviously has to be two main classes of emotions, positive and negative, that deal respectively with significative *gain* or *loss* in resources (leading respectively to *joy* or *sadness*). *Positive emotions* act so as to reinvest the gain (that triggered them in the first place) in order to buy access to further resources : they operate as accumulators or *amplifiers* [Isen 93]. *Negative emotions*, on the other hand, are used so as to patch the breach, slow down the running waste, and eventually to call for help so as to replace the incurred loss : they operate as *regulators*.

Of course, these processes are themselves costly and it might not seem too adaptive to spend so much resources when one is already losing some. Yet, even if one has to pay for the plumber, it might well be worth to do so before completely running out of water! Sometimes, this protection function of negative emotions against the loss would rather be met by setting the agent in economy mode, i.e. by isolating it from the others and reducing its activity level, as it often happens with people suffering from grief or severe distress.

Uncertainty and Temporal Dynamics. On the other hand, emotions being (as motivations) intrinsically related to the goal structure of an agent, they forcefully have to be related also to planning and expectations. That is to say, emotions are necessarily subject to a *temporal dynamics*, and could then be triggered by actual as well as by *anticipated* gain or loss (leading to *hope* or *fear*). While actual gains would be reinvested to obtain further resources, anticipated gains would rather insure goal persistence, by acting so as to justify sustaining the actual investment, or even spending more resources in the pursuit of the current goal. While actual loss would trigger calling for extra resources from other agents, anticipated loss would rather induce significative change in the current planning strategy. In order to do so, the required resources will generally have to be substracted from other current goal-pursuing processes that would then get temporarily (or even definitively) suspended.

Agency : Causal Attribution of Events to Other Agents. Moreover, in multi-agent societies, gains and losses are most frequently caused by the action of agents (self or others). In other words, due to the very structure of commitments as second-order resources, agency is, in those societies, the general cause that a resource management system should naturally (i.e. *evolutionarily*) get a grip upon!

Before classifying emotions according to their appraisal structure, let's first recall what is agency in the psychology of emotions. *Agency* is understood as *causal attribution* [Weiner 85] [Shultz 91]: if something important happens to agent A, this one tries to attribute the responsibility to some other agent B. This is a way, for A, to get a grip on who can be held responsible for the considered upcoming event in order to react efficiently.

Anger is the process that gets control over situations when a significant loss of resources is attributable to the action of another agent [Hutchinson 72] [Averill 83]. On the other hand, if the loss is caused by self, it is *guilt* that steps in [McGraw 87]. When someone else is seen as responsible for some noticeable gain, *gratitude* is triggered. Finally, *pride* takes charge when it is self that appears clearly responsible for the gain.

Joy, sadness, hope or *fear* are triggered either when no attributable agency could be found as a cause for the loss or gain, or when there appears to be no possible control over the corresponding event. From the *point of view* of control structures over commitments, non-controllable agency is tantamount to no agency at all, and there is no point spending resources against overpowerful agents : better call for help then or fly away (and alert relatives to flee as well)! For instance, in cases of anticipated loss attributable to others, anger would be triggered *only if* there is something to be done against the agents to prevent their wrongdoing, while fear would be triggered if nothing could be envisioned to prevent it.

3.2 A Taxonomy Of Emotions

Figure 1 summarizes the preceding categorization of emotions. Although much refinement could be introduced within each category (such as distinguishing between guilt and shame), this taxonomy is pretty much congruent with the intersecting aspects of the current *appraisal theories* in the psychology of emotions [Ortony, Clore & Collins 88] [Roseman 91] [Scherer 88] [Smith & Ellsworth 85] .

A G E		POSITIVE		NEGATIVE	
		actual	anticipated	actual	anticipated
E	none	Joy	Hope	Sadness	Fear
N	others	Gratitude		Anger	
C Y	self	Pride		Guilt	

Fig. 1. The appraisal structure for the basic categories of emotions.

The first four emotions (joy, hope, sadness and fear) act so as to set up or generate new commitments (through giving and sharing resources, strengthening affiliation, building up trust and confidence, calling for help and support...) between agents. The last four emotions (pride, guilt, gratitude and anger) act so as to handle or prevent the breaking of current commitments between agents (through praising or threatening...) or to strengthen and sustain them.

It is perhaps mandatory to stress here some theoretical consequence of having restricted emotions to being *commitments operators*. This means that we would not count as *fear proper* the escaping reactions of lower organisms such as fish, amphibians and most of the reptiles (that happen not to have evolved limbic structures), but as being part of a simpler *need structure*. Our basic criterion for counting a motivational process as an emotion, is that it should provide for some communicative means in the service of interagent binding (such as alarm or distress calls, warning growls, tail waving...).

Figure 2 illustrates the model we have sketched above for the flow of control relative to the management of resources. It could be seen from this diagram that needs could themselves activate emotions in their attempt to regulate a significant variation of resources, for instance when a hungry baby gets distressed or even angered at not being fed.

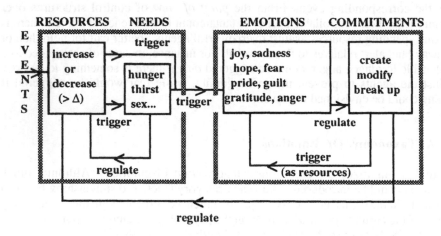

Fig. 2. The flow of control in the management of resources.

It also seems to be the case that first-order resources could activate emotions directly, when the variation is large enough to cross the critical threshold so as to *launch* emotional expression *evolutionarily* designed to commit others to set in and react (so they would help or flee, applaud or repent...) : states of exhaustion often lead to distress, and sudden intense pain is a well documented releaser of anger [Berkowitz 93].

4 Emotions in the Context of Agent Communication

4.1 Agent Communication Deals with Commitments

In the context of MAS, communication has to be about interagent binding, resource sharing, cooperation or conflict, and then has to rest upon establishing and managing commitments. In other words, communication has to be very closely related to the emotional control mechanisms. Obviously, communications will not all be emotional : variations in commitments (as resources) do not always exceed the critical threshold (as stated above) beyond which emotions are triggered. But all emotions - as commitment operators - sure have to be communicative (i.e. they have to make use of communication methods)!

4.2 Speech Acts are Communication Primitives

Both linguistic and DAI communities [Cohen & Perrault 79] [Winograd & Flores 86] [Cohen & Levesque 90] [Singh 94] agree that, in human languages, the basic units of communication are *speech acts*, i.e. various ways of specifying *intentions*. Classically [Searle 79] and later [Vanderveken 90], reformulating [Austin 62] both provide a taxonomy for these communication primitives.

4.3 A Taxonomy of Illocutionary Speech Acts

Speech acts capture categories of statements (typically centered around verbs in human languages) as various ways of specifying intentions - and, as a consequence, commitments [Winograd & Flores 86] among communicating agents, and thereby introduce a taxonomy of communication primitives :

• Assertives *commit* the speaker to some information being reliable.
• Directives request from someone to *commit* to accomplish some action.
• Promissives *commit* oneself to accomplish some action for someone else.
• Declaratives *commit*, and request that others do as well, to some change in status.
• Expressives express some feelings or emotions.

Expressive speech acts. However there are a few well documented problems with this taxonomy. On the one hand, [Austin 62] and [Searle 79] themselves argue that the expressive category has indeed a special character ("a very funny one"), and most further formalisms of speech acts bluntly ignored it [Cohen & Perrault 79] [Cohen & Levesque 90] [Singh 94]. We claim that expressive speech acts cluster intentions that should not belong to the same processing level as those from other categories, in particular because they correspond to different processing priorities. We would rather consider the expressive category as *emotional acts* (vs speech acts). Our contention is that, although this category also has to do with managing and conveying intentions, it simply does not stand on the same level as the others, and rather corresponds, on the verbal level, to a *vestigial* form of a more primitive underneath layer for the handling of commitments in social animals! It amounts to the verbal aspect of a much wider channel of emotional expression (emotional acts) that already flows through various facial, postural, or sound (v.g. crying, yelling, growling, laughing...) behaviors.

We contend that agent communication should *shift back from speech acts to emotional acts* whenever the threshold in the variation of second-order resources is exceeded or crossed over. Hence, communication between agents should non only reflect the verbal aspect of typical human communication but most importantly emotional non-verbal aspects as well. The choice of a platform for a testbed should take this into account : each script used by an agent for communicating with others would have to embody the specific way - in terms of speech acts or emotional acts - through which it operates upon commitments. One critical point here about the *ontology* of communicating agents is that they should be hardly able to ignore (or escape from responding to) emotional signals emitted by other agents, so that those signals could, for instance, *generate interrupts* or *reset computation.*

Declarative speech acts. On the other hand, the case for declaratives is also peculiar : it looks like a very special device of using some authority (i.e. agents with a high status - like judges in our societies) as a third party or witness to guarantee that a whole community of agents would at once subscribe to (i.e. get bound to) a new commitment (which for instance happens when a new status is ascribed to some agent - "I name you President" - or when some object of collective usage is given a new name - "From now on, this street will be called Kennedy Avenue"). This peculiar kind of commitment, shared by a whole community at once, is closely related to what [Shoham & Tennenholtz 95] termed a *useful social law* in computational environments.

Assertive, directive and promissive speech acts. It then looks as if classical categories of speech acts did in fact encompass three different *layers* of communicating tools for setting up and managing commitments between interacting agents. In the middle lay the categories most frequently referred to and formalized within DAI literature and practice, namely assertives, directives and promissives, that deal with common ongoing transactions between agents : exchanging information, requesting and promising, bidding and contracting...

Underneath lies the more primitive (but also more powerful, controlwise) layer of emotional acts, that sometimes emerge as expressive speech acts when they reach the verbal level. Emotional acts are triggered when there is serious risk of breaking ongoing commitments or unforeseen opportunities of establishing new ones. Serious risk here means that the variation in second-order resources is exceeding some predefined threshold.

Finally, the top layer has to do with declaratives, that are used to set up new social laws : they hence provide a mechanism for establishing and *distributing* new commitments at once across a whole community of agents. They rest on the essential condition that the emitter's status should be high enough to enforce the new regulation, so that receivers belonging to the same community would as such be constrained to respect it.

5 Future Work : What Kind of Implementation?

The choice of a proper testbed for the kind of control structure we have in mind is not obvious. First, the problem has to be complex enough so as to require distributing computation over a small community of agents, yet it has to remain manageable enough so we could draw useful conclusions from its implementation. It also seems interesting that it would be resonant or consonant with the kind of problems inhabiting the DAI culture. Finally, we feel that the nature of the problem should - when raised in human or animal societies - frequently, if not inherently, call for *emotional means of resolution*. Distributed meeting scheduling emerges as a rare case satisfying enough with respect to all such criteria.

In the context of meeting scheduling (agendas), relevant first-order resources are : periods of time (to be allocated for the various meetings); processing priority; knowledge (about self or others' available periods of time, or constraints, or preferences or commitments...). Relevant second-order resources are : commitments over time periods reserved for the meetings; reliability of the knowledge exchanged. Special kinds of commitments have to do with : *alliances* (or affiliation between agents that would then feel committed to cooperate with each other); *status* (i.e. allocated roles and power, that could sometimes enable obtaining, or even imposing, consensus among subordinates).

From what we said in the beginning of this article regarding motivations, it should be clear that goals (for instance, setting some specific meeting) are basically about *getting resources* (and from then on, preserving them) or about *setting commitments* (and from then on, keeping them). But this does not preclude that they could also bear upon exchanging resources (i.e. give away some resources in order to *buy* other ones that are required for the current activity), especially when this leads to creating new commitments. Plans are means to achieve goals, i.e. sequences of primitives or procedures (methods) owned by the agent, that could be assembled and executed so as to get to the expected results. As such, plans could be counted as part of the knowledge resource. From the above, it is easy to see that an agent's emotions are to be very closely related to its goal structure. For instance, blocking access to a required resource, would generally amount to goal blocking, which sure is one universal way (i.e. wide across cultures - and even across species!) of triggering anger [Averill 83] [Hutchinson 72] [Oatley 92].

In the context of meeting scheduling, there forcefully has to be many agents involved at the same time, each pursuing many different goals, having to keep and fulfill various commitments, sometimes requiring help and additionnal resources from a small set of intervening emotions. In terms of implementation, this means that not only agents should be represented as dynamic entities and operate in parallel, but this should be the case as well for goals, commitments and emotions! That is, all four concepts have to be represented as actors operating concurrently by sending and receiving messages asynchronously [Agha 86].

An agent does set a goal when asked for a new meeting, or as a subgoal of a current goal (while following a plan). Achieving goals could mainly be done through communicating with other agents and making commitments with them. Of course, some checks and bookkeeping also have to be performed within the agent's internal state, be it only to make sure that the target period is free, or that the request does not interfere with other commitments. Sometimes, meetings could be settled quite easily, when there is no conflict as to the allotted period of time. But with many people from many different groups, there are problems to be solved (and plans to be unfolded) often enough, especially as time goes and as more periods get allocated (hence becoming unavailable for further meetings). Then an agent might think of reconsidering a commitment concerning some *minor* meeting, or try make use of alliances and status as resources in convincing others to revoke theirs. This is typically on such occasions that emotions do step in!

In the spirit of this testbed, one should envision that some requests have high enough priority (as when the meeting is about getting a doctor for an urgency or if the requester owns a much higher status than self) so that reactions such as fear or distress would appear practically unavoidable. In order to be able to interrupt ongoing activity, emotions actors should be allocated a higher processing priority than goals actors or commitments actors. Emotions are to be triggered when current goals or commitments go awry.

The implementation will be using the Actalk actor platform built on top of ST-80 [Briot 94]. It should take profit of the Smalltalk exception handling system in which an exception is defined as a situation when computation could not be completed [Dony 90]. When such a situation can be clearly described, it could also be foreseen and prevented by having a signal watch for its occurrence. Again, as was stated before, proper signals to raise for the triggering of emotions have to do with significant variations in the stock of resources, more precisely those involved within the critical goal or commitment (the one which caused problem). Once a signal is caught, control is to be transferred to a well-tailored handler that could execute some appropriate piece of code before resuming or halting computation.

6 Conclusion

Effective resource management in a distributed system requires powerful control structure yet to be founded. We proposed a model of control, rooted in the psychology of human emotions, that introduces *emotion-like control structures* in the context of multi-agent systems. We pointed out how such control structures fit naturally into an inter-agent communication scheme. Their introduction improves the potential autonomy of agents by taking explicitly into account the management of the resources that are the core of their activity and that should hence be part of the fundamental definition of more autonomous and adaptive multi-agent systems.

References

[Agha 86] Gul Agha. *Actors*. Cambridge, MA : MIT Press, 1986.

[Austin 62] J.L. Austin. *How to do things with words*. Cambridge, MA : Harvard University Press, 1962.

[Averill 83] James R. Averill. Studies in Anger and Agression : Implications for Theories of Emotion. *American Psychologist*, 38, 1145-1160, 1983.

[Berkowitz 93] Leonard Berkowitz. Pain and Agression : Some Findings and Implications. *Motivation and Emotion*, 17, 277-293, 1993.

[Bond 90] Alan H. Bond. A Computational Model for Organizations of Cooperating Intelligent Agents. *SIGOIS Bulletin*, 11, 21-30, 1990.

[Briot 94] Jean-Pierre Briot. Modélisation et Classification de Langages de Programmation Concurrente à Objets : L'Expérience Actalk, *Actes du colloque "Langages et Modèles à Objets"*. Grenoble, France, 1994.

[Cohen & Levesque 90a] Philip R. Cohen and Hector. J. Levesque. Intention is Choice with Commitment. *Artificial Intelligence*, 42, 213-261, 1990.

[Cohen & Levesque 90b] Philip R. Cohen and Hector. J. Levesque. Rational Interaction as the Basis for Communication. In Philip R. Cohen, Jerry Morgan & Martha E. Pollack, editors, *Intentions in Communications*, pages 221-255, Cambridge : MIT Press, 1990.

[Cohen & Perrault 79] Philip R. Cohen and C. Raymond Perrault. Elements of a Plan-Based Theory of Speech Acts. *Cognitive Science*, 3, 177-212, 1979.

[Dongha 94] Paul Dongha. Toward a Formal Model of Commitment for Resource Bounded Agents. In Michael J. Wooldridge and Nicholas R. Jennings, editors, *Intelligent Agents, ECAI-94 Workshop on Agent Theories, Architectures, and Languages*, pages 86-101. New York : Springer-Verlag, 1994.

[Dony 90] Christophe Dony. Exception Handling and Object-Oriented Programming : Towards a Synthesis. In Norman Meyrowitz, editor, *OOPSLA ECOOP'90 Proceedings, Ottawa, October 21-25 1990, Sigplan Notices*, 25 (10), 322-330, 1990.

[Fikes 82] Richard E. Fikes. A Commitment-Based Framework for Describing Informal Cooperative Work. *Cognitive Science*, 6, 331-347, 1982.

[Gasser 91] Les Gasser. Social Conceptions of Knowledge and Action : DAI Foundations and Open Systems Semantics. *Artificial Intelligence*, 47, 107-138, 1991.

[Gerson 76] Elihu M. Gerson. On «Quality Of Life». *American Sociological Review*, 41, 793-806, 1976.

[Hutchinson 72] Ronald R. Hutchinson. The Environmental Causes of Aggression. In James K. Coles & Donald D. Jensen, editors, *Nebraska Symposium on Motivation 1972*, pages 155-181, Lincoln : University of Nebraska Press, 1972.

[Isen 93] Alice M. Isen. Positive Affect and Decision Making. In M. Lewis & J. M. Haviland, editors, *Hanbook of Emotion*, pages 261-277, New York : The Guilford Press, 1993.

[Maes 91] Pattie Maes. Situated Agents Can Have Goals. In Pattie Maes, editor, *Designing Autonomous Agents : Theory and Practice from Biology to Engineering and Back,* pages 49-70. Cambridge, MA : MIT Press, 1991.

[McGraw 87] Kathleen M. McGraw. Guilt Following Transgression : An Attribution of Responsibility Approach. *Journal of Personality and Social Psychology,* 53, 247-256, 1987.

[Norman & Long 95] Timothy J. Norman and Derek Long. *Alarms : An Implementation of Motivated Agency.* Research Note RN/95/24, Department of Computer Science, University College London, London, UK, April 6, 1995.

[Oatley 92] Keith Oatley. *Best Laid Schemes : The Psychology of Emotions.* Cambridge, England : Cambridge University Press, 1992.

[Ortony, Clore & Collins 88] Andrew Ortony, G. L. Clore & Allan Collins. *The Cognitive Structure of Emotions.* Cambridge : Cambridge University Press, 1988.

[Roseman 91] Ira J. Roseman. Appraisal Determinants of Discrete Emotions. *Cognition and Emotion,* 5, 161-200, 1991.

[Scherer 88] Klaus R. Scherer. Criteria for Emotion-Antecedent Appraisal : A Review. In V. Hamilton, G. H. Bower & N. H. Frijda, editors, *Cognitive Perspectives on Emotion and Motivation*, pages 89-126. Dordrecht : Kluwer, 1988.

[Searle 79] John R. Searle. *Speech Acts.* Cambridge, England : Cambridge University Press, 1969.

[Shoham & Tennenholtz 95] Yoav Shoham & Moshe Tennenholtz. On Social Laws for Artificial Agent Societies : Off-Line Design. *Artificial Intelligence*, 73, 231-252, 1995.

[Shultz 91] Thomas R. Shultz. From Agency to Intention : A Rule-Based, Computational Approach. In Andrew Whiten, editor, *Natural Theories of Mind.*

Evolution, Development and Simulation of Everyday Mindreading, pages 79-95. Basic Blackwell, 1991.

[Singh 94] Munindar P. *Singh. Multiagent Systems. A Theoretical Framework for Intentions, Know-How, and Communications.* New York : Springer-Verlag, 1994.

[Smith & Ellsworth 85] Craig A. Smith & Phoebe C. Ellsworth. Patterns of Cognitive Appraisal in Emotion. *Journal of Personality and Social Psychology*, 48, 813-838, 1985.

[Toates 86] Frederick Toates. *Motivational Systems.* Cambridge, England : Cambridge University Press, 1986.

[Vanderveken 90] Daniel Vanderveken. On the Unification of Speech Act Theory and Formal Semantics. In Philip R. Cohen, Jerry Morgan & Martha E. Pollack, editors, *Intentions in Communications*, pages195-220. Cambridge, MA : MIT Press, 1990.

[Weiner 85] Bernard Weiner. An Attributional Theory of Achievement Motivation and Emotion. *Psychological Review*, 92, 548-573, 1985.

[Winograd & Flores 86] Terry Winograd & Fernando Flores. *Understanding Computers and Cognition*, New York : Addison Wesley, 1986.

A Logical and Operational Model of Scalable Knowledge- and Perception-Based Agents*

Gerd Wagner[†]

Abstract We propose a model of an agent which is both logical and operational. Our model of *vivid agents* takes into account that agents need not only the ability to draw inferences but also to update their current knowledge state, to represent and to perform (and to simulate the execution of) actions in order to generate and execute plans, and to react and interact in response to perception and communication events. We illustrate our formalization of this basic functionality of an agent by means of examples. We also show how our model fits into the transition system semantics of concurrent reactive systems by identifying the five basic transitions of vivid agent systems: perception, reaction, planning, action, and replanning.

1 Introduction

A *vivid agent* is a software-controlled entity whose state is represented by a knowledge base, and whose behavior is represented by means of *action* and *re-action rules*. Following [Sho93], we shall view the state of an agent as consisting of mental components, such as beliefs and intentions. The basic functionality of a vivid agent comprises an update and an inference operation, and the possibility to represent and perform actions in order to be able to generate and execute plans. Since a vivid agent is 'situated' in an environment with which it has to be able to communicate, it also needs the ability to react in response to perception events, and in response to communication events created by the communication acts of other agents. We formalize the combination of these reactive and proactive aspects of agent behavior by nondeterministic interleaving of perception, reaction, planning and plan execution, resp. action. Notice that we make the important distinction between action and reaction: actions are deliberatively planned in order to solve a task or to achieve a goal, while reactions are triggered by perception and communication events.

We do not assume a fixed formal language and a fixed logical system for the knowledge-base of an agent.[1] Rather, we believe that it is more appropri-

---

*This work has been done during a stay at Univ. Nova de Lisboa under an HCM research grant of the EU. The author wants to thank Luis M. Pereira for his hospitality and support.

[†]`gw@inf.fu-berlin.de`, Institut für Informatik, Universität Leipzig, Augustusplatz 10-11, D-04109 Leipzig, Germany.

[1]It is important to recognize that for information and knowledge processing, unlike classical first-order logic for mathematics, there is no ONE TRUE LOGIC, but many different logical

ate to choose a suitable knowledge system for each agent individually according to its domain and its tasks. In simple cases, a relational database system will do the job, while in more involved cases one might need the ability to process, in addition to simple facts, (disjunctive or gradual) uncertain information, or temporal information, or even such advanced capabilities as deductive query answering and inconsistency handling. The knowledge system of a vivid agent will be nonmonotonic, since one needs the Closed-World Assumption, and negation-as-failure, in any practical system. Notice that this departs from the use of standard logics (enriched by various modalities) which is common in many other logical approaches to agent modeling. Vivid agents can be obtained by extending vivid knowledge systems through the addition of action and reaction rules. Since vivid knowledge systems are scalable, one can 'plug in' any suitable one for constructing a specific agent system. In any case, our definition of action and reaction rules is general enough to apply to all kinds of knowledge bases, and thus makes vivid agents scalable.

The combination of a knowledge base with action and reaction rules yields an *executable specification* of an agent, resp. of a multi-agent system. This is similar to the idea of PROgramming in LOGic where programs have both a procedural and a declarative reading. Our concept of vivid agents thus is able to narrow the gap between agent theory and practical systems, a gap which seems to be insuperable in many other logic-based approaches.

2 Knowledge Systems

The language of knowledge systems consists of the logical functors conjunction ($\land$), disjunction ($\lor$), weak negation (alias negation-as-failure, denoted by $-$), strong negation ($\sim$), and the truth constant 1; predicate symbols, constant symbols and variables. An *atom a* is an atomic formula, it is called *proper*, if $a \neq 1$. *Literals* are either atoms or strongly negated atoms, $l = a|\sim a$. We use $a, b, \ldots$, $l, k, \ldots$, and $F, G, H, \ldots$ as metavariables for atoms, literals, and well-formed formulas, respectively. A variable-free expression is called *ground*. The set of all proper atoms of a given language is denoted by At. If $\mathcal{F}$ is a set of logical functors, say $\mathcal{F} \subseteq \{1, -, \sim, \land, \lor, \rightarrow, \exists, \forall, \ldots\}$, then $L(\mathcal{F})$ denotes the respective set of well-formed formulas. Where L is a language (a set of formulas), L^0 denotes its restriction to closed formulas. Free(F) denotes the set of free variables of F.

We shall use three specific languages: L_{KB} is the set of all admissible knowledge bases of a knowledge system,[2] L_{Query} is the query language, and L_{Input} is the set of all admissible inputs, i.e. those formulas representing new information a KB may be updated with. Elements of L^0_{Query}, i.e. closed query formulas, are also called *if-queries*.

---

systems accounting for different kinds of knowledge such as temporal, uncertain, secure, partial, disjunctive, deductive, active, etc.

[2]It seems to be unrealistic to allow for arbitrary formulas in a KB for a number of reasons: a KB concept has to be a conservative extension of that of relational databases; it has to provide for negation-as-failure and for some kind of CWA mechanism; the amount of 'disjunctiveness' of a KB needs special care; there will be null values rather than existential quantifiers; etc.

Definition 1 (Knowledge System)   *An abstract knowledge system K is a quintuple:*[3]

$$K = \langle L_{KB}, \vdash, L_{Query}, \mathsf{Upd}, L_{Input} \rangle$$

where the inference relation $\vdash \subseteq L_{KB} \times L^0_{Query}$, together with the update operation $\mathsf{Upd} : L_{KB} \times L^0_{Input} \to L_{KB}$, satisfy for any $X \in L_{KB}$,

(KS1) $X \vdash 1$, *and* $\mathsf{Upd}(X, 1) = X$.

(KS2) $L_{Input} \subseteq L_{Query}$.

(KS3) $\mathsf{Upd}(X, F) \vdash F$, *for any $F \in L^0_{Input}$ which is consistent with X.*

In the sequel, we shall sometimes simply write 'KB' in formal expressions standing for an arbitrary knowledge base $X \in L_{KB}$.

In many cases, it is useful to be able to update by a set of inputs and we 'overload' the symbol Upd to denote also this more general update operation

$$\mathsf{Upd} : L_{KB} \times 2^{L_{Input}} \to L_{KB}$$

which has to be defined in such a way that for any finite $A \subseteq L_{Input}$, $\mathsf{Upd}(KB, A) = \mathsf{Upd}(KB, \bigwedge A)$. We sometimes write $KB + F$ as an abbreviation of $\mathsf{Upd}(KB, F)$, resp. $KB - F$ as an abbreviation of $\mathsf{Upd}(KB, -F)$.

Example 1 (Relational Databases)   *A KB consisting of ground atoms corresponds to a relational database. For instance, $X_1 = \{r(S), r(P), m(P, L)\}$, may represent the information that both Peter and Susan are residents, and that Peter is married to Linda. As a kind of natural deduction from positive facts an inference relation $\vdash$ between a database $X \subseteq At$ and an if-query is defined in the following way:*

$$
\begin{array}{lll}
(\vdash a) & X \vdash a & \textit{if } a \in X \\
(\vdash -a) & X \vdash -a & \textit{if } a \notin X \\
(\vdash \wedge) & X \vdash F \wedge G & \textit{if } X \vdash F \; \& \; X \vdash G \\
(\vdash \vee) & X \vdash F \vee G & \textit{if } X \vdash F \textit{ or } X \vdash G
\end{array}
$$

This inductive definition is completed by DeMorgan-style rewrite rules. We obtain, e.g., $X_1 \vdash m(P, L) \wedge r(P) \wedge -r(L)$.

Updates are insertions, $\mathsf{Upd}(X, a) := X \cup \{a\}$, and deletions, $\mathsf{Upd}(X, -a) := X - \{a\}$, of atoms $a \in At$. For a consistent $E \subseteq At \cup \overline{At}$, we have $\mathsf{Upd}(X, E) = X \cup E^+ - E^-$. For instance,

$$\mathsf{Upd}(X_1, -m(P, L) \wedge m(P, S)) = \{r(S), r(P), m(P, S)\}$$

---

[3]The formulation of a KS in terms of query and input processing was already implicitly present in Belnap's [1977] view of a KS. In [Lev84] it was proposed as a 'functional approach to knowledge representation'. In [Wag94a, Wag95] the concept of knowledge systems was further extended and used as an integrating framework for knowledge representation and logic programming.

describes a possible transaction. The KS of relational databases, denoted by $\mathbf{A}$, is then defined as

$$\mathbf{A} = \langle 2^{At}, \vdash, L(-, \wedge, \vee), \mathsf{Upd}, At \cup \overline{At} \rangle$$

Knowledge systems extending $\mathbf{A}$ conservatively are called *vivid*. Positive vivid knowledge systems have only negation-as-failure and use a general Closed-World Assumption, whereas general vivid knowledge systems employ two kinds of negation and specific Closed-World Assumptions. For instance, $\mathbf{A}$ can be extended to a general vivid knowledge system, called *factbases*, by allowing for literals instead of atoms as information units. In factbases, one can represent inexact predicates which is a particular form of incomplete knowledge. Further important examples of positive vivid knowledge systems are temporal, uncertain and disjunctive databases, which can be extended to corresponding general vivid knowledge systems called temporal, uncertain and disjunctve factbases. All these kinds of knowledge bases can be extended to *deductive knowledge bases* by adding deduction rules of the form $F \leftarrow G$ where $F \in L_{\mathrm{Input}}$ and $G \in L_{\mathrm{Query}}$ (see, e.g., [Wag94b]).

3   Action Rules and Planning

Action rules have the general form of *Action ← Condition*.[4] We shall distinguish between action and reaction rules. While action rules are used to represent the elementary action types of an agent, and to generate and execute plans, thus determining the *proactive* behavior, reaction rules are used to specify the *reactive* behavior of an agent which is based on both perception and knowledge in our account.

3.1   Representing Actions

Depending on the resp. domain and the capabilities and tasks of an agent, only certain actions can be performed by it. Besides communication acts, an agent can perform *private actions* by means of its effectors. An action type corresponds to a set of *action rules* which represent the different execution conditions and effects of different situation contexts. We denote the set of all elementary private action types available to an agent by L_{Act}. They correspond to private action rules of the form

$$r_\alpha \; : \; \mathsf{do}(\alpha), \; \mathit{Eff} \; \leftarrow \; \mathit{Cond}$$

In addition, there are communicative action rules

$$r_\eta \; : \; \mathsf{sendMsg}[\eta, R], \; \mathit{Eff} \; \leftarrow \; \mathit{Cond}$$

where $\mathit{Eff} \in L_{\mathrm{Input}}$, and $\mathit{Cond} \in L_{\mathrm{Query}}$, are logical formulas expressing the epistemic effects, resp. precondition, of the elementary action; $\mathsf{do}(\alpha)$ is a procedure

---

[4]Action rules (in the form of 'event-condition-action' rules) were also proposed as an extension to databases, now called *active databases*, see e.g. [McCD89].

call in order to execute the private action $\alpha \in L_{\text{Act}}$, and r_α is the name of the private action rule; and likewise $\mathsf{sendMsg}[\eta, R]$ is a procedure call to execute the communicative action $\eta \in L_{\text{CEvt}}$ where R identifies the receiver of the outgoing message, and r_η is the name of the communicative action rule.

We require that the precondition *Cond* is an evaluable formula and that all free variables of the epistemic effect formula *Eff* occur also in *Cond*.[5] If we are only interested in the epistemic representation of an action we omit the execution command $\mathsf{do}(\alpha)$, resp. $\mathsf{sendMsg}[\eta, R]$, in the resp. action rule r, thus obtaining its *epistemic projection* $\dot{r}$ which is called an *epistemic action rule*.

Action rules combine declarative queries (or inference) with state change (or update). Since in general, the effects of an action may be context-dependent, an action is represented by a set of action rules expressing the dependence of different effects on different preconditions. The execution of an action in a situation described by the knowledge base X is realized by firing the corresponding action rule whose precondition *Cond* applies to X, i.e. $X \vdash Cond$.

Definition 2 (Rule Application)   *Let $E \in L_{\text{Input}}, C \in L_{\text{Query}}$. An epistemic action rule $r : E \leftarrow C$ represents an update function, i.e. a mapping $r : L_{\text{KB}} \to L_{\text{KB}}$, whose application is defined as*

$$r(X) := \mathsf{Upd}(X, \{E\sigma : \sigma \text{ is a substitution s.th. } X \vdash C\sigma\})$$

Notice that in the case of a non-applicable rule, we get by definition

$$r(X) = \mathsf{Upd}(X, \emptyset) = \mathsf{Upd}(X, \bigwedge \emptyset) = \mathsf{Upd}(X, 1) = X$$

The execution of an action which is represented by the action rule r in a situation described by a knowledge base X corresponds on the epistemic level to the application of $\dot{r}$ to the current knowledge state X, and yields the updated knowledge state $\dot{r}(X)$.

Example 2 (Elevator Actions)   *In an elevator scenario, we have the elementary actions of going one floor up, or one floor down:*

$$\mathsf{oneup} : \quad at(x+1) \wedge -at(x) \leftarrow at(x) \wedge x < topfloor$$
$$\mathsf{onedown} : \quad at(x-1) \wedge -at(x) \leftarrow at(x) \wedge x > 0$$

Let the current situation, where the elevator is halting at the 3rd floor, be described by $X_0 = \{at(3)\}$, and let $topfloor = 10$. Then, performing the action oneup *corresponds to the rule application*

$$\mathsf{oneup}(X_0) = X_0 - at(3) + at(4) = \{at(4)\}$$

In this example, it is assumed that the action of moving one floor upwards is immediate, i.e. without duration. In a more realistic modeling, such as the one below, one would rather define the action of *starting* to move upwards.

---

[5] Rules of this form, where all free variables of the conclusion occur in the premise, and the premise is evaluable, are called *range-restricted*. In the sequel, we assume that rules are always range-restricted.

3.2 Planning

In order to achieve a goal $G \in L^0_{\text{Query}}$, in a situation described by $X_0 \in L_{\text{KB}}$, an agent generates a suitable plan P being a sequence of action rules $r_1, \ldots, r_n$, such that when the corresponding sequence of actions is performed in X_0, it leads to a situation $P(X_0) \in L_{\text{KB}}$ where G holds. Formally,

$$P = r_n \circ \ldots \circ r_1 , \quad \text{and} \quad P(X_0) \vdash G$$

where P is applied to X_0 as a composed function.[6]

Example 3 (The Deliberative Elevator) *Let $L_{\text{Act}} = \{\text{oneup}, \text{onedown}\}$ consist of the two actions defined above, and let the current situation be described by $X_0 = \{at(3)\}$. If the elevator has to perform the task $at(7)$ in order to pick up a passenger at the seventh floor, it could generate the following (admittedly not very exciting, but optimal) plan:*

$$P = \text{oneup} \circ \text{oneup} \circ \text{oneup} \circ \text{oneup}$$

the execution of which solves the task:

$$P(X_0) = \text{oneup}(\text{oneup}(\text{oneup}(\text{oneup}(\{at(3)\})))) = \{at(7)\}$$

4 Reaction and Interaction Rules

Reaction rules control the behaviour of a vivid agent in response to perception events related to the environment, or to communication events caused by other agents. We distinguish between private and communicative reaction rules, and call the latter *interaction rules*. *PEvt* and *CEvt* denote the resp. sets of perception and communication event schemas, *Evt* denotes their union, and L_{PEvt}, L_{CEvt}, and L_{Evt} the resp. event languages.

4.1 Private Reaction Rules

A private reaction rule has the form $\text{do}(\alpha)$, *Eff* $\leftarrow$ recvMsg$[\varepsilon, S]$, *Cond*, where

1. *Eff* $\in L_{\text{Input}}$, and *Cond* $\in L_{\text{Query}}$, are logical formulas expressing the epistemic effects, resp. the precondition, of the reaction;

2. $\alpha \in L_{\text{Act}}$ is an elementary action expression;

3. ε represents either an elementary perception event created by the perception subsystem with identifier S, i.e. $\varepsilon \in L_{\text{PEvt}}$, or a communication event created by another agent identified by S, i.e. $\varepsilon \in L_{\text{CEvt}}$. If there is only one perception subsystem, the identifier S will be omitted, i.e. we write recvMsg$[\varepsilon]$ when $\varepsilon \in L_{\text{PEvt}}$.

---

[6]Notice that our concept of planning on the basis of action rules in knowledge systems can be viewed as a generalization of the STRIPS[7] paradigm which corresponds to planning on the basis of A, the knowledge system of relational databases. Therefore, the frame problem is solved in the same way as in STRIPS: by means of a *minimal change* policy incorporated in the update operation of a knowledge system.

The premise recvMsg[ε, S] is simply a test whether the event queue contains the incoming message ε addressed to the agent either by the perception subsystem, or by another agent, identified by S. Thus, perception and communication events will be represented by incoming messages.[8]

In general, reactions are based both on perception and on knowledge. Immediate reactions do not allow for deliberation. They are represented by rules with an empty epistemic premise, i.e. $Cond = 1$. Timely reactions can be achieved by guaranteeing fast response times for checking the precondition of a reaction rule. This will be the case, for instance, if the precondition can be checked by simple table look-up (such as in relational databases). It will be more difficult in knowledge systems with deduction rules (e.g. deductive databases).

4.2 Interaction Rules

An interaction rule has the form sendMsg[η, R], *Eff* $\leftarrow$ recvMsg[ε, S], *Cond*, where ε, S, *Eff*, and *Cond*, i.e. the triggering event, the sender, the epistemic effect and the precondition formula are defined like for private reaction rules, and the action sendMsg[η, R] represents a communication act realized by asynchronous message passing, such that $\eta \in L_{CEvt}$, and R identifies the receiver of the message. We identify a communication act with the corresponding communication event which is perceived by the addressee of the communication act. Typically, the set of possible communication acts includes *telling*, *asking*, *replying*, and more.

Example 4 (Communicating Elevators) *In the communicating elevator scenario, we assume that two elevators a and b operate in the same shaft and must not collide. For simplicity, we shall consider the case with three floors. Elevator a serves floors 1 and 2, while elevator b serves floors 2 and 3, and hence the critical zone is floor 2. In addition to perception events, $L_{PEvt} = \{req(x), arrAt(x), timeout\}$, we now also have communication events in order to avoid collisions and deadlocks, i.e. for guaranteeing safety and progress. The elevators use two communication acts for coordination: requesting the permission to approach, and granting the permisssion, expressed by $L_{CEvt} = \{reqPerm, grantPerm\}$. This leads to the following specification, including a communication protocol:*

a_1 :   sendMsg[reqPerm, b], $req(2)$ $\leftarrow$ recvMsg[$req(2)$], $at(1)$
b_1 :   sendMsg[reqPerm, a], $req(2)$ $\leftarrow$ recvMsg[$req(2)$], $at(3)$

a_2 :   sendMsg[grantPerm, b] $\leftarrow$ recvMsg[reqPerm, b], $at(1) \lor down(2)$
b_2 :   sendMsg[grantPerm, a] $\leftarrow$ recvMsg[reqPerm, a], $at(3) \lor up(2)$

a_3 : $permreq(b)$ $\leftarrow$ recvMsg[reqPerm, b], $at(2) \lor up(1)$
b_3 : $permreq(a)$ $\leftarrow$ recvMsg[reqPerm, a], $at(2) \lor down(3)$

---

[8]In a robot, for instance, appropriate perception subsystems, operating concurrently, will continuously monitor the environment and interpret the sensory input. If they detect a relevant event pattern in the data, they report it to the knowledge system of the robot in the form of a perception event message.

a_4 :   sendMsg[req(1), a] $\leftarrow$ recvMsg[timeout], $at(2) \wedge permreq(b)$
b_4 :   sendMsg[req(3), b] $\leftarrow$ recvMsg[timeout], $at(2) \wedge permreq(a)$

a_5 :   do(mvup), $up(1) \wedge -at(1) \leftarrow$ recvMsg[grantPerm, b], $at(1) \wedge req(2)$
b_5 :   do(mvdown), $down(3) \wedge -at(3) \leftarrow$ recvMsg[grantPerm, a], $at(3) \wedge req(2)$

a_6 :   do(mvdown), $req(1) \wedge down(2) \wedge -at(2) \leftarrow$ recvMsg[req(1)], $at(2)$
b_6 :   do(mvup), $req(3) \wedge up(2) \wedge -at(2) \leftarrow$ recvMsg[req(3)], $at(2)$

a_7 :   sendMsg[grantPerm, b], $-permreq(b)$
      $\leftarrow$ recvMsg[req(1)], $at(2) \wedge permreq(b)$
b_7 :   sendMsg[grantPerm, a], $-permreq(a)$
      $\leftarrow$ recvMsg[req(3)], $at(2) \wedge permreq(a)$

a_8, b_8 :   do(halt), $at(x) \wedge -req(x) \wedge -up(x-1)$
      $\leftarrow$ recvMsg[arrAt(x)], $req(x) \wedge up(x-1)$

a_9, b_9 :   do(halt), $at(x) \wedge -req(x) \wedge -down(x+1)$
      $\leftarrow$ recvMsg[arrAt(x)], $req(x) \wedge down(x+1)$

Elevator a needs only the rules $a_1, \ldots, a_9$, while elevator b needs only the rules $b_1, \ldots, b_9$. Notice that when one of the elevators is at(2), the timeout mechanism of rule 4 avoids a deadlock by simulating a request to depart.

In all elevator examples we have tacitly used the knowledge system **A** of relational databases. This was sufficient for the simple forms of elevator knowledge where we do not have to deal with incomplete information. Other domains, where incomplete and possibly inconsistent information has to be processed, would require more sophisticated knowledge systems (such as uncertain or defeasible factbases).

5   Formal Specification of Single-Agent Systems

A vivid agent consists of

1. a mental state $M = \langle X, TL, CI \rangle$, comprising

   (a) a knowledge base X representing its *beliefs*,

   (b) a list of *tasks* TL the agent has to carry out,

   (c) a list of goal/plan pairs $CI = [G_1/P_1, \ldots, G_n/P_n]$, where P_i is a plan to achieve G_i, called *current intentions*;

2. an event queue EQ recording perception and communication events in the form of incoming mesages,

3. a set AR of *action rules* describing the available action types which together with the goal list and task list are the basis for planning and plan execution, and

4. a set RR of *reaction rules*, consisting of private reaction and interaction rules which code the reactive and communicative behavior.

In a single-agent domain, there is no need for interaction rules, since there is no inter-agent communication.

Every knowledge system $K = \langle L_{\text{KB}}, \vdash, L_{\text{Query}}, \text{Upd}, L_{\text{Input}} \rangle$ can be extended to an *agent knowledge system AgK* by adding a set of private action schemes *Act*, and a set of perception event schemes *PEvt*, which together with a knowledge base schema form the schema of a single-agent domain. In *AgK*, an agent is specified as a 4-tuple $\langle M, EQ, AR, RR \rangle$, consisting of a *mental state M*, an event queue *EQ*, and a set of action and reaction rules

$$AR \subseteq L_{\text{Act}} \times L_{\text{Input}} \times L_{\text{Query}}$$
$$RR \subseteq L_{\text{Act}} \times L_{\text{Input}} \times L_{\text{PEvt}} \times L_{\text{Query}}$$

The *mental state M* of an agent comprises its beliefs, its tasks, and its current intentions: $M = \langle X, TL, CI \rangle$, such that $X \in L_{\text{KB}}$, and $TL \subseteq L_{\text{Query}}^0$, and for each goal/plan pair G/P from CI, $G \in L_{\text{Query}}^0$, and P is a sequence of action rules, $P \in AR^*$. The tuple $\langle TL, CI \rangle$ is called *intention state*. The *agent state* consist of the mental state and the event queue of the agent, i.e. it is a pair $\langle M, EQ \rangle$, such that EQ is a sequence (list) of instantiated event expressions from L_{Evt}^0. We use the Prolog style list notation for event queues: $EQ = [\varepsilon | RestQ]$, where the head of the list, $\varepsilon = head(EQ)$, denotes the current event, and $RestQ = tail(EQ)$ denotes the tail of EQ. We write $EQ_1 + EQ_2$ for the concatenation of EQ_1 and EQ_2.

In the next sections, we shall show that agent specifications $\langle M, EQ, AR, RR \rangle$ are directly executable.

5.1 Operational Semantics of Private Reaction Rules

We now make the parameters of private actions and of events explicit by writing $\alpha(V) \in L_{\text{Act}}^x$, and $\varepsilon(U) \in L_{\text{Evt}}^x$, such that U, V are suitable list of parameters. For brevity, we use the following notation for a private reaction rule:

$$\text{do}(\alpha(V)), E \leftarrow \text{rM}[\varepsilon(U), S], C$$

Let u be any list of ground terms, such that $\varepsilon(u)$ is an admissible event expression. Whenever there is a new message, say $\varepsilon(u)$, it is popped from the event queue, i.e. $\text{rM}[\varepsilon(u), s]$ holds, where s is the sender responsible for the event,

The concurrent execution of all private reactions triggered by the event $\langle \varepsilon(u), s \rangle$ corresponds to the following transition of the agent state $\langle M, EQ \rangle$:

$$RR(M, [\langle \varepsilon(u), s \rangle | RestQ]) = \langle RR_{\varepsilon(u),s}(M),\ RestQ \rangle$$

where the set $RR_{\varepsilon(u),s}$ of private action rules triggered by the event $\langle \varepsilon(u), s \rangle$ is defined as

$$RR_{\varepsilon(u),s} = \{\text{do}(\alpha(V\sigma)), E\sigma \leftarrow C\sigma \ : \ (\text{do}(\alpha(V)), E \leftarrow \text{rM}[\varepsilon(U), S], C) \in RR$$
$$\&\ u = U\nu \ \&\ \sigma = \nu \cup \{S/s\}\}$$

and the concurrent execution of a set of action rules R in the mental state M yields the update

$$R(M) = \mathsf{Upd}(M, \{E\sigma : E \leftarrow C \in \dot{R} \ \& \ M \vdash C\sigma\})$$

where $\dot{R} = \{\dot{r} : r \in R\}$ denotes the epistemic projection of R.

6 Formal Specification of Multi-Agent Systems

An agent knowledge system AgK can be extended to a homogeneous *multiagent knowledge system* MAK by adding a set of communication event schemas $CEvt$ which represents the language of inter-agent communication. In MAK, the knowledge base of an agent is a 4-tuple $\mathcal{A} = \langle M, EQ, AR, RR \rangle$, such that AR and RR now also comprise communicative (re)action rules:

$$AR \subseteq (L_{\text{Act}} \cup L_{\text{CEvt}}) \times L_{\text{Input}} \times L_{\text{Query}}$$
$$RR \subseteq (L_{\text{Act}} \cup L_{\text{CEvt}}) \times L_{\text{Input}} \times L_{\text{Evt}} \times L_{\text{Query}}$$

A multi-agent system $\mathcal{S}$ is a tuple of agents:

$$\mathcal{S} = \langle \mathcal{A}_1, \ldots, \mathcal{A}_m \rangle$$

The state of agent $\mathcal{A}_i$ is denoted by $\mathcal{A}_i = \langle M_i, EQ_i \rangle$. The global state S of a multi-agent system $\mathcal{S}$ is the corresponding tuple of agent states: $S = \langle A_1, \ldots, A_m \rangle$.

In the next section, we shall show that $\mathcal{S}$ is not only a formal, but also an *executable specification* of a multi-agent system.

6.1 Operational Semantics of Interaction Rules

We briefly describe the operational semantics of interaction rules

$$\mathsf{sM}[\eta(T), R], E \ \leftarrow \ \mathsf{rM}[\varepsilon(U), S], C$$

The concurrent execution of a set of action rules R in the mental state M yields the update

$$R(M) = \mathsf{Upd}(M, \{E\sigma : E \leftarrow C \in \dot{R} \ \& \ M \vdash C\sigma\})$$

where $\dot{R} = \{\dot{r} : r \in R\}$. In addition, we shall need the set of all communication events created by a set of action rules R, and addressed to agent i

$$CE_i(R, M) = \{\eta(T\sigma) \ : \ [\mathsf{sM}[\eta(T), R], E \leftarrow C] \in R \ \& \ M \vdash C\sigma \ \& \ R\sigma = i\}$$

We can now define the concurrent execution of a set of actions by agent $\mathcal{A}_i$ as the application of the resp. set of action rules R to the multi-agent system state S at component i by setting $R(i, \langle A_1, \ldots, A_m \rangle) = \langle A'_1, \ldots, A'_m \rangle$, where

$$
\begin{aligned}
A'_i &= \langle R(M_i), \ EQ_i + CE_i(R, M_i) \rangle \\
A'_j &= \langle M_j, \ EQ_j + CE_j(R, M_i) \rangle \qquad (j \neq i)
\end{aligned}
$$

Given a set of reaction rules RR, the set of action rules triggered by the event $\langle \varepsilon(u), s \rangle$ is defined as $RR^{\varepsilon(u),s}$, where

$$RR^{\varepsilon(u),s} = \{A\sigma, E\sigma \leftarrow C\sigma \;\; : \;\; [A, E \leftarrow \mathsf{rM}[\varepsilon(U), S], C] \in RR$$
$$\& \;\; u = U\nu \;\; \& \;\; \sigma = \nu \cup \{S/s\}\}$$

where $A\sigma = \mathsf{sM}[\eta(T\sigma), R\sigma]$, or $A\sigma = \mathsf{do}(\alpha(V\sigma))$. Finally, the concurrent execution of all reactions of agent i triggered by an event Evt corresponds to a transition of $\mathcal{S}$, denoted $RR(i, S)$, which is given by the application of the set of action rules RR_i^{Evt} at component i:

$$RR(i, S) = RR(i, \langle A_1, \ldots, \langle M_i, [Evt|RestQ]\rangle, \ldots, A_m\rangle)$$
$$= RR_i^{Evt}(i, \langle A_1, \ldots, \langle M_i, RestQ\rangle, \ldots, A_m\rangle)$$

Example 5 *In the communicating elevator scenario, where $\mathcal{S} = \langle A_1, A_2\rangle$, the initial agent states are $A_1^0 = \langle\{at(1)\}, [req(2)]\rangle$, resp. $A_2^0 = \langle\{at(2)\}, [req(3)]\rangle$, and the reaction rules are $RR_1 = \{a_1, \ldots, a_9\}$, resp. $RR_2 = \{b_1, \ldots, b_9\}$, we obtain the following transitions:*

$$RR(1, S_0) = R_1^{req(2)}(1, \langle\langle\{at(1)\}, []\rangle, \langle\{at(2)\}, [req(3)]\rangle\rangle)$$
$$= \langle\langle a_1(\{at(1)\}), []\rangle, \langle\{at(2)\}, [req(3), reqPerm]\rangle\rangle$$
$$= \langle\langle\{at(1), req(2)\}, []\rangle, \langle\{at(2)\}, [req(3), reqPerm]\rangle\rangle$$

$$RR(2, S_0) = R_2^{req(3)}(2, \langle\langle\{at(1)\}, [req(2)]\rangle, \langle\{at(2)\}, []\rangle\rangle)$$
$$= \langle\langle\{at(1)\}\rangle, [req(2)]\rangle, \langle b_6(\{at(2)\}), []\rangle\rangle$$
$$= \langle\langle\{at(1)\}\rangle, [req(2)]\rangle, \langle\{req(3), up(2)\}, []\rangle\rangle$$

$$S_1 = RR(1, RR(2, S_0)) = RR(2, RR(1, S_0))$$
$$= \langle\langle\{at(1), req(2)\}\rangle, []\rangle, \langle\{req(3), up(2)\}\rangle, [reqPerm]\rangle\rangle$$

$$S_2 = RR(2, S_1)$$
$$= \langle\langle\{at(1), req(2)\}\rangle, [grantPerm]\rangle, \langle\{req(3), up(2)\}\rangle, []\rangle\rangle$$

$$S_3 = RR(1, S_2)$$
$$= \langle\langle\{up(1), req(2)\}\rangle, []\rangle, \langle\{req(3), up(2)\}\rangle, []\rangle\rangle$$

Since by assumption, $up(x) \rightsquigarrow \mathsf{recvMsg}[arrAt(x+1)]$ holds, elevator a will receive the message $arrAt(2)$, and elevator b will receive $arrAt(3)$, i.e.

$$S_4 = \langle\langle\{up(1), req(2)\}\rangle, [arrAt(2)]\rangle, \langle\{req(3), up(2)\}\rangle, [arrAt(3)]\rangle\rangle$$

$$S_5 = RR(1, RR(2, S_4))$$
$$= \langle\langle\{at(2)\}\rangle, []\rangle, \langle\{at(3)\}\rangle, []\rangle\rangle$$

6.2 Multi-Agent Systems as State Transition Systems

Assuming the principle of *nondeterministic interleaving* of (possibly concurrent) state changing events, the temporal behavior of a multi-agent system can be described by means of a *labelled transition system*. As in the case of single-agent systems, we have five kinds of transitions transforming a mulit-agent system state $S = \langle A_1, \ldots, A_m \rangle$ with $A_i = \langle M_i, EQ_i \rangle$, and $M_i = \langle X_i, TL_i, CI_i \rangle$:

(Perception) An incoming event message ε at agent i yields the transition $S \xrightarrow{i,\varepsilon} S'$, where $S' = S$, except that for A_i, $EQ'_i = EQ_i + \varepsilon$.

(Reaction) A (possibly concurrent) reaction RR_i^ε of agent i in response to an event $\varepsilon = head(EQ_i)$ yields the transition $S \xrightarrow{RR_i^\varepsilon} S'$, where $S' = RR_i^\varepsilon(i, \hat{S})$, and $\hat{S} = S$ except that $\hat{A}_i = \langle M_i, tail(EQ_i) \rangle$.

(Planning) If $CI_i = []$, or for all G/P in CI_i, $head(P)$ is not executable, then deliberative planning by agent i for the topmost goal G from $TL_i = [G|RestT]$, yields the transition $S \xrightarrow{plan(i,G)} S'$, where $S' = S$, except that $CI'_i = G/P + CI_i$ such that P is a plan to achieve G, i.e. $P(X_i) \vdash G$. If there is no such plan for G, the task list is exhaustively shifted, $TL_i = tail(TL_i) + head(TL_i)$ in order to search an achievable goal.

(Action) If $G/P = head(CI)$, an action $r = head(P)$ which is executable, i.e. $X_i \vdash Cond(r)$, and planned by agent i, yields the transition $S \xrightarrow{i,r} S'$, where $S' = S$, except that for A_i, $X'_i = \dot{r}(X_i)$, $P' = tail(P)$, and $CI'_i = G/P' + tail(CI_i)$ if $P' \neq []$, otherwise $CI'_i = tail(CI_i)$, and finally TL'_i is cleaned up: every task T from TL'_i which is now solved, $X'_i \vdash T$, is deleted from TL'_i.

(Replanning) If $G/P = head(CI_i)$, a planned action $r = head(P)$ which is not executable by agent i, i.e. $X_i \nvdash Cond(r)$, yields the transition $S \xrightarrow{i,r} S'$, where $S' = S$, except that $CI'_i = G/P' + tail(CI_i)$ such that $P' = N + P$, if there is a plan $N \in AR_i^*$ such that $N(X_i) \vdash Cond(r)$, or otherwise $CI'_i = tail(CI_i) + G/P$ (i.e. the currently unachievable goal G is postponed).

Notice that we assume that planning and plan execution may only take place if there is no need to react in response to an event, and that planning, (planned) actions, and (concurrent) reactions can be atomically executed.

Definition 3 (Execution History)   *An execution history of a multi-agent system is a chain of state transitions $S_0 \xrightarrow{t_0} S_1 \xrightarrow{t_1} \ldots$, where each t_i corresponds to one of the transitions listed above. A history can be finite or infinite. By definition, a finite history ends in a state. The set of all histories of a multi-agent system S is denoted by* Hist(S).

For multi-agent system histories, we need the notion of *fairness*.

Definition 4 (Enabled Agent)   *We say that an agent A_i is enabled if its event queue, its list of current intentions, or its task list is nonempty.*

Definition 5 (Fairness) [9]

1. *A finite history of a multi-agent system S is called* fair, *if in its final state no agent is enabled.*

2. *An infinite history H of S is called* fair, *if for all agents A_i, either H contains an infinite number of non-perception transitions of A_i, or it contains an infinite number of states where A_i is not enabled.*

We shall denote the set of all fair histories of S by FHist(S).

6.3 Assertional Reasoning

Definition 6 (S-Queries) *Let S be a homogeneous multi-agent system, and let $L = \{B_i F : F \in L_{\text{Query}}\} \cup \{T_i F : F \in L_{\text{Query}}\} \cup \{rM_i[\varepsilon] : \varepsilon \in L_{\text{Evt}}\}$. Then, $L_{SQ} = L(-, \wedge, \vee)$ denotes the set of multi-agent system query formulas.*

Inference for S-queries on the basis of a state $S = \langle A_1, \ldots, A_m \rangle$ with $A_i = \langle M_i, EQ_i \rangle$, and $M_i = \langle X_i, TL_i, CI_i \rangle$, is defined as follows.

$$
\begin{array}{llll}
S & \vdash & B_i F & \text{iff} \quad X_i \vdash F \\
S & \vdash & -B_i F & \text{iff} \quad X_i \not\vdash F \\
S & \vdash & T_i F & \text{iff} \quad F \in TL_i \\
S & \vdash & -T_i F & \text{iff} \quad F \notin TL_i \\
S & \vdash & rM_i[\varepsilon] & \text{iff} \quad \varepsilon = head(EQ_i) \\
S & \vdash & -rM_i[\varepsilon] & \text{iff} \quad \varepsilon \neq head(EQ_i)
\end{array}
$$

In order to be able to state fairness assumptions for the environment of an agent, and to prove correctness assertions with respect to an agent specification, we define two operators Inv, and $\rightsquigarrow$, which represent a fragment of linear-time temporal logic.[10] Assertions about multi-agent systems refer only to fair histories.

Definition 7 (Invariance and Leads-To Assertions) *Let $H \in$ Hist(S), and let $F, G \in L^0_{SQ}$. We say that H satisfies the invariance assertion Inv(F), symbolically $H \models$ Inv(F), iff for all $S \in H$, $S \vdash F$. We say that H satisfies the leads-to assertion $F \rightsquigarrow G$, symbolically $H \models F \rightsquigarrow G$, if for all states $S \in H$ with $S \vdash F$, there is a later state $S' \in H$, $S \leq S'$, such that $S' \vdash G$. An assertion ϕ holds in S, symbolically $S \models \phi$, if for all fair histories $H \in$ FHist(S), $H \models \phi$.*

Definition 8 (Multi-Agent Domain Description) *A multi-agent domain description S, Φ consists of a multi-agent system specification S, and a set of assertions Φ expressing assumptions about the environment of the agents. Such a domain description satisfies an assertion ϕ, if ϕ is satisfied by all fair histories of S satisfying Φ. Formally,*

$$
S, \Phi \models \phi \quad \text{iff} \quad \text{f.a. } H \in \text{FHist}(S) : H \models \Phi \Rightarrow H \models \phi
$$

---

[9]In [Sha93], this is called *weak fairness* as opposed to a stronger notion of fairness which we shall not consider.

[10]See [MP92], where $\Box F$ corresponds to Inv(F), and $\Box(F \to \Diamond G)$ corresponds to $F \rightsquigarrow G$.

Example 6   *For the communicating elevators system from example 4, we might want to prove the safety property, that it is never the case that the lower elevator goes up to the second floor while the upper one goes down to the second floor, or is currently halting at the second floor, expressed as*

$$S, \Phi \models \mathsf{Inv}(-[\mathsf{B}_1 up(1) \wedge (\mathsf{B}_2 down(3) \vee \mathsf{B}_2 at(2))])$$

where $\Phi = \{up(k) \leadsto \mathsf{rM}_i[\mathrm{at}(k+1)], down(k) \leadsto \mathsf{rM}_i[\mathrm{at}(k-1)]\}$. Also we might want to prove

$$S, \Phi \models \mathsf{rM}_i[\mathrm{req}(2)] \leadsto \mathsf{B}_i at(2)$$

expressing the progress property that both elevators will eventually serve every request from floor 2.

7   Related Work

Although we depart considerably from it, our present work has been much inspired by Shoham's [Sho93] proposal of *agent-oriented programming (AOP)*. Our action rules may be compared with Shoham's *conditional action statements*. The major differences seem to be that 1) our work is based on our theory of knowledge systems (allowing for negation-as-failure in the query language, and for various forms of updating, including deletion/contraction), while Shoham's AGENT-0 system is defined on the basis of temporal fact knowledge using a kind of standard logical inference and recency-preferring revision of facts; 2) there is no genuine concept of actions in Shoham's AOP, actions are simply represented as facts, and therefore conditional action statements in AOP are not able to account for the epistemic effects of an action which is, on the other hand, essential in our account of actions; 3) AOP is much more ambitious about temporal reasoning using appropriate modalities, and it uses a system clock for synchronization purposes, while our communication acts are realized by asynchronous message passing.

In [Woo92], Wooldridge has defined a formal model of a multi-agent system along the same lines we have followed. Instead of a knowledge system in our sense, he uses the 'deduction model of belief' from [Kon86], and extends it by adding a *belief revision function* corresponding to the update operation of our knowledge systems. His *action rules* correspond to our epistemic action rules, and his *message rules* correspond to our communicative action rules. However, perception and reaction are not explicitly considered. Also, the mental state of an agent in this model consists only of beliefs, and since there is no consideration of goals, or tasks, the agent model does not account for planning and plan execution. Wooldridge presents an interleaved execution model for his multi-agent system model, but he does not define fairness conditions for it.

Our framework of assertional reasoning for multi-agent systems is a generalization of the approach of [Sha93] for concurrent systems based on the temporal logic concepts of Hoare [Hoa69], and Manna and Pnueli [MP92]. Since in the theory of concurrent systems, knowledge states consist of the values of state variables, there is no consideration of more complex states such as those of knowledge bases and the related concepts of inference and update. While the system model of [Sha93] contains only one kind of state changing event, corresponding to assignment statements, we have to consider five kinds of transitions in order to take into account all relevant state changes of a multi-agent system: perception, reaction, planning, plan execution, and replanning.

In recent years, 'hybrid' agent architectures combining reactive and deliberative behavior have become increasingly important (see, e.g., [Mue94]). This indicates that, in practice, neither the traditional purely deliberative logic-based approaches, nor the more recently fashionable purely reactive approaches are appropriate for the design and validation of agent systems. Our proposal of *vivid agents* with action and reaction rules provides a theoretical foundation for such hybrid architectures.

8 Conclusion

The concept of vivid agents is a powerful extension of the concept of knowledge bases. It combines static knowledge in the form of a declarative knowledge base with dynamic knowledge in the form of action and reaction rules. We have shown how to model deliberative, reactive and communicative behavior in this framework. We also outlined methods of assertional reasoning for single-agent and multi-agent systems. We hope that our model can serve as a basis for the formalization of more high-level concepts such as values, emotions, social structures, social laws, etc.

Acknowledgements: Thanks to J.J. Alferes, J.N. Aparicio, C. Damasio, R. Li, and L.M. Pereira for stimulating discussions in our working group.

References

[Bel77] N.D. Belnap: A Useful Four-valued Logic, in G. Epstein and J.M. Dunn (Eds.), *Modern Uses of Many-valued Logic*, Reidel 1977, 8–37.

[FN71] R.E. Fikes and N. Nilsson: "STRIPS: A New Approach to the Application of Theorem Proving to Problem Solving", *Artificial Intelligence* **5**:2 (1971), 189–208.

[Hoa69] C.A.R. Hoare: An Axiomatic Basis for Computer Programming, *Communications of the ACM* **12**:10 (1969), 576–583.

[Kon86] K. Konolige: *A Deduction Model of Belief*, Pitman and Morgan Kaufmann, San Mateo (CA), 1986.

[Lev84] H.J. Levesque: Foundations of a Functional Approach to Knowledge Representation, *AI* **23**:2 (1984), 155-212.

[McCD89] D.R. McCarthy and U. Dayal: The Architecture of an Active Database Management System, *Proc. ACM SIGMOD-89*, 1989, 215–224.

[MP92] Z. Manna and A. Pnueli: *The Temporal Logic of Reactive and Concurrent Systems*, Springer-Verlag, New York, 1992.

[Mue94] J.P. Müller: A Conceptual Model of Agent Interaction, in S.M. Deen (Ed.), *Proc. 2nd Int. Working Conf. on Cooperating Knowledge-Based Systems*, DAKE Centre, Univ. of Keele, 1994, 213–233.

[Sha93] A.U. Shankar: An Introduction to Assertional Reasoning for Concurrent Systems, *ACM Computing Surveys* **25**:3 (1993), 225–262.

[Sho93] Y. Shoham: Agent-Oriented Programming, *Artificial Intelligence* **60** (1993), 51–92.

[Wag94a] G. Wagner: *Vivid Logic – Knowledge-Based Reasoning with Two Kinds of Negation*, Springer Lecture Notes in AI **764** (1994).

[Wag94b] G. Wagner: *Disjunctive, Deductive and Active Knowledge Bases*, LWI Report 22/1994, Freie Universität Berlin; available as ddakbs.dvi.gz, resp. ddakbs.ps.gz, via ftp from ftp.inf.fu-berlin.de in the directory /pub/reports/wagner (notice that the file has to be 'gunzip'ed).

[Wag95] G. Wagner: From Information Systems to Knowledge Systems, in E. Falkenberg (Ed.), *Proc. of IFIP Conf. on Information System Concepts (ISCO-3)*, Chapman & Hall, London, 1995.

[Woo92] M. Wooldridge: *The Logical Modelling of Computational Multi-Agent Systems*, PhD thesis, Dep. of Computation, Manchester Metropolitan University, Manchester, UK, 1992.

AgentSpeak(L): BDI Agents Speak Out in a Logical Computable Language

Anand S. Rao

Australian Artificial Intelligence Institute
Level 6, 171 La Trobe Street, Melbourne
Victoria 3000, Australia
Email: anand@aaii.oz.au

Abstract. Belief-Desire-Intention (BDI) agents have been investigated by many researchers from both a theoretical specification perspective and a practical design perspective. However, there still remains a large gap between theory and practice. The main reason for this has been the complexity of theorem-proving or model-checking in these expressive specification logics. Hence, the implemented BDI systems have tended to use the three major attitudes as data structures, rather than as modal operators. In this paper, we provide an alternative formalization of BDI agents by providing an operational and proof-theoretic semantics of a language AgentSpeak(L). This language can be viewed as an abstraction of one of the implemented BDI systems (i.e., PRS) and allows agent programs to be written and interpreted in a manner similar to that of horn-clause logic programs. We show how to perform derivations in this logic using a simple example. These derivations can then be used to prove the properties satisfied by BDI agents.

1 Introduction

The specification, design, verification, and applications of a particular type of agents, called BDI agents, have received a great deal of attention in recent years. BDI agents are systems that are situated in a changing environment, receive continuous perceptual input, and take actions to affect their environment, all based on their internal mental state. Beliefs, desires, and intentions are the three primary mental attitudes and they capture the informational, motivational, and decision components of an agent, respectively. In addition to these attitudes, other notions such as commitments, capabilities, know-how, etc. have been investigated. Sophisticated, multi-modal, temporal, action, and dynamic logics have been used to formalize some of these notions [2, 6, 8, 13, 18, 20, 21]. The complexity of theorem-proving and the completeness of these logics have not been clear [12, 23].

On the other hand, there are a number of implementations of BDI agents [1, 3, 10, 17] that are being used successfully in critical application domains. These implementations have made a number of simplifying assumptions and modelled the attitudes of beliefs, desires, and intentions as data structures. Also, user written plans or programs speed up the computation in these systems. The complexity of the code written for these systems and the simplifying assumptions made by them have meant that the implemented systems have lacked a strong theoretical underpinning. The specification logics have shed very little light on the practical problems. As a result the two streams of work seem to be diverging.

Our earlier attempt to bridge this gap between theory and practice has concentrated on providing an abstract BDI architecture [14], that serves both as an idealization of an implemented system and also as a vehicle for investigating certain theoretical properties. Due to its abstraction this work was unable to show a one-to-one correspondence between the model theory, proof theory, and the abstract interpreter. The holy grail of BDI agent research is to show such a one-to-one correspondence with a reasonably useful and expressive language.

This paper makes another attempt at specifying such a logical language. Unlike some of the previous attempts, it takes as its starting point one of the implemented systems and formalizes its operational semantics. The implemented system being considered is the Procedural Reasoning System (PRS) [5] and its more recent incarnation, the Distributed Multi-Agent Reasoning System (dMARS). The language AgentSpeak(L) can be viewed as a simplified, textual language of PRS or dMARS. The language and its operational semantics are similar to the implemented system in their essential details. The implemented system has more language constructs to make the task of agent programming easier.

AgentSpeak(L) is a programming language based on a restricted first-order language with events and actions. The behaviour of the agent (i.e., its interaction with the environment) is dictated by the programs written in AgentSpeak(L). The beliefs, desires, and intentions of the agent are not explicitly represented as modal formulas. Instead, we as designers can ascribe these notions to agents written in AgentSpeak(L). The current state of the agent, which is a model of itself, its environment, and other agents, can be viewed as its current belief state; states which the agent wants to bring about based on its external or internal stimuli can be viewed as desires; and the adoption of programs to satisfy such stimuli can be viewed as intentions. This shift in perspective of taking a simple specification language as the execution model of an agent and then ascribing the mental attitudes of beliefs, desires, and intentions, from an external viewpoint is likely to have a better chance of unifying theory and practice.

In Section 2 we discuss the agent language AgentSpeak(L). The specification language consists of a set of basc beliefs (or facts in the logic programming sense) and a set of plans. Plans are context-sensitive, event-invoked recipes that allow hierarchical decomposition of goals as well as the execution of actions. Although syntactically plans look similar to the definite clauses of logic programming languages, they are quite different in their behaviour.

Section 3 formalizes the operational semantics of AgentSpeak(L). At run-time an agent can be viewed as consisting of a set of beliefs, a set of plans, a set of intentions, a set of events, a set of actions, and a set of selection functions. The selection of plans, their adoption as intentions, and the execution of these intentions are described formally in this section. An interpreter for AgentSpeak(L) is given and a simple example is used to illustrate some of the definitions and the operational semantics of the language.

In Section 4, we provide the proof theory of the language. The proof theory is given as a labeled transition system. Proof rules define the transition of the agent from one configuration to the next. These transitions have a direct relationship to the operational semantics of the language and hence help to establish the strong correspondence between the AgentSpeak(L) interpreter and its proof theory.

The primary contribution of this work is in opening up an alternative, restricted, first-order characterization of BDI agents. We hope that the operational and proof-theoretic semantics of AgentSpeak(L) will stimulate research in both the pragmatic and theoretical aspects of BDI agents.

2 Agent Programs

In this section, we introduce the language for writing agent programs. The *alphabet* of the formal language consists of variables, constants, function symbols, predicate symbols, action symbols, connectives, quantifiers, and punctuation symbols. Apart from first-order connectives, we also use ! (for achievement), ? (for test), ; (for sequencing), and ← (for implication)[1]. Standard first-order definitions of terms, first-order formulas, closed formulas, and free and bound occurrences of variables are used.

Definition 1. If b is a predicate symbol, and $t_1,...,t_n$ are terms then $b(t_1,...,t_n)$ or $b(\mathbf{t})$ is a belief atom. If $b(\mathbf{t})$ and $c(\mathbf{s})$ are belief atoms, $b(\mathbf{t}) \wedge c(\mathbf{s})$, and $\neg b(\mathbf{t})$ are *beliefs*. A belief atom or its negation will be referred to as a *belief literal*. A ground belief atom will be called a *base belief*.

For example, let us consider a traffic-world simulation, where there are four adjacent lanes and cars can appear in any lane and move in the same lane from north to south. Waste paper can appear on any of the lanes and a robot has to pick up the waste paper and place it in the bin. While doing this the robot must not be in the same lane as the car, as it runs the risk of getting run over by the car. Consider that we are writing agent programs for such a robot.

The beliefs of such an agent represent the configuration of the lanes and the locations of the robot, cars, waste, and the bin (i.e., adjacent(X,Y), location(robot, X), location(car, X), etc.). The base beliefs of such an agent are ground instances of belief atoms (i.e., adjacent(a,b), location(robot, a), etc.).

A goal[2] is a state of the system which the agent wants to bring about. We consider two types of goals: an *achievement goal* and a *test goal*. An achievement goal, written as !$g(\mathbf{t})$ states that the agent wants to achieve a state where $g(\mathbf{t})$ is a true belief. A test goal, written as ?$g(\mathbf{t})$ states that the agent wants to test if the formula $g(\mathbf{t})$ is a true belief or not. In our example, clearing the waste on a particular lane can be stated as an achievement goal, i.e., !cleared(b), and seeing if the car is in a particular lane can be stated as a test goal, i.e., ?location(car, b).

Definition 2. If g is a predicate symbol, and $t_1,...,t_n$ are terms then !$g(t_1,...,t_n)$ (or !$g(\mathbf{t})$) and ?$g(t_1,...,t_n)$ (or ?$g(\mathbf{t})$) are *goals*.

---

[1] In the agent programs we use & for $\wedge$, not for $\neg$, <- for ←. Also, like PROLOG, we require that all negations be ground when evaluated. We use the convention that variables are written in upper-case and constants in lower-case.

[2] In this paper, we discuss only goals, and not desires. Goals can be viewed as adopted desires.

When an agent acquires a new goal or notices a change in its environment, it may trigger additions or deletions to its goals or beliefs. We refer to these events as *triggering events*. We consider the addition/deletion of beliefs/goals as the four triggering events. Addition is denoted by the operator + and deletion is denoted by the operator −. In our example, noticing the waste in a certain lane X, written as +location(waste, X) or acquiring the goal to clear the lane X, written as +!cleared(X) are example of two triggering events.

Definition 3. If $b(t)$ is a belief atom, $!g(t)$ and $?g(t)$ are goals, then $+b(t)$, $-b(t)$ $+!g(t)$, $+?g(t)$, $-!g(t)$, $-?g(t)$ are *triggering events*.

The purpose of an agent is to observe the environment, and based on its observation and its goals, execute certain actions. These actions may change the state of the environment. For example, if move is an action symbol, the robot moving from lane X to lane Y, written as move(X,Y), is an action. This action results in an environmental state where the robot is in lane Y and is no longer in lane X.

Definition 4. If a is an action symbol and $t_1,...,t_n$ are first-order terms, then $a(t_1,...,t_n)$ or $a(t)$ is an action.

An agent has plans which specify the means by which an agent should satisfy an end. A plan consists of a head and a body. The head of a plan consists of a triggering event and a context, separated by a ":". The triggering event specifies why the plan was triggered, i.e., the addition or deletion of a belief or goal. The context of a plan specifies those beliefs that should hold in the agent's set of base beliefs, when the plan is triggered. The body of a plan is a sequence of goals or actions. It specifies the goals the agent should achieve or test, and the actions the agent should execute. For example, we want to write a plan that gets triggered when some waste appears on a particular lane. If the robot is in the same lane as the waste, it will perform the action of picking up the waste, followed by achieving the goal of reaching the bin location, followed by performing the primitive action of putting it in the bin. This plan can be written as:

```
+location(waste,X):location(robot,X) &
                 location(bin,Y)
                 <- pick(waste);
                    !location(robot,Y);
                    drop(waste).            (P1)
```

Consider the plan for the robot to change locations. If it has acquired the goal to move to a location X and it is already in location X, it does not have to do anything and hence the body is true. If the context is such that it is not at the desired location then it needs to find an adjacent lane with no cars in it, and then move to that lane.

```
+!location(robot,X):location(robot,X) <- true.   (P2)

+!location(robot,X):location(robot,Y) &
                 (not (X = Y)) &
```

```
                 adjacent(Y,Z) &
                 (not (location(car, Z)))
                         <- move(Y,Z);
                         +!location(robot,X). (P3)
```

More formally, we have the following definition of plans.

Definition 5. If e is a triggering event, $b_1,...,b_m$ are belief literals, and $h_1,...,h_n$ are goals or actions then $e:b_1 \wedge ... \wedge b_m \leftarrow h_1;...;h_n$ is a *plan*. The expression to the left of the arrow is referred to as the *head* of the plan and the expression to the right of the arrow is referred to as the *body* of the plan. The expression to the right of the colon in the head of a plan is referred to as the *context*. For convenience, we shall rewrite an empty body with the expression *true*.

With this we complete the specification of an agent. In summary, a designer specifies an agent by writing a set of base beliefs and a set of plans. This is similar to a logic programming specification of facts and rules. However, some of the major differences between a logic program and an agent program are as follows:

- In a pure logic program there is no difference between a goal in the body of a rule and the head of a rule. In an agent program the head consists of a triggering event, rather than a goal. This allows for a more expressive invocation of plans by allowing both data-directed (using addition/deletion of beliefs) and goal-directed (using addition/deletion of goals) invocations.
- Rules in a pure logic program are not context-sensitive as plans.
- Rules execute successfully returning a binding for unbound variables; however, execution of plans generates a sequence of ground actions that affect the environment.
- While a goal is being queried the execution of that query cannot be interrupted in a logic program. However, the plans in an agent program can be interrupted.

3 Operational Semantics

Informally, an agent consists of a set of base beliefs, B, a set of plans, P, a set of events, E, a set of actions, A, a set of intentions, I, and three selection functions, $S_\mathcal{E}$, $S_\mathcal{O}$, and $S_\mathcal{I}$. When the agent notices a change in the environment or an external user has asked the system to adopt a goal, an appropriate triggering event is generated. These events correspond to external events. An agent can also generate internal events. Events, internal or external, are asynchronously added to the set of events E. The selection function $S_\mathcal{E}$ selects an event to process from the set of events E. This event is removed from E and is used to unify with the triggering events of the plans in the set P. The plans whose triggering events so unify are called relevant plans and the unifier is called the relevant unifier. Next, the relevant unifier is applied to the context condition and a correct answer substitution is obtained for the context, such that the context is a logical consequence of the set of base beliefs, B. Such plans are called applicable plans or options and the composition of the relevant unifier with the correct answer substitution is called the applicable unifier.

For each event there may be many applicable plans or options. The selection function $\mathcal{S}_O$ chooses one of these plans. Applying the applicable unifier to the chosen option yields the intended means of responding to the triggering event. Each intention is a stack of partially instantiated plans or intention frames. In the case of an external event the intended means is used to create a new intention, which is added to the set of intentions I. In the case of an internal event to add a goal the intended means is pushed on top of an existing intention that triggered the internal event.

Next, the selection function $\mathcal{S}_I$ selects an intention to execute. When the agent executes an intention, it executes the first goal or action of the body of the top of the intention. Executing an achievement goal is equivalent to generating an internal event to add the goal to the current intention. Executing a test goal is equivalent to finding a substitution for the goal which makes it a logical consequence of the base beliefs. If such a substitution is found the test goal is removed from the body of the top of the intention and the substitution is applied to the rest of the body of the top of the intention. Executing an action results in the action being added to the set of actions, A, and it being removed from the body of the top of the intention.

The agent now goes to the set of events, E, and the whole cycle continues until there are no events in E or there is no runnable intention. Now we formalize the above process[3].

The state of an agent at any instant of time can be formally defined as follows:

Definition 6. An *agent* is given by a tuple $<E,B,P,I,A,\mathcal{S}_\mathcal{E},\mathcal{S}_O,\mathcal{S}_I>$, where E is a set of events, B is a set of base beliefs, P is a set of plans, I is a set of intentions, and A is a set of actions. The selection function $\mathcal{S}_\mathcal{E}$ selects an event from the set E; the selection function $\mathcal{S}_O$ selects an option or an applicable plan (see Definition 10) from a set of applicable plans; and $\mathcal{S}_I$ selects an intention from the set I.

The sets B, P, and A are as defined before and are relatively straightforward. Here we describe the sets E and I.

Definition 7. The set I is a set of intentions. Each *intention* is a stack of *partially instantiated plans*, i.e., plans where some of the variables have been instantiated. An intention is denoted by $[p_1\ddagger\ldots\ddagger p_z]$, where p_1 is the bottom of the stack and p_z is the top of the stack. The elements of the stack are delimited by $\ddagger$. For convenience, we shall refer to the intention [+!true:true <- true] as the *true intention* and denote it by T.

Definition 8. The set E consists of events. Each event is a tuple $<e, i>$, where e is a triggering event and i is an intention. If the intention i is the *true intention*, the event is called an *external event*; otherwise it is an *internal event*.

Now we can formally define the notion of relevant and applicable plans and unifiers. As we saw earlier, a triggering event d from the set of events, E, is to be unified with the triggering event of all the plans in the set P. The *most general unifier (mgu)* that unifies these two events is called the relevant unifier. The intention i could be wither the true intention or an existing intention which triggered this event. More formally,

---

[3] The reader can refer to the Appendix for some basic definitions from first-order logic and horn clause logic.

Definition 9. Let $\mathcal{S}_{\mathcal{E}}(E) = \epsilon = <d, i>$ and let p be $e : b_1 \wedge \ldots \wedge b_m \leftarrow h_1; \ldots; h_n$. The plan p is a *relevant plan* with respect to an event ϵ iff there exists a most general unifier σ such that $d\sigma = e\sigma$. σ is called the *relevant unifier* for ϵ.

For example, assume that the triggering event of the event selected from E is

```
+!location(robot,b).
```

The two plans P2 and P3 are relevant for this event with the relevant unifier being $\{X/b\}$.

A relevant plan is also applicable if there exists a substitution which, when composed with the relevant unifier and applied to the context, is a logical consequence of the set of base beliefs B. In other words, the context condition of a relevant plan needs to be a logical consequence of B, for it to be an applicable plan. More formally,

Definition 10. A plan p, denoted by $e : b_1 \wedge \ldots \wedge b_m \leftarrow h_1; \ldots; h_n$ is an *applicable plan* with respect to an event ϵ iff there exists a relevant unifier σ for ϵ and there exists a substitution θ such that $\forall(b_1 \wedge \ldots \wedge b_m)\sigma\theta$ is a logical consequence of B. The composition $\sigma\theta$ is referred to as the *applicable unifier* for ϵ and θ is referred to as the *correct answer substitution*.

Continuing with the same example, consider that the set of base beliefs is given by

```
adjacent(a,b).
adjacent(b,c).
adjacent(c,d).
location(robot,a).
location(waste,b).
location(bin,d).
```

The applicable unifier is $\{X/b, Y/a, Z/b\}$ and only plan P3 is applicable.

Depending on the type of the event (i.e., internal or external), the intention will be different. In the case of external events, the intended means is obtained by first selecting an applicable plan for that event and then applying the applicable unifier to the body of the plan. This intended means is used to create a new intention which is added to the set of intentions I.

Definition 11. Let $\mathcal{S}_{\mathcal{O}}(O_\epsilon) = p$, where O_ϵ is the set of all applicable plans or options for the event $\epsilon = <d, i>$ and p is $e : b_1 \wedge \ldots \wedge b_m \leftarrow h_1; \ldots; h_n$. The plan p is *intended* with respect to an event ϵ, where i is the true intention iff there exists an applicable unifier σ such that $[+!true : true \leftarrow true\ddagger(e : b_1 \wedge \ldots \wedge b_m \leftarrow h_1; \ldots; h_n)\sigma] \in I$.

In our example, the only applicable plan P3 will be intended with the intention I now being

```
[+!location(robot,b): location(robot,a) &
                       not(b = a) &
                       adjacent(a, b) &
                       not(location(car,b)) <-
                          move(a,b);
                          +!location(robot,b)].
```

In the case of internal events the intended means for the achievement goal is pushed on top of the existing intention that triggered the internal event.

Definition 12. Let $\mathcal{S}_O(O_\epsilon) = p$, where O_ϵ is the set of all applicable plans or options for the event $\epsilon = <d, [p_1\ddagger\ldots\ddagger f : c_1 \wedge \ldots \wedge c_y \leftarrow !g(\mathbf{t}); h_2; \ldots; h_n] >$, and p is $+!g(\mathbf{s}): b_1 \wedge \ldots \wedge b_m \leftarrow k_1; \ldots; k_j$. The plan p is *intended* with respect to an event ϵ iff there exists an applicable unifier σ such that $[p_1\ddagger\ldots\ddagger f : c_1 \wedge \ldots \wedge c_y \leftarrow !g(\mathbf{t}); h_2; \ldots; h_n\ddagger(+!g(\mathbf{s}) : b_1 \wedge \ldots \wedge b_m)\sigma \leftarrow (k_1; \ldots; k_j)\sigma; (h_2; \ldots; h_n)\sigma] \in I$.

The above definition is very similar to SLD-resolution of logic programming languages. However, the primary difference between the two is that the goal g is called indirectly by generating an event. This gives the agent better real-time control as it can change its focus of attention, if needed, by adopting and executing a different intention. Thus, one can view agent programs as multi-threaded interruptible logic programming clauses.

When an intention is selected and executed, the first formula in the body of the top of the intention can be: (a) an achievement goal; (b) a test goal; or (c) an action; or (d) *true*. In the case of an achievement goal the system executes it by generating an event; in the case of a test goal it looks for a mgu that will unify the goal with the set of base beliefs of the agent, and if such an mgu exists it applies it to the rest of the means; in the case of an action the system adds it to the set of actions A; and in the last case the top of the intention and the achievement goal that was satisfied are removed and the substitution is applied to the rest of the body of that intention.

Definition 13. Let $\mathcal{S}_\mathcal{I}(I) = i$, where i is $[p_1\ddagger\ldots\ddagger f : c_1 \wedge \ldots \wedge c_y \leftarrow !g(\mathbf{t}); h_2; \ldots; h_n]$. The intention i is said to have been *executed* iff $< +!g(\mathbf{t}), i > \in E$.

Definition 14. Let $\mathcal{S}_\mathcal{I}(I) = i$, where i is $[p_1\ddagger\ldots\ddagger f : c_1 \wedge \ldots \wedge c_y \leftarrow ?g(\mathbf{t}); h_2; \ldots; h_n]$. The intention i is said to have been *executed* iff there exists a substitution θ such that $\forall g(\mathbf{t})\theta$ is a logical consequence of B and i is replaced by $[p_1\ddagger\ldots\ddagger(f : c_1 \wedge \ldots \wedge c_y)\theta \leftarrow h_2\theta; \ldots; h_n\theta]$.

Definition 15. Let $\mathcal{S}_\mathcal{I}(I) = i$, where i is $[p_1\ddagger\ldots\ddagger f : c_1 \wedge \ldots \wedge c_y \leftarrow a(\mathbf{t}); h_2; \ldots; h_n]$. The intention i is said to have been *executed* iff $a(\mathbf{t}) \in A$, and i is replaced by $[p_1\ddagger\ldots\ddagger f : c_1 \wedge \ldots \wedge c_y \leftarrow h_2; \ldots; h_n]$.

Definition 16. Let $\mathcal{S}_\mathcal{I}(I) = i$, where i is $[p_1\ddagger\ldots\ddagger p_{z-1}\ddagger!g(\mathbf{t}) : c_1 \wedge \ldots \wedge c_y \leftarrow true]$, where p_{z-1} is $e : b_1 \wedge \ldots \wedge b_x \leftarrow !g(\mathbf{s}); h_2; \ldots; h_n$. The intention i is said to have been *executed* iff there exists a substitution θ such that $g(\mathbf{t})\theta = g(\mathbf{s})\theta$ and i is replaced by $[p_1\ddagger\ldots\ddagger p_{z-1}\ddagger(e : b_1 \wedge \ldots \wedge b_x)\theta \leftarrow (h_2; \ldots; h_n)\theta]$.

Continuing our example, we would execute I and by Definition 15 we would add {move (a, b) } to A and change I to be as follows:

```
[+!location(robot,b): location(robot,a) &
                      not(b = a) &
                      adjacent(a, b) &
                      not(location(car,b)) <-
                        +!location(robot,b)].
```

In the next iteration, after the robot moves from a to b the environment will send the agent a belief update event to change the location of the robot to b. This will result in the belief location(robot,b) being added to the set B and the event +location (robot,b) being added to the set of events, E. As there are no relevant plans for this the system will choose the above intention to execute. Executing this will result in an intention add event being generated and added to the set of events, E; in other words E is {<+!location (robot,b),i>}, where i is the same intention as before. By Definition 12 the relevant plan in this case is P1 with the relevant unifier {X/b}. This plan is also applicable and the applicable unifier is the same. As the body of this plan is true, the intention is satisfied and the set of events is empty. This terminates the execution until the next event is added into the set E.

From the above definitions and description of the operational semantics of the language AgentSpeak(L) we can write an interpreter for AgentSpeak(L). Figure 1 describes such an interpreter. We use the function *top* to return the top of an intention stack; the function *head* to return the head of an intended plan; the function *body* to return the body of an intended plan. In addition, the functions *first* and *rest* are used to return the first element of a sequence, and all but the first element of a sequence. The function *push* takes an intention frame and an intention (i.e., stack of intention frames) and pushes the intention frame on to the top of the intention. The function *pop* takes an intention as an argument and returns the top of the intention.

4 Proof Theory

So far we have presented the operational semantics of AgentSpeak(L). Now we briefly discuss its proof theory based on labeled transition systems.

Definition 17. A *BDI transition system* is a pair $\langle \Gamma; \vdash \rangle$ consisting of:

- A set Γ of *BDI configurations*; and
- A binary transition relation $\vdash \subseteq \Gamma \times \Gamma$.

We define a BDI configuration as follows:

Definition 18. A *BDI configuration* is a tuple of $\langle E_i, B_i, I_i, A_i, i \rangle$, where $E_i \subseteq E$, $B_i \subseteq B$, $I_i \subseteq I$, $A_i \subseteq A$, and i is the label of the transition.

Note that we have not taken the set of plans, P, in the configuration as we have assumed it to be constant. Also, we do not explicitly keep track of goals as they appear as intentions when adopted by the agent. Now we can write transition rules that take an agent from one configuration to its subsequent configuration.

The following proof rule *IntendEnd* gives the transition for intending a plan at the top level. It states how the agent's set of intentions I changes in response to an external event that has been chosen (by the $\mathcal{S}_{\mathcal{E}}$ function) to be processed.

$$(IntendEnd) \frac{< \{\ldots, < +!g(\mathbf{t}), T >, \ldots\}, B_i, I_i, A_i, i >}{< \{\ldots\}, B_i, I_i \cup \{[p\sigma\theta]\}, A_i, i+1 >}$$

Algorithm Interpreter()
```
while E ≠ ∅ do
    ε = < d, i > = S_ℰ(E);
    E = E/ε;
    O_ε = {pθ | θ is an applicable unifier for event ε and plan p}
    if external-event(ε) then I = I ∪ [S_O(O_ε)];
    else push(S_O(O_ε)σ, i), where σ is an applicable unifier for ε;
    case first(body(top(S_I(I)))) = true
        x = pop(S_I(I));
        push(head(top(S_I(I)))θ ← rest(body(top(S_I(I))))θ, S_I(I)),
        where θ is an mgu such that xθ = head(top(S_I(I)))θ;
    case first(body(top(S_I(I)))) = !g(t)
        E = E ∪ <+!g(t), S_I(I)>
    case first(body(top(S_I(I)))) = ?g(t)
        pop(S_I(I));
        push(head(top(S_I(I)))θ ← rest(body(top(S_I(I))))θ, S_I(I)),
        where θ is the correct answer substitution
    case first(body(top(S_I(I)))) = a(t)
        pop(S_I(I));
        push(head(top(S_I(I))) ← rest(body(top(S_I(I)))), S_I(I));
        A = A ∪ {a(t)};
endwhile.
```

Fig. 1. Algorithm for the BDI Interpreter

where $p = +!g(s) : b_1 \wedge \ldots \wedge b_m \leftarrow h_1; \ldots; h_n \in P$, $S_ℰ(E) = < +!g(t), T >$, $g(t)\sigma = g(s)\sigma$ and $\forall (b_1 \wedge \ldots \wedge b_m)\theta$ is a logical consequence of B_i.

The proof rule *IntendMeans* is similar to the previous proof rule, except that the applicable plan is pushed at the top of the intention given as the second argument of the chosen event. More formally we have,

$$(IntendMeans) \frac{< \{\ldots, < +!g(t), j >, \ldots\}, B_i, \{\ldots, [p_1‡ \ldots ‡p_z], \ldots\}, A_i, i >}{< \{\ldots\}, B_i, \{\ldots, [p_1‡ \ldots ‡p_z‡p\sigma\theta], \ldots\}, A_i, i+1 >}$$

where $p_z = f : c_1 \wedge \ldots \wedge c_y \leftarrow !g(t); h_2; \ldots; h_n$, $p = +!g(s) : b_1 \wedge \ldots \wedge b_m \leftarrow k_1; \ldots; k_x$, $S_ℰ(E) = < +!g(t), j >$, j is $[p_1‡ \ldots ‡p_n] >$, $g(t)\sigma = g(s)\sigma$ and $\forall (c_1 \wedge \ldots \wedge c_y)\theta$ is a logical consequence of B_i.

Next, we have four proof rules for execution. The four proof rules are based on the type of the goal or action that appears as the first literal of the body of the top of an intention chosen to be executed by the function S_I. We give the execution proof rule for achieve *ExecAch*, the other proof rules can be written analogously.

$$(ExecAch) \frac{< E_i, B_i, \{\ldots, [p_1‡ \ldots ‡f : c_1 \wedge \ldots \wedge c_y \leftarrow !g(t); h_2; \ldots; h_n], \ldots\}, A_i, i >}{< E_i \cup \{< +!g(t), j >\}, B_i, \{\ldots, [p_1‡ \ldots ‡p_z], \ldots\}, A_i, i+1 >}$$

where $S_I(I_i) = j = [p_1‡ \ldots ‡p_z]$ and $p_z = f : c_1 \wedge \ldots \wedge c_y \leftarrow !g(t); h_2; \ldots; h_n$.

Although we have given the proof rules only for additions of goals, similar proof rules apply for deletion of goals, and addition and deletion of beliefs.

With these proof rules one can formally define derivations and refutations. The definition of derivations is straightforward and is a sequence of transitions using the above proof rules.

Definition 19. A *BDI derivation* is a finite or infinite sequence of BDI configurations, i.e., $\gamma_0, \ldots, \gamma_i, \ldots$.

The notion of refutation in AgentSpeak(L) is with respect to a particular intention. In other words, the refutation for an intention starts when an intention is adopted and ends when the intention stack is empty. Thus, using the above proof rules we can formally prove certain behavioural properties, such as safety and liveness of agent systems, as was done elsewhere [15]. Furthermore, there is a one-to-one correspondence between the proof rules discussed in this section and the operational semantics discussed in the previous section. Such a correspondence has not been possible before, because the proof theory (usually based on multi-modal logics) has been far removed from the realities of the operational semantics.

In addition to the internal events considered in this paper (i.e., addition of intentions), one can extend the operational semantics and proof rules with respect to other internal events, such as deletion of intentions, and success and failure events for actions, plans, goals, and intentions.

The body of the plans considered in this paper includes only sequences of goals or actions. Other dynamic logic operators, such as non-deterministic or, parallel, and iteration, operators can be allowed in the body of plans. In addition, assertion and deletion of beliefs in plan bodies can also be included. Another useful feature of the implemented system dMARS is different post-conditions for successful and failure executions of plans. The operational semantics and proof rules can once again be modified to account for the above constructs.

5 Comparisons and Conclusion

A number of agent-oriented languages such as AGENT0 [17], PLACA (PLAnning Communicating Agents) [19], AgentSpeak [22], SLP [16, 4], and CONGOLOG [9] have been proposed in the literature.

AGENT0 and its successor PLACA can model beliefs, commitments, capabilities, and communications between agents. These attitudes are treated as data structures of an agent program. An interpreter that can execute such agent programs are described. However, the authors do not provide a formal proof theory or justify how the data structures capture the model-theoretic semantics of beliefs, commitments, and capabilities. In contrast, the work described here discusses the connections between the interpreter and a proof theory based on labeled transition systems.

SLP or Stream Logic Programming is based on reactive, guarded, horn clauses. A clause in SLP consists of a guard and a behaviour. The guard is further decomposed into an head and a boolean constraint. The boolean constraint is similar to our context. The head in SLP is an object and the body is a network of concurrent objects connected by communication message slots. Behaviour is specified by object replacement. The execution model of SLP and AgentSpeak(L) are fundamentally different. The behaviour of an agent to a particular external stimuli is captured in a single intention, as a stack of committed sub-behaviours. This provides a global coherence absent in SLP. For example, consider an agent that wants to drop its intention because it no longer needs to achieve a given top-level goal. Killing such an intention would be much easier in AgentSpeak(L) than in SLP.

The semantics of CONGOLOG is based on situation calculus. Although it provides a richer set of actions than what has been discussed here, it is essentially a single intention (or single-threaded) system, unlike AgentSpeak(L). The language AgentSpeak [22] is an object-oriented analogue of AgentSpeak(L).

AgentSpeak(L) is a textual and simplified version of the language used to program the Procedural Reasoning System [3] and its successor dMARS. These implementations have been in use since the mid-1980s. Other agent-oriented systems, such as COSY [1], INTERRAP [10], and GRATE* [7], have been built based on the BDI architecture. The formal operational semantics given here could apply to some of these systems as well. However, a more thorough analysis of these systems and their relation to AgentSpeak(L) is beyond the scope of this paper.

Bridging the gap between theory and practice in the field of agents, and in particular the area of BDI agents, has proved elusive. In this paper, we provide an alternative approach by providing the operational semantics of AgentSpeak(L) which abstracts an implemented BDI system. The primary contribution of this work is in opening up an alternative, restricted, first-order characterization of BDI agents and showing a one-to-one correspondence between the operational and proof-theoretic semantics of such a characterization. We are confident that this approach is likely to be more fruitful than the previous approaches in bridging the gap between theory and practice in this area and will stimulate research in both the pragmatic and theoretical aspects of BDI agents.

Acknowledgements: The research reported in this paper was funded partly by the Generic Industry Research and Development Grant on *Distributed Real-Time Artificial Intelligence* and partly by the *Cooperative Research Centre for Intelligent Decision Systems*. The author wishes to thank Michael Georgeff and Lawrence Cavedon for their valuable input and comments on this paper.

Appendix

Definition 20. An atom of the form $s = t$, where s and t are terms is called an *equation*.

Definition 21. A *substitution* is a finite set $\{x_1/t_1,...,x_n/t_n\}$, where $x_1,...,x_n$ are distinct variables, and $t_1,...,t_n$ are terms such that $x_i \neq t_i$ for any i from 1..n.

Definition 22. The application of a substitution $\theta = \{x_1/t_1,...,x_n/t_n\}$ to a variable x_i, written as $x_i\theta$, yields t_i iff $x_i/t_i \in \theta$ and x_i otherwise. The application of θ to a term or formula is the term or formula obtained by simultaneously replacing every occurrence of x_i by t_i for all i from 1 to n.

Definition 23. Let $\theta = \{x_1/t_1,...,x_n/t_n\}$ and $\sigma = \{y_1/s_1,...,y_m/s_m\}$. The *composition* $\theta\sigma$ of θ and σ is the substitution obtained from the set: $\{x_1/t_1\sigma,...,x_n/t_n\sigma\} \cup \theta$ by removing all $x_i/t_i\sigma$ for which $x_i = t_i\sigma$ ($1 \leq i \leq n$)and removing those y_j/t_j for which $y_j \in \{x_1,...,x_n\}$ ($1 \leq j \leq m$) [11].

Definition 24. A substitution σ is a *solution* or *unifier* of a set of equations $\{s_1 = t_1, ..., s_n = t_n\}$ iff $s_i\sigma = t_i\sigma$ for all $i = 1,...,n$. A substitution σ is *more general* than θ iff there is a substitution ω such that $\sigma\omega = \theta$. A *most general unifier (mgu)* of two terms (atoms) is a maximally general unifier of the terms.

References

1. B. Burmeister and K. Sundermeyer. Cooperative problem-solving guided by intentions and perception. In E. Werner and Y. Demazeau, editors, *Decentralized A.I. 3*, Amsterdam, The Netherlands, 1992. North Holland.
2. P. R. Cohen and H. J. Levesque. Intention is choice with commitment. *Artificial Intelligence*, 42(3), 1990.
3. M. P. Georgeff and A. L. Lansky. Procedural knowledge. In *Proceedings of the IEEE Special Issue on Knowledge Representation*, volume 74, pages 1383–1398, 1986.
4. M. M. Huntbach, N. R. Jennings, and G. A. Ringwood. How agents do it in stream logic programming. In *Proceedings of the International Conference on Multi-Agent Systems (ICMAS-95)*, San Francisco, USA, June, 1995.
5. F. F. Ingrand, M. P. Georgeff, and A. S. Rao. An architecture for real-time reasoning and system control. *IEEE Expert*, 7(6), 1992.
6. N. R. Jennings. On being responsible. In Y. Demazeau and E. Werner, editors, *Decentralized A.I. 3*. North Holland, Amsterdam, The Netherlands, 1992.
7. N. R. Jennings. Specification and implementation of belief, desire, joint-intention architecture for collaborative problem solving. *Journal of Intelligent and Cooperative Information Systems*, 2(3):289–318, 1993.
8. D. Kinny, M. Ljungberg, A. S. Rao, E. A. Sonenberg, G. Tidhar, and E. Werner. Planned team activity. In *Artificial Social Systems, Lecture Notes in Artificial Intelligence (LNAI-830)*, Amsterdam, Netherlands, 1994. Springer Verlag.
9. Y. Lesperance, H. J. Levesque, F. Lin, D. Marcu, R. Reiter, and R. B. Scherl. Foundations of a logical approach to agent programming. In *Working notes of the IJCAI-95 Workshop on Agent Theories, Architectures, and Languages*, Montreal, Canada, 1995.
10. J. P. Muller, M. Pischel, and M. Thiel. Modelling reactive behaviour in vertically layered agent architectures. In *Intelligent Agents: Theories, Architectures, and Languages. Lecture Notes in Artificial Intelligence LNAI 890*, Heidelberg, Germany, 1995. Springer Verlag.
11. U Nilsson. Abstract interpretations and abstract machines. Technical Report Dissertation No 265, Department of Computer and Information Science, Linkoping University, Linkoping, Sweden, 1992.
12. A. S. Rao. Decision procedures for propositional linear-time belief-desire-intention logics. In *Working notes of the IJCAI-95 Workshop on Agent Theories, Architectures, and Languages*, Montreal, Canada, 1995.
13. A. S. Rao and M. P. Georgeff. Modeling rational agents within a BDI-architecture. In J. Allen, R. Fikes, and E. Sandewall, editors, *Proceedings of the Second International Conference on Principles of Knowledge Representation and Reasoning*. Morgan Kaufmann Publishers, San Mateo, CA, 1991.

14. A. S. Rao and M. P. Georgeff. An abstract architecture for rational agents. In C. Rich, W. Swartout, and B. Nebel, editors, *Proceedings of the Third International Conference on Principles of Knowledge Representation and Reasoning.* Morgan Kaufmann Publishers, San Mateo, CA, 1992.

15. A. S. Rao and M. P. Georgeff. A model-theoretic approach to the verification of situated reasoning systems. In *Proceedings of the Thirteenth International Joint Conference on Artificial Intelligence (IJCAI-93)*, Chamberey, France, 1993.

16. G. A. Ringwood. A brief history of stream parallel logic programming. *Logic Programming Newsletter*, 7(2):2–4, 1994.

17. Y. Shoham. Agent-oriented programming. *Artificial Intelligence*, 60(1):51–92, 1993.

18. M. Singh and N. Asher. Towards a formal theory of intentions. In J. van Eijck, editor, *Logics in AI*, volume LNAI:478, pages 472–486. Springer Verlag, Amsterdam, Netherlands, 1990.

19. S. R. Thomas. The PLACA agent programming language. In *Intelligent Agents: Theories, Architectures, and Languages. Lecture Notes in Artificial Intelligence LNAI 890*, Amsterdam, Netherlands, 1995. Springer Verlag.

20. W. van der Hoek, B. van Linder, and J.-J. Ch. Meyer. A logic of capabilities. In *Proceedings of the Third International Symposium on the Logical Foundations of Computer Science (LFCS'94), Lecture Notes in Computer Science LNCS 813*. Springer Verlag, Heidelberg, Germany, 1994.

21. B. van Linder, W. van der Hoek, and J. J. Ch. Meyer. How to motivate your agents? In *Working notes of the IJCAI-95 Workshop on Agent Theories, Architectures, and Languages*, Montreal, Canada, 1995.

22. D. Weerasooriya, A. S. Rao, and K. Ramamohanarao. Design of a concurrent agent-oriented language. In *Intelligent Agents: Theories, Architectures, and Languages. Lecture Notes in Artificial Intelligence LNAI 890*, Amsterdam, Netherlands, 1995. Springer Verlag.

23. M. Wooldridge and M. Fisher. A decision procedure for a temporal belief logic. In *Proceedings of the First International Conference on Temporal Logic*, Bonn, Germany, 1994.

A Methodology and Modelling Technique for Systems of BDI Agents

David Kinny   Michael Georgeff   Anand Rao

Australian Artificial Intelligence Institute
171 Latrobe Street, Melbourne 3000, Australia
{ *dnk,georgeff,anand* }*@aaii.oz.au*

Abstract. The construction of large-scale embedded software systems demands the use of design methodologies and modelling techniques that support abstraction, inheritance, modularity, and other mechanisms for reducing complexity and preventing error. If multi-agent systems are to become widely accepted as a basis for large-scale applications, adequate agent-oriented methodologies and modelling techniques will be essential. This is not just to ensure that systems are reliable, maintainable, and conformant, but to allow their design, implementation, and maintenance to be carried out by software analysts and engineers rather than researchers. In this paper we describe an agent-oriented methodology and modelling technique for systems of agents based upon the Belief-Desire-Intention (BDI) paradigm. Our models extend existing Object-Oriented (OO) models. By building upon and adapting existing, well-understood techniques, we take advantage of their maturity to produce an approach that can be easily learnt and understood by those familiar with the OO paradigm.

1 Introduction

Managing complexity is perhaps the most challenging task facing designers of large-scale embedded software systems. It is now widely accepted that the construction of reliable, maintainable, and extensible systems that conform to their specifications requires, *inter alia*, the use of design methodologies and modelling techniques that support abstraction, structuring, inheritance, modularity, and other mechanisms for managing their inherent complexity.

Perhaps foremost amongst the methodologies that have been developed for the design, specification, and programming of conventional software systems are various Object-Oriented (OO) approaches, based upon the central notion of *objects* which encapsulate state information as a collection of data values and provide *behaviours* via well-defined interfaces for operations upon that information. OO methodologies guide the key steps of object identification, design, and refinement, permitting abstraction via *object classes* and inheritance within *class hierarchies*.

OO methodologies provide a uniform paradigm which is useful across a range of system scales and implementation languages. They have achieved a considerable degree of maturity, and there is widespread acceptance of their advantages. A large community of software developers familiar with their use now exists. The OO design and development environment is well supported by diagram editors and visualization tools. There is even, perhaps, a convergence of viewpoints amongst the major proponents of different variations on the OO theme.

The *agent* paradigm in AI is based upon the notion of reactive, autonomous, internally-motivated entities embedded in changing, uncertain worlds which they perceive and in which they act. It supports a flourishing research community which has made substantial progress in recent years in providing a theoretical and practical understanding of many aspects of agents and multi-agent systems. Currently, many flowers bloom — there is a multitude of viewpoints on what exactly constitutes an agent, on how they should be structured, and how collections of agents interacting with each other and the environment can be used to implement complex systems. Despite this healthy lack of consensus, the benefits of implementing agent systems are little disputed, and several agent architectures have progressed to being useable technologies.

As yet, however, there are not many examples of the successful application of agent system technologies on a significant scale. In part this is due to the absence of mature languages and software tools, but our experience suggests that the absence of methodologies that allow system complexity to be effectively managed is a greater obstacle. OO methodologies are not directly applicable to agent systems — agents are usually significantly more complex than typical objects, both in their internal structure and in the behaviours they exhibit. We believe that if multi-agent systems are to become widely accepted as a basis for large-scale commercial and industrial applications, adequate design methodologies and modelling techniques will be essential. This is not just to guarantee that such systems are sufficiently reliable, maintainable, and conformant, but to allow their design, implementation, and maintenance to be carried out by software analysts and engineers rather than AI researchers. Others have reached similar conclusions about the need for familiar, intuitive modelling techniques [22].

Our research program has centred upon the design, implementation and theoretical understanding of a particular Belief-Desire-Intention (BDI) agent architecture [10, 23] which has now achieved considerable maturity. Recently, we have been applying this technology as the basis of a number of medium to large-scale software systems. The application domains of these systems include air-traffic management [20], air-combat simulation [30], and business process management.

Realizing that existing formalisms for describing and reasoning about agents do not provide adequate support for the *process* of agent design, we have been attempting to develop suitable methodologies and models. Our approach, pragmatically motivated, has been to explore how existing OO modelling techniques can be extended to apply to BDI agent systems. By building upon and adapting existing, well-understood techniques, we take advantage of the maturity of the OO approach and aim to develop models and a methodology that will be easily learnt and understood by those familiar with the OO paradigm.

In this paper we present an overview of our agent-oriented methodology, focussing upon the models we have developed. Elsewhere [18], we provide a more detailed description of the methodology and the process of multi-agent system design. In the sections that follow we will outline the models and methodology, present an application domain which illustrates their use, describe particular models in more detail, and compare our approach to other work in this area.

2 An Agent-Oriented Methodology

A methodology to support design and specification of agent systems should provide a clear conceptual framework that enables the complexity of the system to be managed by decomposition and abstraction. OO methodologies [2, 25] advocate the decomposition of a system by identification of the key *object classes* in the application domain, focussing upon their *behaviour* and their relationships with other classes. The essential details of a system design are captured by three different types of models.

1. An *Object Model* captures information about objects within the system, describing their data structure, relationships and the operations they support.
2. A *Dynamic Model* describes the states, transitions, events, actions, activities and interactions that characterize system behaviour.
3. A *Functional Model* describes the flow of data during system activity, both within and between system components.

The dynamic and functional models serve to guide the refinement of the object model; in particular, the refinement of the operations that an object will provide. A fully refined object model is a complete specification of an object based system. The object concept is applied uniformly at all levels of abstraction.

By contrast, in specifying an agent system, we have found that it is highly desirable to adopt a more specialized set of models which operate at two distinct levels of abstraction. Firstly, from the *external viewpoint*, the system is decomposed into agents, modelled as complex objects characterized their purpose, their responsibilities, the services they perform, the information they require and maintain, and their external interactions. Secondly, from the *internal viewpoint*, the elements required by a particular agent architecture must be modelled for each agent. In our case, these are an agent's beliefs, goals, and plans.

2.1 Agents from the External Viewpoint

Our agent-oriented methodology advocates the decomposition of a system based on the key *roles* in an application. The identification of roles and their relationships guides the specification of an *agent class hierarchy*; agents are particular instances of these classes. Analysis of the *responsibilities* of each agent class leads to the identification of the *services* provided and used by an agent, and hence its external interactions. Consideration of issues such as the creation and duration of roles and their interactions determines *control relationships* between agent classes. These details are captured in two models.

1. An *Agent Model* describes the hierarchical relationship among different abstract and concrete agent classes, and identifies the agent instances which may exist within the system, their multiplicity, and when they come into existence.
2. An *Interaction Model* describes the responsibilities of an agent class, the services it provides, associated interactions, and control relationships between agent classes. This includes the syntax and semantics of messages used for inter-agent communication and communication between agents and other system components, such as user interfaces.

These models are largely independent of our BDI architecture. The methodology for their elaboration and refinement can be expressed as four major steps.

1. Identify the roles of the application domain. There are several dimensions in which such an analysis can be undertaken; roles can be organizational or functional, they can be directly related to the application, or required by the system implementation. Identify the lifetime of each role. Elaborate an agent class hierarchy. The initial definition of agent classes should be quite abstract, not assuming any particular granularity of agency.

2. For each role, identify its associated responsibilities, and the services provided and used to fulfill those responsibilities. As well as services provided to/by other agents upon request, services may include interaction with the external environment or human users. For example, a responsibility may require an agent to monitor the environment, to notice when certain events occur, and to respond appropriately by performing actions, which may include notifying other agents or users. Conversely, a responsibility may induce a requirement that an agent be notified of conditions detected by other agents or users. Decompose agent classes to the service level.

3. For each service, identify the interactions associated with the provision of the service, the performatives (speech acts) required for those interactions, and their information content. Identify events and conditions to be noticed, actions to be performed, and other information requirements. Determine the control relationships between agents. At this point the internal modelling of each agent class can be performed.

4. Refine the agent hierarchy. Where there is commonality of information or services between agent classes, consider introducing a new agent class, which existing agent classes can specialize, to encapsulate what is common. Compose agent classes, via inheritance or aggregation, guided by commonality of lifetime, information and interfaces, and similarity of services. Introduce concrete agent classes, taking into account implementation dependent considerations of performance, communication costs and latencies, fault-tolerance requirements, etc. Refine the control relationships. Finally, based upon considerations of lifetime and multiplicity, introduce agent instances.

Roles, responsibilities, and services are just descriptions of purposeful behaviours at different levels of abstraction; roles can be seen as sets of responsibilities, and responsibilities as sets of services. Services are those activities that it is not natural to decompose further, in terms of *the identity of the performer*. The roles initially identified serve as a starting point for the analysis, not an up-front decision about what agents will result from the process of analysis.

Once roles have been decomposed to the level of services and internal modelling performed, a fine-grained model of agency has been produced. When this is recomposed in accordance with the considerations mentioned above, the concrete agents which result may reflect groupings of services and responsibilities that differ from the original roles. The identification of agent boundaries is deferred until the information and procedures used to perform services have been elaborated. This results in concrete agents whose internal structure is inherently modular.

Simple service relationships and interactions between agents could be represented as associations within the agent model, but we have chosen to describe them in a separate model. Modelling of agent interactions is currently the subject of intensive research, and many modelling techniques, often quite complex, have been proposed and developed (see, for example, [1, 6, 7, 9, 11, 12, 28]). They address issues from information content and linguistic intent through to protocols for coordination and negotiation. We do not hold a strong view on the general suitability of particular techniques for modelling interactions, hence our methodology and modelling framework is designed to allow the selection of models appropriate to the application domain.

The interaction model also captures control relationships between agents, such as responsibilities for agent creation and deletion, delegation, and team formation. Modelling techniques for these relationships are the subject of ongoing research.

2.2 Agents from the Internal Viewpoint

The BDI paradigm provides a "strong" notion of agency; agents are viewed as having certain mental attitudes, Beliefs, Desires and Intentions, which represent, respectively, their informational, motivational and deliberative states. In our BDI architecture an agent can be completely specified by the events that it can perceive, the actions it may perform, the beliefs it may hold, the goals it may adopt, and the plans that give rise to its intentions.[1] These are captured, for each agent class, by the following models.

1. A *Belief Model* describes the information about the environment and internal state that an agent of that class may hold, and the actions it may perform. The possible beliefs of an agent and their properties, such as whether or not they may change over time, are described by a *belief set*. In addition, one or more *belief states* – particular instances of the belief set – may be defined and used to specify an agent's *initial mental state*.

2. A *Goal Model* describes the goals that an agent may possibly adopt, and the events to which it can respond. It consists of a *goal set* which specifies the goal and event domain and one or more *goal states* – sets of ground goals – used to specify an agent's initial mental state.

3. A *Plan Model* describes the plans that an agent may possibly employ to achieve its goals. It consists of a *plan set* which describes the properties and control structure of individual plans.

Implicit in this characterization are the execution properties of the architecture which determine how, exactly, events and goals give rise to intentions, and intentions lead to action and revision of beliefs and goals. These properties, described in detail elsewhere [16], are responsible for ensuring that beliefs, goals, and intentions evolve rationally. For example, the architecture ensures that events are responded to in a timely manner, beliefs are maintained consistently, and that

---

[1] We distinguish beliefs from the notion of knowledge, as defined, for example, in the literature on distributed computing, as beliefs are only required to provide information on the likely state of the environment. The distinction between desires and goals, while important from a philosophical perspective, is not significant in this context.

plan selection and execution proceeds in a manner which reflects certain notions of rational commitment [17, 24]

Our methodology for the development of these models begins from the services provided by an agent and the associated events and interactions. These define its purpose, and determine the top-level goals that the agent must be able to achieve. Analysis of the goals and their further breakdown into subgoals leads naturally to the identification of different means, i.e., plans, by which a goal can be achieved.

The appropriateness of a given plan, and the manner in which a plan is carried out, will in general depend upon the agent's beliefs about the state of the environment and possibly other information available to the agent, i.e., the agent's belief context. This may also include certain beliefs which represent working data. A context is represented in terms of various data entities and their relationships. Analysis of contexts results in the elaboration of the beliefs of an agent. To summarize, the methodology for internal modelling can be expressed as two steps.

1. Analyze the means of achieving the goals. For each goal, analyze the different contexts in which the goal has to be achieved. For each of these contexts, decompose each goal into activities, represented by subgoals, and actions. Analyze in what order and under what conditions these activities and actions need to be performed, how failure should be dealt with, and generate a plan to achieve the goal. Repeat the analysis for subgoals.
2. Build the beliefs of the system. Analyze the various contexts, and the conditions that control the execution of activities and actions, and decompose them into component beliefs. Analyze the input and output data requirements for each subgoal in a plan and make sure that this information is available either as beliefs or as outputs from prior subgoals in the plan.

These steps are iterated as the models which capture the results of analysis are progressively elaborated, revised, and refined. Refinement of the internal models feeds back to the external models; building the plans and beliefs of an agent class clarifies the information requirements of services, particularly with respect to monitoring and notification. Analyzing interaction scenarios, which can be derived from the plans, may lead to the redefinition of services.

Unlike object-oriented methodologies, the primary emphasis of our methodology is on roles, responsibilities, services, and goals. These are the key abstractions that allow us to manage complexity. We analyze the application domain in terms of what needs to be achieved, and in what context. The focus is on the end-point that is to be reached, rather than the types of behaviours that will lead to the end-point, which are the primary emphasis of OO methodologies.

Although this might seem a small paradigm shift, it is quite subtle and leads to a substantially different analysis. This is because goals, as compared to behaviours or plans, are more stable in any application domain. Correctly identifying goals leads to a more robust system design, where changes to behaviours can be accommodated as new ways of achieving the same goal. In other words, a goal-oriented analysis results in more stable, robust, and modular designs.

The context-sensitivity of plans provides modularity and compositionality; plans for new contexts may be added without changing existing plans for the same goal. This results in an extensible design that can cope with frequent changes and special cases, and permits incremental development and testing.

3   An Air-Traffic Management System

In this section we describe informally the structure of the air-traffic management (ATM) system which we have developed. The system is responsible for assisting a human Flow Controller to determine the landing sequence of aircraft on multiple runways at a single airport so as to maintain safety and other constraints while minimizing delay and congestion.

Following the methodology in the previous section, we arrived at a system design consisting of three permanent agents with the roles of Coordinator, Sequencer and Windmodel, and a variable number of aircraft agents, each of which is associated with a particular flight and exists only during the time that the aircraft is under the control of the flow controller.

The Coordinator is responsible for the creation and deletion of Aircraft agents and the distribution to them of initial flight plans. The Sequencer is responsible for determining landing time assignments, which it does by interacting with aircraft agents and the flow controller. The Windmodel maintains a 4-dimensional model of past, present and future wind conditions in the controlled airspace.

An Aircraft agent consists of three active components; a Predictor, Monitor and Planner. Conceptually they were modelled as separate roles, but because of their common lifetimes and close interactions they were aggregated into a single concrete agent. They are generic, i.e., identical in all aircraft agents. Aircraft agents also contain a performance profile component specific to the aircraft type.

The Predictor is responsible for a number of services. Its primary service is to compute the expected time of arrival (TOA) at the waypoints specified in the flight plan, including the final landing point. Inputs to the computation are the flight plan, which may be modified during the flight, the aircraft performance profile, which is determined by the aircraft type, and wind conditions, so it requires the services of the Windmodel agent. Different wind conditions may apply at different stages of the flight, primarily due to altitude change. The TOA computation produces both estimated times and performance envelopes, which are the earliest and latest times that the aircraft could arrive at the waypoint while remaining within its permitted operating profile. The Predictor provides this information to the Monitor and Planner.

The Monitor receives 3-dimensional location information derived from radar data and compares actual TOAs with those predicted. If significant deviations occur, it analyzes the reason for the occurrence and notifies the Predictor and Planner. Deviations may be due to the aircraft not following the planned path, not flying at the assigned altitude, not holding the planned air-speed, or inaccuracies in the wind information. The first two of these are directly detectable from the radar data. To distinguish the latter two the behaviour of multiple aircraft must be compared, so Monitor requests Windmodel to perform this global analysis.

When the Sequencer assigns (or revises) the aircraft's landing time assignment (LTA), the Planner is requested to construct a set of plans that will allow the aircraft to land at that time. A plan here is the future trajectory, air-speed and altitude profile of the aircraft. Acceptable plans are highly constrained; trajectories are restricted, holding points are limited, air-speeds must be multiples of 10 knots; in general, the issuing of instructions to the pilot should be minimized.

The Planner uses various different strategies, algorithmic and heuristic, to produce these plans; moreover, the choice of strategy depends on the stage of the flight. The Planner then sends the set of plans to the flow controller.

Once the flow controller has chosen which plan to adopt, the Planner responds to deviations detected by the Monitor by determining whether the aircraft can still meet its LTA. If so, the current plan is modified as required. If not, the Planner notifies the Sequencer, which computes a new LTA, and the cycle repeats.

4 The Modelling Technique

As mentioned previously, OO modelling techniques are based upon an object model which employs classes and instances uniformly at all levels of abstraction. The dynamic and functional models serve as a description of object behaviour which guides the refinement of the object model.

Our agent system modelling technique employs object classes and instances to describe different kinds of entities within a multi-agent system at different levels of abstraction. Unlike the standard OO approach, the meaning of relationships such as association, inheritance and instantiation is quite distinct for these different kinds of entities. By partitioning different types of entities into separate models we maintain these important distinctions, and simplify the process of consistency checking, within and between models.

As a result of of our commitment to a particular BDI execution architecture, we can employ OO dynamic models, augmented with a notion of failure, as *directly executable* specifications which generate agent behaviour, i.e., as plans. This provides considerable advantages over the OO approach of programming object methods guided by the dynamic model. Moreover, plans are not required to be a *total* specification of behaviour; certain elements, such as successively trying different means to achieve a goal, are inherent in the the architecture.

The OO object and dynamic model representation techniques, suitably extended and constrained, serves as a basis for our representations. Specifications of the models may be supplied by the agent designer in the form of diagrams or text files for input to the compilation process that produces an executable system.

In the following sections we present in more detail the features of the agent, belief, and plan models. A full description appears elsewhere [19].

4.1 Agent Models

An Agent Model has two components.

1. An *Agent Class Model* - a set of class diagrams which define abstract and concrete agent classes and capture the inheritance and aggregation relationships between them.
2. An *Agent Instance Model* - a set of instance diagrams that identify agent instances.

In systems containing only a small number of agent classes and instances they may combined into a single diagram. Figure 1 shows a simplified combined agent diagram from the ATM application domain. Note that the attributes of agent classes do not appear in this diagram.

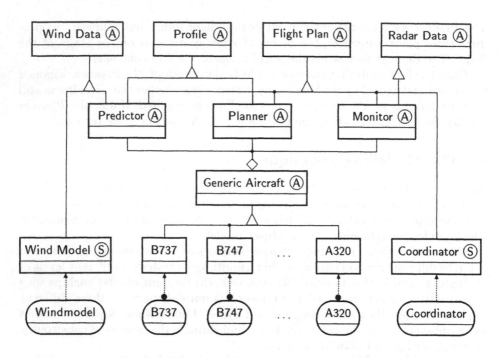

Fig. 1. ATM Agent Class and Instance Diagram

Agent Class Models An agent class model is a directed, acyclic graph containing nodes denoting both *abstract* and *concrete* (instantiable) agent classes. Agent classes are represented by class icons, and abstract classes are distinguished by the presence of the adornment Ⓐ in the upper section of the icon. Edges in the graph denoting inheritance are distinguished by a triangle with a vertex pointing towards the superclass, and edges denoting aggregation by a diamond adjacent to the aggregate class. Other associations between agent classes are not allowed.

Agent classes may have attributes, but not operations. Attributes may not be arbitrary user-named data items, rather they are restricted to a set of predefined *reserved attributes*. For example, each class may have associated belief, goal, and plan models, specified by the attributes beliefs, goals, and plans.

Multiple inheritance is permitted. Inheritance, as usual, denotes an *is-a* relationship, and aggregation a *has-a* relationship, but in the context of an agent model these relationships have a special semantics. Agents inherit and may refine the belief, goal, and plan models of their superclasses. Note that it is, for example, the set of plans which is refined, rather than the individual plans. Aggregation denotes the incorporation within an agent of subagents that do **not** have access to each other's beliefs, goals, and plans.

For example, in Figure 1, Monitor is an abstract agent which is a subagent of Generic Aircraft. Monitor is both a Radar Data agent and a Flight Plan agent. Predictor, another subagent of Generic Aircraft, is a Wind Data, aircraft Profile and Flight Plan agent. Monitor and Predictor do not share their beliefs about flight plans, Monitor has no beliefs about wind data or aircraft profiles, and Predictor has no beliefs about radar data.

Other attributes of an agent class include its belief-state-set and goal-state-set, which determine possible initial mental states. Particular elements of these sets may then be specified as the default initial mental state for the agent class, via the initial-belief-state and initial-goal-state attributes. For example, the belief model of the abstract aircraft Profile agent defines belief states corresponding to different aircraft types. A concrete aircraft agent such as B747 inherits these, but would only specify a particular instance, i.e., data values appropriate for a 747, in its belief state set and as its initial belief state.

Abstract agent classes, aggregation, and inheritance provide powerful mechanisms for enforcing modularity of beliefs, goals, and plans within agents, and for sharing them between agents. Related beliefs, goals, and plans may be encapsulated in separate abstract classes which may then, by aggregation or inheritance, be grouped together to form a concrete agent class. Decisions about agent boundaries may be deferred to a late stage of the design process. The ability to take an agent class and refine it by the addition of further beliefs, goals, or plans provides a compositional framework for system design and encourages re-use.

Agent Instance Models An agent instance model is an instance diagram which defines both the *static agent set* – the set of agents that are instantiated at compile-time – and the *dynamic agent set* – the set of agents that may be instantiated at run-time. The former are distinguished by the adornment Ⓢ in the upper section of the icon.

Each agent instance is specified by an instance icon linked to a concrete agent class by an instantiation edge, represented as a dotted vector from instance to class. Static instances must be named, but the naming of dynamic instances may be deferred till their instantiation. A multiplicity notation at the instance end of the instantiation link may be used to indicate whether a dynamic class may be multiply instantiated.

The initial mental state of an agent instance may be specified by the initial-belief-state and initial-goal-state attributes, whose values are particular elements of the belief and goal state sets of the agent class. If not specified, the defaults are the values associated with the agent class. For dynamic agent instances these attributes may be overridden at the time the agent is created.

4.2 Belief Models

A belief model consists of a belief set and one or more belief states. The belief set is specified by a set of object diagrams which define the domain of the beliefs of an agent class. A belief state is a set of instance diagrams which define a particular instance of the belief set.

Belief Sets Formally, a belief set is a set of typed predicates whose arguments are terms over a universe of predefined and user-defined function symbols. These predicates and functions are directly derived from the class and instance definitions in the belief set diagrams. The classes and instances defined therein correspond, in many cases, to real entities in the application domain, but, unlike

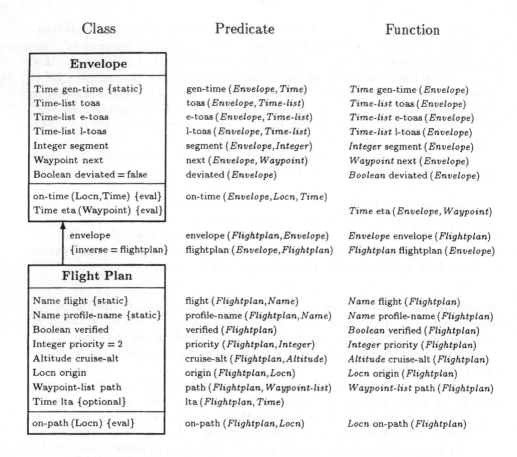

Class	Predicate	Function

Envelope

Time gen-time {static}	gen-time (*Envelope, Time*)	*Time* gen-time (*Envelope*)
Time-list toas	toas (*Envelope, Time-list*)	*Time-list* toas (*Envelope*)
Time-list e-toas	e-toas (*Envelope, Time-list*)	*Time-list* e-toas (*Envelope*)
Time-list l-toas	l-toas (*Envelope, Time-list*)	*Time-list* l-toas (*Envelope*)
Integer segment	segment (*Envelope, Integer*)	*Integer* segment (*Envelope*)
Waypoint next	next (*Envelope, Waypoint*)	*Waypoint* next (*Envelope*)
Boolean deviated = false	deviated (*Envelope*)	*Boolean* deviated (*Envelope*)
on-time (Locn, Time) {eval}	on-time (*Envelope, Locn, Time*)	
Time eta (Waypoint) {eval}		*Time* eta (*Envelope, Waypoint*)
envelope {inverse = flightplan}	envelope (*Flightplan, Envelope*) flightplan (*Envelope, Flightplan*)	*Envelope* envelope (*Flightplan*) *Flightplan* flightplan (*Envelope*)

Flight Plan

Name flight {static}	flight (*Flightplan, Name*)	*Name* flight (*Flightplan*)
Name profile-name {static}	profile-name (*Flightplan, Name*)	*Name* profile-name (*Flightplan*)
Boolean verified	verified (*Flightplan*)	*Boolean* verified (*Flightplan*)
Integer priority = 2	priority (*Flightplan, Integer*)	*Integer* priority (*Flightplan*)
Altitude cruise-alt	cruise-alt (*Flightplan, Altitude*)	*Altitude* cruise-alt (*Flightplan*)
Locn origin	origin (*Flightplan, Locn*)	*Locn* origin (*Flightplan*)
Waypoint-list path	path (*Flightplan, Waypoint-list*)	*Waypoint-list* path (*Flightplan*)
Time lta {optional}	lta (*Flightplan, Time*)	
on-path (Locn) {eval}	on-path (*Flightplan, Locn*)	*Locn* on-path (*Flightplan*)

Fig. 2. ATM Belief Classes and Derived Predicates and Functions

an OO object model, the definitions do not define the behaviours of these enti-ties. This is because they are not implementations of the entities, rather, they represent an agent's beliefs about those entities.

A class in a belief set diagram serves to define the type signatures of attributes of an object, functions that may be applied to the object, and other predicates that apply to the object, including *actions*, which have a special role in plans. Attributes, which define binary predicates, are specified in the usual way. If an at-tribute is never undefined, an accessor function is also generated. Other predicates and functions are defined by specializations of the operation notation. An object of the class upon which the operation is defined is an implicit first argument to the derived function or predicate.

Predicates may also be defined by binary and higher order associations be-tween classes. The multiplicity of these associations is indicated in the usual way. Figure 2 shows two associated belief classes from the ATM domain, and the predicates and functions derived from them. Some predicates and function are not associated with any particular object, i.e. they do not have an implicit first argument. In this case, they can be specified as attributes and operations upon an anonymous (unnamed) class.

We extend the standard notation for attributes and operations by allowing an optional *property list*, which is used to specify certain properties of the derived predicates and functions, such as:

- whether they are abstract, stored in the belief database or computed,
- whether they may change over time, and
- for predicates, whether they have open- or closed-world negation semantics.

Properties may also be associated with classes, instances and associations, and may represented either by property lists or by adornments. For example, in Figure 2, the attribute flight has the property static, indicating that its value may not change, the attribute lta has the property optional, indicating that its value may be undefined, and the predicate on-path has the property eval, indicating that it is computed.

4.3 Plan Models

A plan model consists of a set of plans, known as a *plan set*. Individual plans are specified as plan diagrams, which are denoted by a form of class icon. A generic plan diagram appears in Figure 3. The lower section, known as the *plan graph*, is a state transition diagram, similar to an OO dynamic model. Unlike OO approaches, however, plans are not just descriptions of system behaviour developed during analysis. Rather, they are directly executable prescriptions of how an agent should behave to achieve a goal or respond to an event.

The elements of the plan graph are three types of node; *start states*, *end states* and *internal states*, and one type of directed edge; *transitions*. Start states are denoted by a small filled circle (●). End states may be *pass* or *fail* states, denoted respectively by a small target (◉) or a small no entry sign (⊘).

Internal states may be *passive* or *active*. Passive states have no substructure and are denoted by a small open circle (○). Active states have an associated *activity* and are denoted by instance icons. Activities may be subgoals, denoted by formulae from the agent's goal set, iteration constructs, including do and while loops, or in the case of a *graph state*, an embedded graph called a *subgraph*.

Events, conditions, and actions may be attached to transitions between states. In general, transitions from a state occur when the associated event occurs, provided that the associated condition is true. When the transition occurs any associated action is performed. Conditions are predicates from the agent's belief set. Actions include those defined in the belief set, and built-in actions. The latter include *assert* and *retract*, which update the belief state of the agent.

Failure Unlike conventional OO dynamic models, which are based upon Harel's statecharts [13], plan graphs have a semantics which incorporates a notion of failure. Failure within a graph can occur when an action upon a transition fails, when an explicit transition to a fail state occurs, or when the activity of an active state terminates in failure and no outgoing transition is enabled.

If the graph is the body of a graph state, then the activity of that state terminates in failure. If the graph is a plan graph, then the plan terminates in failure. If the plan has been activated to perform a subgoal activity in another plan, this may result in that activity terminating in failure, depending on the availability of alternative plans to perform the activity.

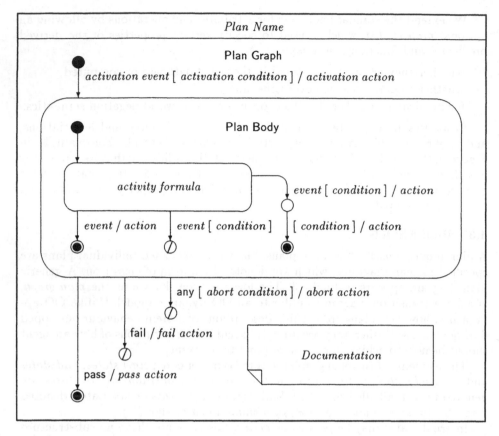

Fig. 3. Generic Plan Diagram

Plan Execution The initial transition of the plan graph is labelled with an an *activation event* and *activation condition* which determine when and in what context the plan should be activated. The activation event may be a belief event which occurs when an agent's beliefs change or when certain external changes are sensed, leading to event-driven activation, or a goal event which occurs as a result of the execution of a subgoal activity in another plan, leading to goal-driven activation. If multiple plans are applicable to a given event in a given context, they are activated in parallel if activation is event-driven, or sequentially until successful termination if activation is goal-driven. An optional *activation action* permits an action to be taken when a plan is activated.

Transitions from active states may be labelled with the events **pass** and **fail** which denote the success or failure of the activity associated with the state. Transitions from active states that are labelled with the event **any** may occur whenever their condition becomes true, allowing activities to be interrupted. A special case of this is the abort transition of a plan. Once the plan is activated, if at any time during the execution of its body the abort condition becomes true then it terminates in failure. The final transitions of the plan graph may be labelled with actions to be taken upon the success, failure or aborting of the plan.

5 Comparison and Conclusions

A number of agent-oriented systems based on BDI architectures have been developed, including PRS [10], COSY [5], GRATE* [14], ARCHON [15], INTERRAP [21], and dMARS[16]. Likewise, agent-oriented languages, such as AGENT0 [26, 27] and PLACA [29], have been proposed as languages for programming agents.

However, there is very little work on how to analyze and design agent-oriented systems. Brazier *et al.* [3] discuss a formal specification framework for multi-agent system design, called DESIRE (DEsign and Specification of Interacting REasoning components). DESIRE emphasizes hierarchical task-based decomposition. It captures the task structure, sequences of subtasks, information exchange between tasks, knowledge decomposition, and role delegation. As with our agent model, DESIRE provides a compositional framework for modelling agents. However, the plan model discussed herein allows greater expressive power for describing task structure. In addition, our methodology emphasizes the importance of goals and services as opposed to tasks.

The object-oriented methodology proposed by Wirfs-Brock *et al.* [31] views a *subsystem* as a set of object classes which collaborate to fulfill a set of responsibilities. The notion of responsibility conveys a sense of the purpose of the objects in a subsystem and is characterized by the services provided by the subsystem. Thus, our notion of role is very similar to the notion of subsystem. The crucial difference is that, in an object-oriented paradigm, there is no programming construct that supports the realization of a subsystem whereas, in the agent-oriented paradigm, agents are used to realize particular instances of roles which then take on a separate identity and existence.

Within the object-oriented community, the notion of agents has also been used to capture user requirements. Dubois *et al.* [8] employ temporal logic to specify the behaviours of agents, called *agent level* modelling, and the interactions between them, called *society level* modelling.

Burkhard [4] considers a number of design choices for agent-oriented languages and the consequences of these for programming open systems. Our methodology and agent modelling formalism provide one way of achieving many of the desired features for a class of such languages.

In summary, the primary contribution of this paper has been to provide the elements of a rigorous framework for analyzing and building complex, distributed, multi-agent systems. We have presented a methodology and modelling technique to describe the external and internal perspective of multi-agent systems based on a BDI architecture, and have illustrated the approach using an implemented air-traffic management system. Our agent-oriented methodology, with its emphasis on roles, responsibilities, services, and goals, permits a fine-grained analysis that allows agent boundaries to be chosen flexibly and results in system designs that are robust, modular, and extensible. Our agent system modelling technique builds upon and adapts existing, well-understood object-oriented models.

6 Acknowledgements

The authors wish to thank the anonymous referees for their helpful suggestions.

References

1. Mihai Barbuceanu and Mark S. Fox. COOL: A language for describing coordination in multi-agent systems. In *Proceedings of the International Conference on Multi-Agent Systems, ICMAS-95*, San Francisco, CA, 1995.
2. Grady Booch. *Object-Oriented Analysis and Design with Applications*. Benjamin/Cummings, Redwood City, CA, 2nd edition, 1994.
3. F. Brazier, B. D. Keplicz, N. R. Jennings, and J. Treur. Formal specification of multi-agent systems: A real-world case. In *Proceedings of the International Conference on Multi-Agent Systems, ICMAS-95*, San Francisco, CA, 1995.
4. Hans-Dieter Burkhard. Agent-oriented programming for open systems. In *Intelligent Agents: Theories, Architectures, and Languages. Lecture Notes in Artificial Intelligence LNAI 890*. Springer Verlag, 1995.
5. B. Burmeister and K. Sundermeyer. Cooperative problem-solving guided by intentions and perception. In E. Werner and Y. Demazeau, editors, *Decentralized A.I. 3*, Amsterdam, 1992. North Holland.
6. Jennifer Chu-Carrol and Sandra Carberry. Generating information-sharing subdialogues in expert-user consultation. In *Proceedings of the Fourteenth International Joint Conference on Artificial Intelligence, IJCAI-95*, pages 1243–1250, Montreal, 1995.
7. Philip R. Cohen and Hector J. Levesque. Communicative actions for artificial agents. In *Proceedings of the International Conference on Multi-Agent Systems, ICMAS-95*, San Francisco, CA, 1995.
8. E. Dubois, P. Du Bois, and M. Petit. OO requirements analysis: An agent perspective. In *ECOOP'93 - Object-Oriented Programming. Lecture notes in Computer Science LNCS 707*, pages 458–481. Springer Verlag, 1993.
9. Tim Finin *et al.* Specification of the KQML agent communication language. Technical report, DARPA Knowledge Sharing Initiative, External Working Group, 1992.
10. Michael P. Georgeff and Amy L. Lansky. Procedural knowledge. In *Proceedings of the IEEE Special Issue on Knowledge Representation*, volume 74, 1986.
11. Barbara J. Grosz and Candace L. Sidner. Plans for discourse. In P. R. Cohen, J. Morgan, and M. E. Pollack, editors, *Intentions in Communication*. MIT Press, Cambridge, MA, 1990.
12. Afsaneh Haddadi. *Reasoning About Interactions in Agent Systems: A Pragmatic Theory*. PhD thesis, University of Manchester Institute of Science and Technology, United Kingdom, 1995.
13. D. Harel and C. Kahana. On statecharts with overlapping. *ACM Transactions on Software Engineering and Methodology*, 1(4), 1992.
14. N. R. Jennings. Specification and implementation of belief, desire, joint-intention architecture for collaborative problem solving. *Journal of Intelligent and Cooperative Information Systems*, 2(3):289–318, 1993.
15. N. R. Jennings, J. M. Corera, and I. Laresgoiti. Developing industrial multi-agent systems. In *Proceedings of the International Conference on Multi-Agent Systems, ICMAS-95*, San Francisco, CA, 1995.
16. David Kinny. *The Distributed Multi-Agent Reasoning System Architecture and Language Specification*. Australian Artificial Intelligence Institute, Melbourne, Australia, 1993.
17. David Kinny and Michael Georgeff. Commitment and effectiveness of situated agents. In *Proceedings of the Twelfth International Joint Conference on Artificial Intelligence, IJCAI-91*, pages 82–88, Sydney, 1991.

18. David Kinny and Michael Georgeff. A design methodology for BDI agent systems. Technical Report 55, Australian Artificial Intelligence Institute, Melbourne, Australia, 1995.

19. David Kinny and Michael Georgeff. Modelling techniques for BDI agent systems. Technical Report 54, Australian Artificial Intelligence Institute, Melbourne, Australia, 1995.

20. Magnus Ljungberg. The OASIS air traffic management system. Technical Report 28, Australian Artificial Intelligence Institute, Melbourne, Australia, 1992.

21. J. P. Muller, M. Pischel, and M. Thiel. Modelling reactive behaviour in vertically layered agent architectures. In *Intelligent Agents: Theories, Architectures, and Languages. Lecture Notes in Artificial Intelligence LNAI 890*. Springer Verlag, 1995.

22. J. Y. C. Pan and J. M. Tenenbaum. An intelligent agent framework for enterprise integration. *IEEE Transactions on Systems, Man and Cybernetics*, 21(6), 1991.

23. Anand S. Rao and Michael P. Georgeff. Modeling rational agents within a BDI architecture. In *Proceedings of the Second International Conference on Principles of Knowledge Representation and Reasoning, KR '91*, pages 473–484, Cambridge, MA, 1991.

24. Anand S. Rao and Michael P. Georgeff. An Abstract Architecture for Rational Agents. In *Proceedings of the Third International Conference on Principles of Knowledge Representation and Reasoning, KR '92*, pages 439–449, Boston, MA, 1992.

25. James Rumbaugh, Michael Blaha, William Premerlani, Frederick Eddy, and William Lorensen. *Object-Oriented Modeling and Design*. Prentice Hall, Englewood Cliifs, NJ, 1991.

26. Yoav Shoham. AGENT0: a simple agent language and its interpreter. In *Proceedings of the Ninth National Conference on Artificial Intelligence, AAAI-91*, pages 704–709, San Jose, CA, 1991.

27. Yoav Shoham. Agent-oriented programming. *Artificial Intelligence*, 60(1):51–92, 1993.

28. Candace L. Sidner. An artificial discourse language for collaborative negotiation. In *Proceedings of the Twelfth National Conference on Artificial Intelligence, AAAI-94*, pages 814–819, Seattle, WA, 1994.

29. S. Rebecaa Thomas. The placa agent programming language. In *Intelligent Agents: Theories, Architectures, and Languages. Lecture Notes in Artificial Intelligence LNAI 890*. Springer Verlag, 1995.

30. Gil Tidhar, Mario Selvestrel, and Clinton Heinze. Modelling teams and team tactics in whole air mission modelling. Technical Report 60, Australian Artificial Intelligence Institute, Melbourne, Australia, 1995.

31. R. Wirfs-Brock, B. Wilkerson, and L. Wiener. *Designing Object-Oriented Software*. P T R Prentice Hall, Englewood Cliffs, New Jersey, 1990.

Formalising the Contract Net as a Goal-Directed System

Mark d'Inverno[1] and Michael Luck[2]

[1] School of Computer Science, University of Westminster, London, W1M 8JS, UK.
Email: dinverm@westminster.ac.uk
[2] Department of Computer Science, University of Warwick, Coventry, CV4 7AL, UK.
Email: mikeluck@dcs.warwick.ac.uk

Abstract. In response to the problems that have arisen regarding the terminology and concepts of agent-oriented systems, previous work has described a formal framework for understanding agency and autonomy. In this paper we outline the framework and refine it by adding further levels of detail to develop a formal model of the *Contract Net Protocol*. The model serves to make precise both the operations of nodes in the contract net, and the state of the net at various points during the protocol. In particular, the nature of the dependencies between the nodes in the net is explicated. Finally, we generalise the relationships that can be found in the contract net which are brought out by the formalisation, and introduce more general concepts such as *cooperation* and *engagement*.

1 Introduction

There are many threads of research in Distributed Artificial Intelligence but, to a greater or lesser extent, they can be grouped under the banner either of experimental work, or of formal, theoretical work. Recently, however, some efforts have been made to provide a greater harmony between these two camps, and to integrate the complementary aspects (e.g. [19]). The current work is one such effort. Previously, we have developed a principled theory of agency and autonomy through the provision of a formal framework which defines and characterises these concepts, and specifies the relationship between them [9]. In this paper, we refine that framework so that it may be applied to the Contract Net Protocol which is very firmly situated in the experimental camp. In so doing, we seek to provide a bridge between the formality on the one hand and the practical work on the other.

The current work uses the Z specification language [15] which is increasingly being used for specifying frameworks and systems in AI (e.g. [6, 11]). Z provides the modularity, abstraction and expressiveness that allows a structured account of a computer system and its associated operations to be given at different levels of detail, with system complexity being added at successively lower levels. In addition, Z schemas are particularly suitable in squaring the demands of formal modelling with the need for implementation, by providing clear and unambiguous definitions of state and operations on state which provide a basis for program development. These qualities satisfy our needs for preciseness through formality but do not detract from our desire to remain connected to issues of implementation.

The paper begins with a brief review of the agent hierarchy framework specified previously. The next section introduces the Contract Net Protocol, and extends the formal specification of the framework to cover the components of, and relationships within, the Contract Net. Then we examine these relationships to provide more general definitions of *cooperation* and *engagement*, and finally we very briefly review related work.

2 The Agent Hierarchy

In this section, we briefly review the agent hierarchy framework for agency and autonomy. Our treatment will be sketchy and will lack many examples due to space constraints. For full details, the reader is referred to [9]. In short, we propose a three-tiered hierarchy of entities comprising *objects*, *agents* and *autonomous agents*. The basic idea underlying this hierarchy is that all known entities are objects. Of this set of objects, some are agents, and of these agents, some are autonomous agents. Below, we define what is required for each of the entities in the hierarchy. First we must define some primitives.

An *action* is a discrete event which changes the state of the environment. An *attribute* is a perceivable feature. It is the only characteristic of the world which is manifest.

[*Action, Attribute*]

A *goal* is a state of affairs to be achieved in the environment. It is just a set of attributes that describe a state of affairs in the world:

$$Goal == \mathbb{P}\, Attribute$$

A *motivation* is any desire or preference that can lead to the generation and adoption of goals and which affects the outcome of the reasoning or behavioural task intended to satisfy those goals. (This draws on the definition used by Kunda [8].)

[*Motivation*]

Now we can provide a *template* for all the entities in the world and use it to construct formal definitions and specifications of agency and autonomy.

An *entity* is something that comprises a set of attributes, a set of actions, a set of goals and a set of motivations. This is defined in Z using the *state schema* below that has a *declarative* part which contains four variables and their types. First, *attributes* is the set of features of the entity. Second, *capableof* is the set of actions of the entity, and is sometimes referred to as the *competence* of the entity. Next, *goals* and *motivations* are the sets of goals and motivations of the entity respectively.

```
┌─ Entity ────────────────────────────────────────────────
│  attributes : P Attribute
│  capableof : P Action
│  goals : P Goal
│  motivations : P Motivation
└─────────────────────────────────────────────────────────
```

The type of any schema can be considered as the cartesian product of the types of each of its variables, without any notion of order, but constrained by predicates.

An *object* is an entity with non-empty sets of actions and attributes, and no further defining characteristics. The *Object* schema below has a declarative part that simply includes the previously defined template schema, *Entity*. In addition, it has a *predicate* part which relates and constrains those variables. This specifies that an object must have non-empty sets of attributes and actions. Objects are therefore defined by their ability in terms of their actions, and their configuration in terms of their attributes. The configuration of an object includes references to the body of the object and its position, similar to the notion of Goodwin [6].

```
┌─ Object ────────────────────────────────────────────────
│  Entity
│ ─────────────────────────────────────────────
│  attributes ≠ { }
│  capableof ≠ { }
└─────────────────────────────────────────────────────────
```

Agents are just objects with certain dispositions. An object is an agent if it serves a useful purpose either to a different agent, or to itself, in which case the agent is *autonomous*. Specifically, an agent is something that 'adopts' or satisfies a goal or set of goals (often of another). Thus if I want a robot to make me a cup of coffee, then the robot is my agent for making coffee since it has *adopted* my goal to make coffee. An *agent* is thus defined in relation to its goals, and is an instantiation of an object together with an associated goal or set of goals.

```
┌─ Agent ─────────────────────────────────────────────────
│  Object
│ ─────────────────────────────────────────────
│  goals ≠ { }
└─────────────────────────────────────────────────────────
```

An agent has or is *ascribed* a set of goals which it retains over any instantiation. One object may give rise to different instantiations of agents; an agent is instantiated from an object in response to another agent. Agency is *transient*, and an object which becomes an agent at some time may subsequently revert to being an object.

In order to ground this goal adoption, there must be some agents which can generate their own goals. These are *autonomous* agents since they are not dependent on the goals of others. Instead of adopting goals from other agents, autonomous agents possess goals which they *generate* themselves from *motivations* which are higher-level non-derivative internal components characterising the nature of the agent. However, since they are not describable states of affairs in the environment, motivations are distinct from goals. For example, the motivation *survival* does not specify a state of affairs to be achieved, nor is it describable in terms of the environment, but it may (if other motivations permit) give rise to the generation of a goal to flee from danger. The difference between the motivation of survival and the goal of fleeing is clear, with the former providing a reason for doing the latter.

Thus, a *motivated agent* is one which pursues its own agenda for reasoning and behaviour in accordance with its internal motivation. It is this that is the critical factor in achieving autonomy and, consequently, an *autonomous agent* must necessarily be a *motivated* agent.

An *autonomous agent* is any agent which has its own set of motivations. In other words, the behaviour of the agent is determined by both external and internal factors. This is qualitatively different from an agent with goals because motivations are non-derivative and governed by internal inaccessible rules, while goals are derivative and relate directly to motivations.

$$
\begin{array}{|l|}
\hline
\;AutonomousAgent \\
\;\;Agent \\
\hline
\;\;motivations \neq \{\,\} \\
\hline
\end{array}
$$

3 Formalising the Contract Net Protocol

Now we consider the Contract Net as described by Smith [13, 14, 3], which can be distilled to the basic components described here. Essentially, a *contract net* is a collection of nodes that cooperate in achieving goals which, together, satisfy some high-level goal or task. Each node may be either a *manager*, who monitors task execution and processes the results, or a *contractor*, who performs the actual execution of the task.

Negotiation to undertake and satisfy tasks arises when new tasks are generated. These tasks are decomposed into sub-tasks and, when there may be inadequate knowledge or data to undertake these sub-tasks directly, they are offered for bidding by other agents. A *task announcement* message is broadcast, detailing the task requirements. In response to a task announcement, agents can evaluate their interest using *task evaluation procedures* specific to the problem at hand. If there is sufficient interest, then that agent will submit a bid to undertake to perform the task. The *manager* selects nodes using *bid evaluation procedures* based on the information supplied in the bid. It sends *award* messages to successful bidders who then become *contractors* to the manager, and who may in turn subcontract parts of their task. The manager terminates a contract with a *termination* message.

We can refine the framework described above to arrive at a formal specification of the Contract Net Protocol which retains the structure of the framework.

First, we specify the different kinds of entity from which a contract net is constructed, and which participate in it. A node in a contract net is just an object.

```
┌─ CNode ─────────────────────────────────────
│ Object
└─────────────────────────────────────────────
```

A *ContractAgent* is any node currently involved in some task.

```
┌─ ContractAgent ─────────────────────────────
│ CNode
│ Agent
└─────────────────────────────────────────────
```

All nodes in the net are therefore either doing nothing, or doing something, in which case they are agents. The collection of such nodes is given in the following schema.

```
┌─ AllNodes ──────────────────────────────────
│ nodes : ℙ CNode
│ contractagents : ℙ ContractAgent
│─────────────────────────────────────────────
│ contractagents ⊆ nodes
└─────────────────────────────────────────────
```

This completes the definition of the nodes in the net and we now need to consider the function of the net. A manager engages contractors to perform certain tasks. A task is defined to be the same as a goal, as it just specifies a state of affairs to be achieved.

$$Task == Goal$$

In the next schema, we define a contract to comprise a task, a manager and a contractor. The contractor and manager must be different, and the task must be a goal of both the manager and the contractor.

```
┌─ Contract ──────────────────────────────────
│ task : Task
│ manager : ContractAgent
│ contractor : ContractAgent
│─────────────────────────────────────────────
│ manager ≠ contractor
│ task ∈ (manager.goals ∩ contractor.goals)
└─────────────────────────────────────────────
```

Now we can define the set of all contracts currently in operation in the contract net. The schema below includes *AllNodes*, and defines *contracts* to be the set of all contracts currently in the net. The managers are the set of nodes which are managing a contract and the contractors are the set of nodes which are contracted. The union of the contractors and the managers gives the set of contract agents.

```
┌─ AllContracts ─────────────────────────────────────────
│ AllNodes
│ contracts : ℙ Contract
│
│ managers : ℙ ContractAgent
│ contractors : ℙ ContractAgent
├────────────────────────────────────────────────────────
│ managers = { c : Contract | c ∈ contracts • c.manager }
│ contractors = { c : Contract | c ∈ contracts • c.contractor }
│ managers ∪ contractors = contractagents
└────────────────────────────────────────────────────────
```

We also need to introduce the notion of *eligibility*. A node is eligible for a task if its actions and attributes satisfy the task requirements. We define *Eligibility* to be a type comprising a set of actions and attributes representing an eligibility specification. This has just the same type as an object.

$$Eligibility == Object$$

The first step in establishing a contract is to issue a *task announcement*. A *TaskAnnouncement* is issued by a *Sender* to a set of *Recipients* to request bids for a particular *Task* from agents with a given *Eligibility* specification.

$$Sender == CNode$$
$$Recipient == CNode$$

```
┌─ TaskAnnouncement ─────────────────────────────────────
│ sender : Sender
│ recs : ℙ Recipient
│ task : Task
│ eligibility : Eligibility
└────────────────────────────────────────────────────────
```

Notice that the combination of a task together with an eligibility is, in fact, an *agency* requirement.

A bid is issued from some node who describes a subset of itself in response to an eligibility specification which will be used in evaluating the bid.

```
┌─ Bid ──────────────────────────────────────────────────
│ cnode : CNode
│ eligibility : Eligibility
├────────────────────────────────────────────────────────
│ eligibility.capableof ⊆ cnode.capableof
│ eligibility.attributes ⊆ cnode.attributes
└────────────────────────────────────────────────────────
```

The state of the contract net can now be represented as the current set of nodes, contracts, task announcements and bids. Each task announcement will have associated with it some set of bids which are just eligibility specifications as described above. In addition, each node has a means of deciding whether it is capable of, and interested in, performing certain tasks (and so bidding for them). First, we need to define *bool*.

$bool ::= True \mid False$

ContractNet
AllContracts
bids : $TaskAnnouncement \nrightarrow \mathbf{P}\ Bid$
interested : $CNode \longrightarrow Task \longrightarrow bool$

taskannouncements : $\mathbf{P}\ TaskAnnouncement$

taskannouncements = dom *bids*

The operation of a node making a task announcement is then given in the schema below where there is a change to *ContractNet*, but no change to *AllContracts*. A node that issues a task announcement must be an agent. Note that the variables with a ? suffix indicate *inputs* to the operation. The second part of the schema specifies that the recipients and the sender must be nodes, that the task must be in the sender's goals, and that the sender must not be able to satisfy the eligibility requirements of the task alone. Finally, the task announcement is added to the set of all task announcements, and an empty set of bids is associated with it.

MakeTaskAnnouncement
$\Delta ContractNet$
$\Xi AllContracts$
$m?$: $ContractAgent$
$ta?$: $TaskAnnouncement$

$m? \in nodes$
$ta?.recs \subseteq nodes$
$ta?.sender = m?$
$ta?.task \in m?.goals$
$\neg\ ((ta?.eligibility.capableof \subseteq m?.capableof) \land$
$\qquad\qquad (ta?.eligibility.attributes \subseteq m?.attributes))$
$taskannouncements' = taskannouncements \cup \{ta?\}$
$bids' = bids \cup \{(ta?, \{\})\}$

In response to a task announcement, a node may make a bid. The schema below specifies that a node making a bid must be one of the receivers of the task announcement, that it must be eligible for the task, that it is interested in performing the task, and that it is not the sender. As a result of a node making a bid, the set of task announcements does not change, but the bids associated with the task announcement are updated to include the new bid.

MakeBid

$\Delta ContractNet$
$con? : CNode$
$bid? : Bid$
$ta? : TaskAnnouncement$

$bid?.cnode = con?$
$con? \in nodes$
$ta? \in taskannouncements$
$con? \in ta?.recs$
$ta?.eligibility.capableof \subseteq bid?.eligibility.capableof$
$ta?.eligibility.attributes \subseteq bid?.eligibility.attributes$
$interested\ con?\ (ta?.task) = True$
$con? \neq ta?.sender$
$taskannouncements' = taskannouncements$
$bids' = bids \oplus \{(ta?, bids\ ta? \cup \{bid?\})\}$

After receiving bids, the issuer of a task announcement awards the contract
to the highest rated bid. The node that makes the award must be the node
that issued the task announcement, and the bid that is selected must be in the
set of bids associated with the task announcement. In order to choose the best
bid, the *rating* function is used to provide a natural number as an evaluation
of a bid with respect to a task announcement. Thus the bid with the highest
rating is selected. After making an award, the set of all contracts is updated
to include a new contract for the particular task with the issuer of the task
announcement as manager and the awarded bidder as contractor, where the
contractor is instantiated from the old node as a new agent with the additional
task of the contract. The task announcement is now satisfied and removed from
the system, and the set of bids is updated accordingly.

MakeAward

$\Delta ContractNet$
$m? : ContractAgent$
$ta? : TaskAnnouncement$
$bid? : Bid$
$rating : TaskAnnouncement \longrightarrow Bid \longrightarrow \mathbb{N}$

$m? = ta?.sender$
$bid? \in bids\ ta?$
$\forall b : Bid \mid b \in bids\ ta? \bullet rating\ ta?\ bid? \geq rating\ ta?\ b$
$contracts' = contracts$
$\qquad \cup \{makecontract\ ta?.task\ m?\ (newagent\ bid?.cnode\ ta?.task)\}$
$contractagents' = contractagents \setminus \{newagent\ bid?.cnode\ ta?.task\}$
$\qquad \cup \{newagent\ bid?.cnode\ ta?.task\}$
$taskannouncements' = taskannouncements \setminus \{ta?\}$
$bids' = bids \setminus \{(ta?, bids\ ta?)\}$

The functions *makecontract* and *newagent* are defined as follows.

$makecontract : Task \nrightarrow ContractAgent \nrightarrow CNode \nrightarrow Contract$
$newagent : CNode \longrightarrow Task \longrightarrow ContractAgent$

$\forall t : Task;\ c : CNode;\ a : ContractAgent \bullet newagent\ c\ t = a \Leftrightarrow$
$\quad a.attributes = c.attributes \wedge a.capableof = c.capableof \wedge$
$\qquad\qquad\qquad\qquad\qquad\qquad\qquad a.goals = c.goals \cup \{t\}$
$\forall t : Task;\ m : ContractAgent;\ c : CNode;\ con : Contract \bullet$
$\quad makecontract\ t\ c\ m = con \Leftrightarrow t \in (m.goals) \wedge m \neq c \wedge$
$\quad con.task = t \wedge con.manager = m \wedge con.contractor = newagent\ c\ t$

Finally, a manager can terminate a contract as specified below where the contract is removed from the set of all contracts.

Whilst the contractor will remove the task from its set of goals the manager will not, since it will still be a contractor for that task or the monitor of that goal. The goal is therefore removed from the goals of the contractor agent. If this node is still an agent, there will be no change to *contractagents*, but if the node previously had only one goal then it will be removed from *contractagents* since it is no longer an agent.

TerminateContract _____
$\Delta AllContracts$
$m? : ContractAgent$
$con? : ContractAgent$
$t? : Task$

$contracts' = contracts \setminus \{makecontract\ t?\ m?\ con?\}$
$oldagent\ con?\ t? \in ContractAgent \Rightarrow$
$\quad contractagents' = contractagents \setminus \{con?\} \cup \{oldagent\ con?\ t?\}$
$oldagent\ con?\ t? \notin ContractAgent \Rightarrow$
$\quad contractagents' = contractagents \setminus \{con?\}$

The *oldagent* function makes an agent revert to the node it was before adopting the goal of the contract.

$oldagent : CNode \longrightarrow Task \longrightarrow ContractAgent$

$\forall t : Task;\ c : CNode;\ a : ContractAgent \bullet oldagent\ c\ t = a \Leftrightarrow$
$\quad a.attributes = c.attributes \wedge$
$\quad a.capableof = c.capableof \wedge$
$\quad a.goals = c.goals \setminus \{t\}$

Davis and Smith[3] also describe a single processor node in a distributed sensing example called a *monitor* node which starts the initialisation as the first step in net operation. If this is just another node which passes on information to another, then it is no different to the manager specified above. If it generated the goal or task to perform by itself, then it is autonomous.

```
┌─ Monitor ──────────────────────────────────────────────
│  AutonomousAgent
│  ContractAgent
└────────────────────────────────────────────────────────
```

4 Cooperation and Engagement in the Contract Net

The contract net is a useful and effective example of applying the framework proposed earlier because it is a concrete and well-understood system. In addition, many of the relationships that arise in the contract net can be generalised to other goal-directed systems. In this section, we elaborate the framework described earlier by considering cooperation and engagement, especially in the light of the contract net example. Thus we use the contract net case-study as an exemplar which allows us to analyse these relationships, first in a limited and well-defined way, and then by broadening them to define properties of multi-agent systems in general (fuller details of which can be found in [10]).

We now define a new agent, a *server* agent, which is a *non-autonomous* agent.

```
┌─ ServerAgent ──────────────────────────────────────────
│  Agent
│ ───────────────────────────────────────────────────────
│  motivations = { }
└────────────────────────────────────────────────────────
```

Just as a contract net is a collection of *CNodes* and *ContractAgents* we define the world as a collection of objects, agents, and autonomous agents.

```
┌─ World ────────────────────────────────────────────────
│  objects : ℙ Object
│  agents : ℙ Agent
│  autoagents : ℙ AutonomousAgent
│  serveragents : ℙ ServerAgent
│ ───────────────────────────────────────────────────────
│  autoagents ⊆ agents ⊆ objects
│  autoagents ∪ serveragents = agents
└────────────────────────────────────────────────────────
```

Whenever a node that is not autonomous adopts some goal, it is being *engaged*. This is the normal situation in the contract net, where the nodes that participate in a contract need not be autonomous, and the manager *engages* the contractor. In a direct engagement, an agent with some goal, the *client*, uses another agent, the *server*, to assist in achieving that goal. The *server* agent is never autonomous, but the *client* can be either autonomous or non-autonomous.

We can modify the *Contract* schema so that it applies to more general situations. A *direct engagement* consists of a *client*, a *server* and the *goal* that the *server* is satisfying for the *client*. The server and client cannot be the same and, just as in a contract, both agents must possess the goal. The schema below thus captures a generalised version of the information that the *Contract* schema, which refers specifically to contract nets, contains.

```
┌─ DirectEngagement ─────────────────────────────────
│ goal : Goal
│ client : Agent
│ server : ServerAgent
├────────────────────────────────────────────────────
│ client ≠ server
│ goal ∈ (client.goals ∩ server.goals)
└────────────────────────────────────────────────────
```

All of the *direct* engagements in the world are given in the following schema by *dengagement*, analogous to *contracts* in the earlier *AllContracts* schema. The client agents of the world are all those which are the clients for some direct engagement, and the server-agents are those which are the server agent for some direct engagement. All these agents are a subset of the agents in the world. Finally, we can say that an agent, *c*, *directly engages* another server-agent, *s*, if, and only if, there is a direct engagement between *c* and *s*. The set of all such relationships is given by *dengages*. This schema thus captures the same information about the world as the *AllContracts* schema that refers specifically to contract nets.

```
┌─ WorldEngagements ─────────────────────────────────
│ World
│ dengagement : P DirectEngagement
│ clientagents : P Agent
│ dengages : Agent ↔ ServerAgent
├────────────────────────────────────────────────────
│ clientagents = {d : dengagement • d.client}
│ serveragents = {d : dengagement • d.server}
│ {d : dengagement • d.server} ∪ {d : dengagement • d.client} ⊆ agents
│ dengages = {e : dengagement • (e.client, e.server)}
└────────────────────────────────────────────────────
```

We can also consider the case of an agent that is contracted to perform a task who subcontracts that task to another agent. This leads to the possibility of an *engagement chain* which is a sequence of *direct engagements*. Thus an *engagement chain* involves a *goal*, the autonomous client-agent that generated the goal, *autoagent*, and a sequence of server-agents, *chain*, where each is directly engaging the next. Note that in a contract, the autonomous agent (or monitor) who originally generated the goal may belong to the contract net or may be some external entity.

```
┌─ EngagementChain ──────────────────────────────────
│ goal : Goal
│ autoagent : AutonomousAgent
│ chain : seq₁ Agent
├────────────────────────────────────────────────────
│ goal ∈ autoagent.goals
│ goal ∈ ⋃{s : Agent | s ∈ ran chain • s.goals}
│ #(ran chain) = #chain
└────────────────────────────────────────────────────
```

This leads to the specifying of all engagement chains in the world by *engchain* in the schema below. In a contract net, engagement chains involve contracts and subcontracts of agents, all for one task. Every engagement chain, *ec*, has a direct engagement between the autonomous agent, *ec.autoagent*, and the first client, *head ec.chain*, with respect to the goal, *ec.goal*. There must also be a direct engagement between any two agents which follow each other in the chain with respect to the goal.

```
┌─ WorldEngagementChains ─────────────────────────────────────────
│ WorldEngagements
│ engchain : ℙ EngagementChain
├─────────────────────────────────────────────────────────────────
│ ∀ ec : engchain; s₁, s₂ : Agent •
│     (∃ d : dengagement • d.goal = ec.goal ∧ d.client = ec.autoagent
│                    ∧ d.server = head (ec.chain)) ∧
│     ⟨s₁, s₂⟩ in ec.chain ⇒ (∃ d : dengagement •
│                    d.client = s₁ ∧ d.server = s₂ ∧ d.goal = ec.goal)
└─────────────────────────────────────────────────────────────────
```

If an autonomous agent adopts the goal of another autonomous agent, then we say that they are *cooperating* with respect to that goal. The term *cooperation* is reserved for use only when the parties involved are autonomous and potentially capable of resisting. If they are not autonomous (and not capable of resisting), then one simply *engages* the other. We distinguish between these relationships on the basis of the autonomy of the agents involved. Cooperation is a *symmetric* relation between two autonomous agents, in contrast to a normal contract in the contract net which is an engagement, an asymmetric relation between a (client) agent and another server-agent.

Thus, a *cooperation* describes a goal, the autonomous agent that originally generated that goal, and the autonomous agents who have adopted that goal from the original agent. It is a more sophisticated relationship than normally appears in the contract net, because it requires autonomy in all participants, a quality which is not necessary in the simpler engagements prevalent there.

```
┌─ Cooperation ───────────────────────────────────────────────────
│ goal : Goal
│ generatingagent : AutonomousAgent
│ cooperatingagents : ℙ AutonomousAgent
├─────────────────────────────────────────────────────────────────
│ #cooperatingagents ≥ 1
│ ∀ aa : cooperatingagents • goal ∈ aa.goals
│ goal ∈ generatingagent.goals
└─────────────────────────────────────────────────────────────────
```

The set of all cooperations is given in the schema below by *cooperations*. An agent x_1 *cooperates* with agent x_2 if, and only if, both x_1 and x_2 are autonomous, one of them is the generating agent and the other is one of the cooperating agents. In the following schema, *cooperates* describes the set of all such relationships. Since the relationship is symmetric, it is equal to its own inverse.

WorldCooperations
World
$cooperations : \mathbb{P}\ Cooperation$
$cooperates : AutonomousAgent \longleftrightarrow AutonomousAgent$

$cooperates = \bigcup \{a1, a2 : AutonomousAgent\ |$
$\qquad (\exists\ c : cooperations \bullet a1 = c.generatingagent \wedge$
$\qquad\qquad a2 \in c.cooperatingagents) \bullet \{(a1, a2), (a2, a1)\}\}$
$cooperates^{\sim} = cooperates$

---

5   Discussion

The contract net is important both because it was a significant effort to tackle cooperative problem solving, and because it is very definitely situated in the practical and experimental camp. Moreover, it is relatively well-defined and understood, and hence very suitable to be used as an exemplar for the kind of work described here. As a result, there have been several extensions proposed to the basic contract net such as [12, 16], and there have been other attempts at formalisation, by Werner [17], and by Wooldridge [18, 5], for example. However, our approach differs markedly: first, we use a well-known generic specification language which ties in closely with implementation issues, and which has a very large user base; and second, we situate our formalisation in the broader context of a general framework for agency and autonomy. We are not concerned with the development of the formalism, but with its application in a succinct way to the abstract framework proposed, the relationships defined within that framework, and to the specification of concrete systems using the framework to provide structure. Although alternative specification languages such as DESIRE [1], for example, would also have been possible, Z's qualities of encapsulation and abstraction within a formalism used extensively in industry and academia, for both small and large-scale systems (e.g. [2, 11, 7]) and for more theoretical approaches to multi-agent systems (e.g. [4]), provide a more *accessible* method.

In this paper we have outlined previous work on constructing a formal framework for autonomous agent systems, within which particular models and systems can be specified by adding further levels of detail. In that vein, we have described the contract net protocol and specified it formally, making use of the entities defined and described within the framework. The contract net protocol provides exemplars of certain commonly occurring inter-agent relationships such as cooperation and engagement. By using the example of the contract net and generalising the relationships found therein, we have been able to elaborate the formal framework to include definitions of these general relationships, building up a common and general language with which to discuss multi-agent systems and models. A key feature of the work that is illustrated in this paper is the ease with which a particular system, described in detail, can be accommodated by the framework and used to focus further development of the theoretical underpinnings of multi-agent systems.

References

1. F. Brazier, B. Dunin Keplicz, N. Jennings, and J. Treur. Formal specification of multi-agent systems: A real-world case. In *Proceedings of the First International Conference on Multi-Agent Systems*, pages 25–32. AAAI Press / MIT Press, 1995.
2. I. Craig. *Formal Specification of Advanced AI Architectures*. Ellis Horwood, 1991.
3. R. Davis and R. G. Smith. Negotiation as a metaphor for distributed problem solving. *Artificial Intelligence*, 20(1):63–109, 1983.
4. M. d'Inverno and M. Luck. A formal view of social dependence networks. In *Proceedings of the First Australian DAI Workshop*. Springer Verlag, To appear, 1996.
5. M. Fisher and M. Wooldridge. Specifying and executing protocols for cooperative action. In S. Deen, ed., *CKBS-94: Proceedings of the Second International Working Conference on Cooperating Knowledge-Based Systems*. Springer-Verlag, 1994.
6. R. Goodwin. Formalizing properties of agents. Technical Report CMU-CS-93-159, Carnegie-Mellon University, 1993.
7. M. G. Hinchey and J. P. Bowen, editors. *Applications of Formal Methods*. Prentice Hall International Series in Computer Science, 1995.
8. Z. Kunda. The case for motivated reasoning. *Psychological Bulletin*, 108(3):480–498, 1990.
9. M. Luck and M. d'Inverno. A formal framework for agency and autonomy. In *Proceedings of the First International Conference on Multi-Agent Systems*, pages 254–260. AAAI Press / MIT Press, 1995.
10. M. Luck and M. d'Inverno. Engagement and cooperation in motivated agent modelling. In *Proceedings of the First Australian DAI Workshop*. Springer Verlag, To appear, 1996.
11. B. G. Milnes. A specification of the Soar architecture in Z. Technical Report CMU-CS-92-169, School of Computer Science, Carnegie Mellon University, 1992.
12. T. Sandholm. An implementation of the contract net protocol based on marginal cost calculations. In *Proceedings of the Eleventh National Conference on Artificial Intelligence (AAAI-93)*, pages 256–262. AAAI Press / MIT Press, 1993.
13. R. G. Smith. The contract net protocol: High-level communication and control in a distributed problem solver. *IEEE Transactions on Computers*, 29(12), 1980.
14. R. G. Smith and R. Davis. Frameworks for cooperation in distributed problem solving. *IEEE Transactions on Systems, Man and Cybernetics*, 11(1):61–70, 1981.
15. J. M. Spivey. *The Z Notation*. Prentice Hall, Hemel Hempstead, 2nd edition, 1992.
16. H. Van Dyke Parunak. Manufacturing experience with the contract net. In M. Huhns, editor, *Distributed Artificial Intelligence*, pages 285–310. Pitman Publishing: London and Morgan Kaufmann: San Mateo, CA, 1987.
17. E. Werner. Cooperating agents: A unified theory of communication and social structure. In L. Gasser and M. Huhns, editors, *Distributed Artificial Intelligence Volume II*, pages 3–36. Pitman Publishing: London and Morgan Kaufmann: San Mateo, CA, 1989.
18. M. Wooldridge. *The Logical Modelling of Computational Multi-Agent Systems*. PhD thesis, Department of Computation, UMIST, Manchester, UK, October 1992.
19. M. J. Wooldridge and N. R. Jennings. Formalizing the cooperative problem solving process. In *Proceedings of the Thirteenth International Workshop on Distributed Artificial Intelligence*, 1994.

A Coordination Algorithm for Multi-Agent Planning

Amal El Fallah Seghrouchni[1] and Serge Haddad[2]

[1] LIPN - URA 1507, Inst. Galilée, Université Paris-Nord
Av. J.B. Clément, 93430 Villetaneuse, France
elfallah@ura1507.univ-paris13.fr
[2] LAMSADE, Université Paris-Dauphine,
Centre Informatique, Place du Maréchal de Lattre de Tassigny
75775 Paris Cédex 16, France
haddad@lamsade.dauphine.fr

Abstract. One of the major interests of Multi-Agent Systems (MAS), which are able to handle distributed planning, is coordination. This coordination requires both an adequate plan representation and efficient interacting methods between agents. Interactions are based on information exchange (e.g. data, partial or global plan) and allow agents to update their own plans by including the exchanged information. Coordination generally produces two effects: it cancels negative interactions (e.g. resource sharing) and it takes advantage of helpful ones (e.g. handling redundant actions). A coordination model should satisfy the following requirements: domain independence, broad covering of interacting situations, operational coordination semantics and natural expression for the designer. This paper presents an adequate framework for the representation and handling of plans in MAS. It then shows how an approach based on a plan representation by means of a partial order model enables the definition of a coordination algorithm for the possible enrichment of plans.

Keywords: Multi-Agent Systems, Distributed Planning, Coordination, Plan Interactions.

1 Introduction

One of the major interests of Multi-Agent Systems (MAS) is their ability to handle distributed planning by coordinating agents' plans. Such a coordination requires both an adequate plan representation and an efficient interaction between agents. Based on information exchange (e.g. data, plans), the interaction allows agents to update their own plans by considering the exchanged information. Coordination generally produces two effects: cancelling negative interactions (e.g. harmful actions) and taking advantage of helpful interactions (e.g. handling redundant actions). Agents organize their activities and update their plans in order to cooperate and avoid conflicts. The main requirements of coordination can be summarized as follows:

- communication between agents,
- recognition of potential interactions between plans,
- negotiation between agents in the case of conflictual situations.

These aspects have already been studied in numerous papers. In coordination, the use of communication is a part of planning and action. It concerns the development of MAS where speech acts are often involved [15, 16, 3, 4, 9]. The second aspect comes from the study of interactions which have been of continuing interest in multi-agent planning [5, 8, 17, 11, 14, 7]. This mainly focuses on how planning agents can positively cooperate in distributed environments. The last aspect has been studied in [17, 6, 2]. The main criticisms to be made about most of the planning models proposed in Multi-Agent research are:

- The formal cooperation models are theoretical. Although they can be used to prove cooperation theories mathematically and show how assumptions about their domains and characteristics affect their capabilities, these models are often remote from practical systems and provide only a little help in designing MAS.
- The computing methods used to work out dependencies between agents (e.g. between actions, plans, etc.) are often static when they need to be dynamic. Even when they are dynamic, these methods often require a synchronous rhythm between execution and planification whereas the dependencies need to be handled asynchronously (i.e. we want to cover cases where one agent is building a plan while another is executing his own plan).
- The coordination process is generally centralized where it should be distributed and implies two agents where it should imply n agents. (i.e. not just two by two).

This paper focuses on the situation where n agents carry out their already coordinated plans while a new agent produces a new plan which has to be coordinated with the existing ones. A coordinating algorithm is proposed, with solutions to the representation and management of plans in view of distributed planning. The main advantages offered by the algorithm are as follows:

- the algorithm is distributed on each agent, with the result that the coordination is really distributed (i.e. each agent contributes to the coordination process),
- during coordination, no agent is suspended (i.e. each agent pursues his plan without interruption),
- the existing agents do not regenerate their plans (i.e. an agent plans once and once only) since the proposed algorithm allows coordination through the enrichment of plans,
- the algorithm solves the negative and positive interactions,
- the algorithm ensures both concurrent planning and the tolerance of possible agent failure,
- an essential feature of this algorithm is that the coordination is performed without generating all the possible plan overlaps, thus avoiding a combinatorial explosion.

Section two introduces a conceptual framework for plan management based on a classical planification formalism. Section three shows how this framework is adapted to handle a specific planification domain. Section four presents the coordination requirements, describes the specific contribution of this efficient new algorithm which can handle negative and positive interactions by coordinating plans, and gives its proof. Section five is a discussion of possible ways of improving and extending the algorithm.

2 Conceptual Framework for Plan Management

The model used here is made up of cognitive agents which represent the active components of the MAS and which evolve in the environment. The formalism is based on a classical representation often used in planning. Let us now define the framework for the plan management.

2.1 Definition of the environment

The positive or negative interactions depend on the environment, the representation of which includes the modeling of resources. The environment can be completely defined through a set of predicates called $Prop$ such that: $Prop = \{p, \bar{p}, q, \bar{q}, \cdots\}$

Notation: Let p be a positive proposition and $\bar{p}$ the negative one. A Greek letter is used for each item of $Prop$ such as: ξ, ψ, φ, etc. The negation can be extended to any sub-set of $Prop$ in the following way:
if $S \in 2^{Prop}$ then $\bar{S} = \{\bar{\xi}/\xi \in S\}$
Hence, an environment state is defined as a consistent sub-set of $Prop$, a partial state and a global state being distinguished as follows:

Definition 1. S is a partial state if and only if:
$\forall \xi \in Prop, |\{\xi, \bar{\xi}\} \cap S| \leq 1$
(i.e. an execution context which is partially defined)

Definition 2. S is a total state if and only if:
$\forall \xi \in Prop, |\{\xi, \bar{\xi}\} \cap S| = 1$

2.2 Definition of actions

The resolution plan involves actions associated with tasks to be performed. These actions constitute the plan generated by the planner. An action is defined through three components:

- the label or the name of the action,

- the pre-conditions (Pre), which represent a partial state by means of the set of conditions which are necessary (i.e. must be satisfied) to perform the action,
- the post-conditions ($Post$), which are the set of conditions that will be satisfied after the action has been performed (add list and delete list in STRIPS representation, for instance).

Note that these conditions are syntactic constructions expressing some constraints to be satisfied. This is similar to the STRIPS rule.

Definition 3. Let $Act = \{a, b, c, \cdots\}$ be the set of possible actions, and let $a \in Act$, then:
$a \rightarrow Pre(a)$ where $Pre(a)$ is a partial state
$a \rightarrow Post(a)$ where $Post(a)$ is a partial state
The execution of the action a, when the state is S, produces the new state S' such that:

$$S \xrightarrow{a} S' \Leftrightarrow Pre(a) \subset S \text{ and } S' = (S \setminus \overline{Post}(a)) \cup Post(a).$$

2.3 Definition of plans

To reach a given goal, an agent uses a planner to elaborate a local plan. Such a plan organizes a collection of actions which can be performed sequentially or concurrently. Each agent is responsible for generating his local plans and maintaining their consistency. A correct plan execution often requires that actions be taken in some specific partial order. Whatever the total order that extends the partial order obtained from the graph, the plan must remain feasible.

Notation: Let R be an ordering relation, we note R^+ the transitive closing of R and R^* the reflexive and transitive closing of R.

Definition 4. A plan $\Pi = \{A_\pi, R_\pi\}$ is a directed acyclic graph where:
$A_\pi \subset Act$ is the set of nodes,
R_π is the set of arcs such that $R_\pi \subset A_\pi \times A_\pi$

Definition 5. Let π be a plan and $a \in A_\pi$. The necessary post-conditions $PostNec$ of an action a are defined as follows:
$PostNec(a) = \{\xi / \xi \in Post(a), \exists b \text{ such that } a R_\pi^+ b \text{ with } \xi \in Pre(b), \forall c \text{ such that } a R_\pi^+ c \text{ and } c R_\pi^+ b, \xi \notin Post(c)\}$

This definition means that the post-condition ξ which is obtained by the performance of action a is necessary for the performance of action b and that b cannot be sure of obtaining the proposition ξ otherwise. In other words, the $PostNec$ conditions are necessary for the future execution. In order to execute a plan, such post-conditions cannot be deleted. It is important to distinguish such propositions during the coordination process.
Let us note that the $PostNec$ set can be obtained automatically by a planner as

described in [15] using algorithms such as POCL [12] or TOPI [13]. The $PostNec$ are equivalent to the causal links in [1]. If another planner is used to compute the $PostNec$ set, then the cost may be high.

3 Planning Performance

3.1 Definition of a feasible plan

A plan Π is feasible if and only if each action a of Π can be performed whatever the total order that extends the partial order obtained from the graph.
An action a of Π can be performed if each pre-condition ξ of a can be satisfied. This is possible if there exists a strict predecessor b of a which generates the pre-condition ξ, and for all action c which generates $\bar{\xi}$, then c must be a predecessor of b or a successor of a.

Definition 6. A plan Π is feasible if and only if:
$\forall a \in A_\pi$, $\forall \xi \in Pre(a)$, $\exists b \in A_\pi$, such that:

- $\xi \in Post(b)$
- $bR_\pi^+ a$ (strict predecessor)
- $\forall c \in A_\pi$ such that $\bar{\xi} \in Post(c)$ $cR_\pi^* b$ or $aR_\pi^* c$

Hypothesis: We assume that each agent has a set of stable states where an agent is idle. Such states are called homestates and can be defined as a family of states to which an agent can come back and from which he can easily generate a plan. In order to build a structured plan, we also assume that an agent proceeds in two phases.

Phase 1. The agent builds his plan independently of the initial state. An agent starts from the current state and tries to come back to a family of homestates.

Phase 2. The agent tries to build a structured plan from the first phase.

3.2 Definition of a structured plan

Definition 7. A plan $\Pi = \{A_\pi, R_\pi\}$ is a structured plan if and only if:

- $\forall a_i \in Init_\pi$, $\forall a \in A_\pi$ we have not $aR_\pi a_i$
- $\forall a \in A_\pi$, $\exists a_i \in Init_\pi$ such that $a_i R_\pi^* a$
- $\forall a \in A_\pi$, $\exists a_e \in End_\pi$ such that $aR_\pi^* a_e$

where:
$$A_\pi = Init_\pi \uplus Int_\pi \uplus End_\pi$$
and $\uplus$ is the disjoint union of:

- $Init_\pi$: the set of initial actions in the plan Π generated by the first phase,
- Int_π: the set of intermediate actions in Π through which the intermediate results are obtained,
- End_π: the set of the end actions which give the final results of the performed plan.

These constraints mean that no initial action can have a predecessor, and each intermediate action has both an end action as a successor and an initial action as a predecessor.

4 Coordination Requirements

In order to introduce the coordination process, let us consider an MAS with n agents $\{g_1, g_2, \ldots, g_n\}$, to each of which is associated a plan: $g_i \to \Pi_i$. Let us also assume that the plans $\Pi_1, \Pi_2, \ldots, \Pi_{n-1}$, (associated respectively with $g_1, g_2, \ldots, g_{n-1}$) are already coordinated and that the agent g_n produces a new plan Π_n. The problem to be solved here is to coordinate the plan Π_n by enriching it without modifying the existing plans $\Pi_1, \Pi_2, \ldots, \Pi_{n-1}$. Moreover, the coordination process must generate both a feasible plan for g_n and a solution for possible positive and negative interactions.

4.1 The coordination algorithm involving n agents

The coordination algorithm (COA) involves all the agents during the two phases: the first one is a general coordination preparation, the results of which are applied dynamically in the second phase.

Phase 1. 1. $g_1, g_2, \ldots, g_{n-1}$ perform respectively the plans $\Pi_1, \Pi_2, \ldots, \Pi_{n-1}$ which are already coordinated. The agent g_n produces a new plan.

2. g_n sends his plan Π_n to the existing agents.

3. Each agent $g_k (1 \leq k \leq n-1)$ receives Π_n and tries to coordinate it with his own plan Π_k.

4. $g_1, g_2, \ldots, g_{n-1}$ return to g_n the coordination results in the form of arcs representing the possible synchronization between the two plans.

The last two points represent the local coordination for each agent. Let us assume that the agent $g_i (1 \leq i \leq n-1)$ handles his own plan Π_i, and Π_n received from g_n.

To begin with, the agent g_i synchronizes Π_i and Π_n by creating an arc between each pair of actions in $End_{\Pi_i} \times Init_{\Pi_n}$. Each $arc(a_j^i, a_k^n)$ has an action a_j in End_{Π_i} as a source and an action a_k in $Init_{\Pi_n}$ as a target (see Situation 1

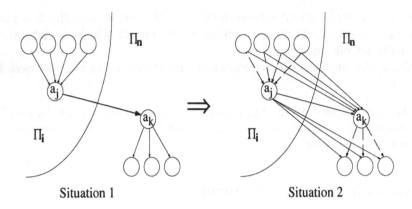

Fig. 1. Moving up arcs.

in Figure. 1). Note that the action index represents the action index in the plan while the action exponent represents the plan index in the system.

Then the agent g_i starts from the synchronization arcs and tries to move up through the arcs in order to constitute the set of possible interactions as follows. While there exists a synchronization arc which verifies the condition

$$Arc = \{arc(a_j^i, a_k^n) \text{ such that:}$$

- $1 \leq i \leq n - 1$ and $1 \leq j \leq | A_i |$ and $1 \leq k \leq | A_n |$,
- $\overline{Post}(a_j^i) \cap PostNec(a_k^n) = \emptyset$,
- $\overline{Pre}(a_j^i) \cap Post(a_k^n) = \emptyset\}$.

move up through the arcs (see Situation 2 in Figure. 1) such that:
$Suc(a_j) = Suc(a_k)$ and the $Pred(a_k) = Pred(a_j)$
where:
$Pred(a) = \{b \in A_{\Pi_i} \text{ such that } bR_{\Pi_i}a\}$
$Suc(a) = \{c \in A_{\Pi_n} \text{ such that } aR_{\Pi_i}c\}$

Phase 2. The agent g_n starts performing his plan Π_n by taking into account the synchronization arcs (i.e. $arc(a_j^i, a_k^n)$). The coordinated plan Π_n' is:
$$\Pi_n' = \Pi_n \cup arc(a_j^i, a_k^n)$$
where
$(1 \leq i \leq n - 1)(1 \leq j \leq | A_i |)$ and $(1 \leq k \leq | A_n |)$

When the action a_j^i is performed the agent g_i sends synchronization messages to g_n indicating that the arcs (a_j^i, a_k^n) are valid. Consequently, an action a_k^n depending on arcs (a_j^i, a_k^n) will be executed by g_n only if all the corresponding messages are received.
Note that if all the $PostNec(a_k^n)$ of an action have already been generated

by the existing agents, the agent g_n does not execute a_k^n. In the following, we will note $Q_{i,j}$ the set of the synchronisation arcs which are created from the plan Π_i to the plan Π_j such that:

$$Q_{i,j} = arc(a_k^i, a_l^j) \text{ where } 1 \le i, j \le n, \ 1 \le k \le |A_i|, \text{ and } 1 \le l \le |A_j|$$

Let us now prove that global performance remains possible. In other words, we must prove that the union of all the plans and the new arcs $Q_{i,j}$ is a feasible plan.

Theorem 8. *The union of the plans (i.e. existing ones and the new plan) and the new sets of $Q_{i,j}$ generated by the algorithm COA:*

$$\left(\bigcup_{i=1}^{n} \Pi_i \right) \bigcup \left(\bigcup_{i=1}^{n} [\bigcup_{j=i+1}^{n} Q_{i,j}] \right)$$

is a feasible plan.

4.2 Proof of the coordination algorithm

Notation:

Let $\Pi^{(1)}, \cdots, \Pi^{(n)}$ be the coordinated plans of the agents $\{1\}, \{1,2\}, \ldots, \{1,\ldots,n\}$. We prove by recurrence that the plan $\Pi^{(n)}$ is feasible. First, we introduce new notations:

- $\Pi_{\{i,j\}} = \Pi_i \cup \Pi_j \cup Q_{i,j} \quad if \ i < j$
- $\Pi_{\{i,i\}} = \Pi_i$

Our recurrence hypothesis for a plan $\Pi^{(i)}$ is:

$\forall a \in A_{\Pi_j}, \ \forall \xi \in Pre(a), \exists b \in A_{\Pi_j}$ such that:

- $\xi \in PostNec(b)$
- $b R_{\Pi_j}^+ a$
- $\forall c \in A_{\Pi_k}$ such that $\bar{\xi} \in Post(c)$ then

$$c R_{\Pi_{\{j,k\}}}^* b \ or \ a R_{\Pi_{\{j,k\}}}^* c$$

Initially, $\Pi^{(1)} = \Pi_1$ is feasible and satisfies the recurrence hypothesis because all the actions belonging to the agent (1) are coordinated. Let us assume that $\Pi^{(n-1)}$ satisfies the recurrence hypothesis and let us prove that $\Pi^{(n)}$ also satisfies it. We can note a series of plans $\Pi^{(n)(1)}, \cdots, \Pi^{(n)(s)}$ where:

- $\Pi^{(n)(1)}$ is the plan which is obtained from $\Pi^{(n-1)}$ by adding Π_n and the initial synchronization arcs $Q_{i,n}$ as follows:

$$\Pi^{(n)(1)} = \Pi^{(n-1)} \cup \Pi_n \bigcup_{i<n} Q_{i,n}$$

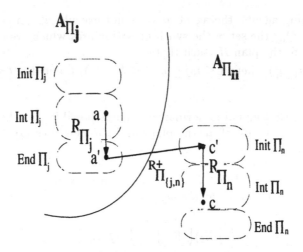

Fig. 2. A structured plan

- $\Pi^{(n)(m+1)}$ is the plan obtained from $\Pi^{(n)(m)}$ by substituting other arcs for the synchronization arc $\alpha \rightarrow \beta$ with $\alpha \in \Pi^{(i)}$ and $\beta \in \Pi^{(n)}$ during examination of the plan.

First, we prove that $\Pi^{(n)(1)}$ satisfies the recurrence hypothesis:
$\forall a \in A_{\Pi_j}, \forall \xi \in Pre(a)$

case 1: If $j \neq n$ then the recurrence hypothesis implies:

$\exists b \in A_{\Pi_j}$ such that:
- $\xi \in PostNec(b)$
- $bR^{+}_{\Pi_j}a$
- $\forall c \in A_{\Pi_k}(k \neq n)$ such that $\bar{\xi} \in Post(c)$ then
$$cR^{*}_{\Pi_{\{j,k\}}}b \text{ or } aR^{*}_{\Pi_{\{j,k\}}}c$$

Let us now benefit from our structured plan definition (see definition 7 and Figure. 2) and let $c \in A_{\Pi_n}$, then:
- $\exists c' \in Init_{\Pi_n} : c'R^{*}_{\Pi_n}c$
- $\exists a' \in End_{\Pi_j} : aR^{*}_{\Pi_j}a'$
- $\exists(a',c') \in Q_{\{j,n\}}$
hence $aR^{*}_{\Pi_{j,n}}c$

case 2: If $j = n$ then, since Π_n is a feasible plan, $\exists b \in A_{\Pi_n}$ such that:

- $\xi \in PostNec(b)$
- $bR^{+}_{\Pi_n}a$
- $\forall c \in A_{\Pi_n}$ such that $\bar{\xi} \in Post(c)$ then

$$cR^*_{\Pi_n} b \text{ or } aR^*_{\Pi_n} c$$

Let $c \in A_{\Pi_k} (k \neq n)$, then:
- $\exists c' \in End_{\Pi_k} : cR^*_{\Pi_k} c'$
- $\exists a' \in Init_{\Pi_n} : a'R^*_{\Pi_{\{k,n\}}} b$
- $\exists (c', a') \in Q_{k,n}$

hence $cR^*_{\Pi_{\{k,n\}}} b$

We conclude then that $\Pi^{(n)(1)}$ satisfies the recurrence hypothesis. All that remains to be down is to prove that if $\Pi^{(n)(m)}$ satisfies the recurrence hypothesis then $\Pi^{(n)(m+1)}$ also satisfies it. Let us call $\alpha \to \beta$ (with $\alpha \in \Pi^{(i)}$ and $\beta \in \Pi^{(n)}$) the substituted arc.
$\forall a \in A_{\Pi_j}$, $\forall \xi \in Pre(a)$, the recurrence hypothesis implies that $\exists b \in A_{\Pi_j}$ such that:

- $\xi \in PostNec(b)$
- $bR^+_{\Pi_j} a$

Let us assume that $\exists c \in A_{\Pi_k}$ such that $\bar{\xi} \in Post(c)$. Let us now consider all the possible cases:

case 1: ($j \neq i$ and $j \neq n$) or ($k \neq i$ and $k \neq n$)
As $\Pi_{\{j,k\}}$ is unchanged by the substitution then $cR^*_{\Pi_{\{j,k\}}} b$ or $aR^*_{\Pi_{\{j,k\}}} c$

case 2: ($j = i$ and $k = i$)
As Π_j is unchanged by the substitution then $cR^*_{\Pi_{\{j,k\}}} b$ or $aR^*_{\Pi_{\{j,k\}}} c$

case 3: ($j = n$ and $k = n$)
As Π_n is unchanged by the substitution then $cR^*_{\Pi_{\{j,k\}}} b$ or $aR^*_{\Pi_{\{j,k\}}} c$

case 4: ($j = n$ and $k = i$)
In $\Pi^{(n)(m)}$ we have $cR^*_{\Pi_{\{j,k\}}} b$ or $aR^*_{\Pi_{\{j,k\}}} c$
since $j = n$ then necessarily $cR^*_{\Pi_{\{j,k\}}} b$ (because in $Q_{i,n}$ the arcs are oriented from i to n).

Let (δ, γ) be the only arc on the path from c to b where $\delta \in \Pi_i$ and $\gamma \in \Pi_n$. The situation in $\Pi^{(n)(m)}$ is then:

case 4.a: $(\delta, \gamma) \neq (\alpha, \beta)$
The situation is unchanged in $\Pi^{(n)(m+1)}$ (see Figure. 3).

case 4.b: $(\delta, \gamma) = (\alpha, \beta)$

case 4.b.1: If $(c \neq \delta)$ then $\exists c'$ such that $cR^*_{\Pi_i} c'$ and $c'R_{\Pi_i}\delta$ then $cR^*_{\Pi_{\{j,k\}}} b$ (see Situation 1 in Figure. 4)

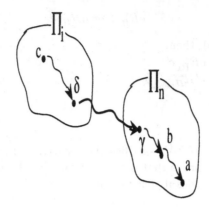

Fig. 3. Unchanged arc

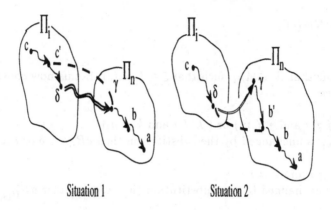

Situation 1   Situation 2

Fig. 4. Substituted arcs

case 4.b.2: If $(b \neq \gamma)$ then $\exists b'$ such that $b' R^*_{\Pi_n} b$ and $\gamma R_{\Pi_n} b'$ then the situation in $\Pi^{(n)(m+1)}$ becomes (see Situation 2 in Figure. 4): $c R^*_{\Pi_{\{j,k\}}} b$

case 4.b.3: If $(c = \delta = \alpha$ and $b = \gamma = \beta)$ then $\xi \in PostNec(\beta)$ and $\bar{\xi} \in Post(\alpha)$ which is an impossible case.

case 5: If $(j = n$ and $k = n)$ then in $\Pi^{(n)(m)}$ we have $c R^*_{\Pi_{\{j,k\}}} b$ or $a R^*_{\Pi_{\{j,k\}}} c$ since $j = n$ then necessarily $a R^*_{\Pi_{\{j,k\}}} c$ (as in case 4).

Let (δ, γ) be an arc as defined before (see case 4), the situation in $\Pi^{(n)(m)}$ (see Figure. 5) presents two sub-cases:

case 5.a: if $(\delta, \gamma) \neq (\alpha, \beta)$ then the $\Pi^{(n)(m+1)}$ situation is unchanged.

case 5.b: if $(\delta, \gamma) = (\alpha, \beta)$ then

    5.b.1: $a \neq \delta$ (as in case 4)

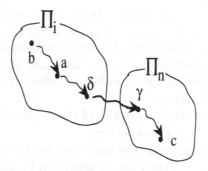

Fig. 5. Unchanged or impossible case

5.b.2: $c \neq \delta$ (as in case 4)
5.b.3: if $(a = \delta = \alpha$ and $c = \gamma = \beta)$
then $\xi \in Pre(\alpha)$ and $\bar{\xi} \in Post(\beta)$ which is an impossible case.

5 Discussion and conclusion

Different research has been done in the area of distributed planning and, in particular, incremental planning. Some of the approaches are similar to the one presented in this paper and include the following.

The approach suggested by V. Martial [11] offers a number of advantages in that the model is a theoretical one which handles both positive and negative interactions. It is however limited by the fact that only two agents (point to point) can be coordinated at a time whereas it would be more useful to be able to coordinate n agents, thus providing a really distributed coordination. The approach put forward by R. Alami [10] is based on the paradigm of plan merging. Although it is robust and handles n agents at a time, it is centralized by the new agent. Moreover, the existing agents are suspended during the process and the new plan is generated in function of existing ones. This is incompatible with the idea of an autonomous agent who can produce his own plan to be coordinated later. Other research focuses on distributed planning [2] but is based rather on organizational structures [18].

The approach described in this paper provides a formal framework to deal with coordinating plans in the area of distributed planning. Both plans and the environment components are defined exactly. A distributed algorithm is proposed to coordinate plans; it is based on the enrichment of plans without modifying existing ones. In this approach the planning and communication aspects are merged, which offers a number of advantages.

- It is a distributed algorithm.
- It coordinates n agents at once.

- It can cancel negative interactions (through the synchronization arcs) and take advantage of positive ones (an action is not executed systematically). In addition, if the different inter-dependencies between agents are specified in advance (predicated) they are only taken into account gradually during execution, thus offering great flexibility and allowing for agent failures.
- No replanning is necessary.
- The approach is generic, independent of the application domain and can be applied to a large range of applications.
- The formalism used is simple and easy to understand.
- The *PostNec* type conditions can be generated by any classical planner.
- The conditions resulting from the planner may cover different sorts of constraints: resource sharing, presence or absence of events, etc. The distinctions have not been drawn here since all the conditions are represented in the predicates where domains of variables can be extended or reduced depending on the domain in question.

This approach can be improved by introducing the notions of abstraction and refinement in the plan. The plan may contain different levels of abstraction used according to the nature of the operation realized on it. Abstraction is necessary to deal with abstract actions which may be refined in order to take into account the favor relations [11].

References

1. A. Barrett and D.S. Weld. Characterizing Subgoal Interactions for Planning. In proceedings of IJCAI-93, pp 1388-1393, 1993.
2. A.H. Bond and L. Gasser. Reading on DAI. Morgan Kauffman Publishers, Inc. 1988.
3. P.R. Cohen and H. Leveque. Teamwork. Tr 503. SRI International, 1991.
4. P.R. Cohen, J. Morgan, and M.E. Pollack (editors). Intentions in communication. MIT Press, 1990.
5. D.D. Corkill. Hierarchical Planning in a Distributed Environment. In Proc. of the sixth International Joint Conference on Artificial Intelligence (IJCAI-79), 1979.
6. R. Davis and R. Smith. Negotiation as a Metaphor for distributed Problem Solving. In Proc. of Artificial Intelligence, vol 20, pp 63-109, 1983.
7. E. Ephrati and J.S. Rosenschein. Constrained Intelligent Action: Planning Under the Influence of a Master Agent. In Proc. of the tenth National Conference on Artificial Intelligence (AAAI-92), 1992.
8. M.P. Georgeff. Communication and interaction in Multi-Agent Planning. In Proc. of the third National Conference on Artificial Intelligence (AAAI-83), 1983.
9. B.J. Grosz and C.L. Sidner. Attention, intentions and structure of discourse. Computational Linguistics, 12(3), 1986.
10. F. Ingrand, R. Alami and F. Robert. Multi-Robot Cooperation through Incremental Plan Merging. Submitted to International Conference on Robotics and Automation, Nagoya. Japan, 1995.

11. V. Martial. Coordination of Plans in a Multi-Agent World by Taking Advantage of the Favor Relation. In Proc. of the tenth International Workshop on Distributed Artificial Intelligence, 1990. and Coordinating plans of autonomous agents, Springer Verlag, 1991.

12. D. McAllester and D. Rosenblitt. Systematic Non-linear Planning. In proceedings of AAAI-91, pp 634-639, 1991.

13. N. Nilsson. Principles of Artificial Intelligence. Tioga Publishing company, Palo Alto, CA, 1980.

14. E. Osawa and M. Tokoro. Collaborative Plan Construction for Multi-Agent Mutual Planning. In E.Werner and Y.Demazeau, DECENTRALIZED A.I.3. Elsevier/North Holland, 1992.

15. J.R. Searle. Collective Intentionality. In Cohen et al, 1990

16. J.R. Searle. Collective intentions and actions. In: PR Cohen, J. Morgan and ME Pollac (eds.), Intentions in Communication, pp 401-416. MIT Press, 1990.

17. G. Zlotkin and J.S. Rosenschein. Negociation and Task Sharing in a Cooperative Domain. In Proceedings of the ninth Workshop on Distributed Artificial Intelligence, 1989.

18. E. Werner. Cooperating agents: a unified theory of communication and social structure. In L. Gasser and MN. Huhns (eds.), Distributed Artificial Intelligence Vol II, pp 3-36. Pitman, 1989.

Modelling Approach and Tool for Designing Protocols for Automated Cooperation in Multi-agent Systems

Omar BELAKHDAR and Jacqueline AYEL

Artificial Intelligence Laboratoiry, Université de Savoie, Chambéry–FRANCE
email: {belakdar, jayel }@lia.univ-savoie.fr

Abstract. The goal of our work is to provide a platform for the development of multi-agent systems. Based on a modelling appoach of cooperation behaviors called COPROM, we have developed a tool called MASCOOF. The latter allows developers to define cooperation protocols in such a way that they are directly usable by the agents to perform cooperative behavior during the problem resolution. Therefore, developers are provided with a language called COOPLAS which allows the specification of protocols for cooperation which the developer desires the agents in his system to use[5,6]. The developer is given via this language the means to define the global structure of the cooperation process in terms of states of conversation and transitions between those states. One problem investigated by our modelling appoach is that of automated meeting scheduling.

1 Introduction

The goal of our work is to provide a platform for the development of multi-agent systems (MAS). This platform provides developers of MAS a certain number of tools and formalisms which allow:

- the specification of the cooperative behaviors of the agents of the SMA using a set of pre-defined protocols initially loaded into the memories of the agents, but which can be eventually modified by the agents during execution.
- the use of these protocols to implement these cooperative behaviors during problem solving.

This platform, called MASCOOF, is based on an interaction modelling approach called COPROM that uses an agent model in which the level of cooperation is clarly identified and a specification language to describe protocols of cooperation.

By studying different approaches of modelling of interaction behaviors (e.g. Contract Net protocol[15], Multistage Negotiation[8], Partial Global Planning[10], Organizational Structuring[9], ...) we have been helped to extract the fundamental concepts of cooperation and to validate our work.

Two applications have been used to test our approach. One is of task attribution using a variation of the Contract Net protocol to achieve a cooperative task of gathering ore by a set of robots [12,6]. The other is the problem of meeting scheduling, which is presented in Section 3.

In Section 2, we present the modelling approach, COPROM. In Section 3, we present the architecture of MASCOOF platform and some of the experiences we have encountred implementing MAS with this framework.

2 COPROM: Cooperation Protocols Modelling

The aim of COPROM is to provide developers of multi–agent systems with a tool allowing them to define cooperation protocols in such a way that they are directly usable by the agents to perform their cooperative behaviors during the problem resolution.

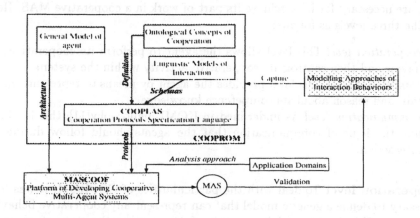

Fig. 1. COOPROM: Cooperative Protocols Modelling in MAS

COOPROM is thus a framework that contains:

- a set of means to define the ontological concepts of cooperation,
- a linguistic model of interaction,
- an agent model, and
- a specification language of cooperation protocols.

Both the set of ontological concepts of cooperation and the linguistic model of interaction have allowed us to define COOPLAS (specification language of cooperation protocols)[5,6].

The linguistic model describes the set of different stages of the agent conversations during the problem resolution.

The ontological concepts of cooperation are defined as objects, relations or functions. They are used by the developers to define the context of use of the protocols.

2.1 Model of agent

From the point of view of our modelling approach, we consider a MAS as a collection of interacting agents in a distributed environment. In such systems, one can always state that there exists many types of interaction but we are only concerned in explicit interactions to acheive a cooperative solution to a problem. To do so, we have found that is necessary to separate clearly the aspects of communication, cooperation and competence in the agent model, some things which has not been done previously in most developed MAS. Firstly, we think that it is neccesary to carry out and to study the functionalities of each aspect independently from the others. Secondly, from this model of agent, it is apparent it is efficient for us to define the real needs of each aspects towards the other ones. So, one can state the interrelationships that may occur between these aspects and then try to model them using the identified interrelationships.

Each of these three levels is associated with certain functionalities of an agent wich are necessary for it to achieve its part of work in a cooperative MAS. Here are the three levels as follows:

- *cooperation level* This level allows the agent to perform its cooperative behavior and then controls its cooperative activity within the system.
- *competence level* This level provides the agent by means to represent, maintain and reason about its competence knowledge.
- *communication level* As underlined in KQML philosophy[11], this level define the logic of communication that the agents should follow during its interaction.

Cooperation level To deal with the particularities of COPROM, it was first necessary to define a generic model that can represent any cooperative behavior or process. This model must be capable of representing the state of an agent within a cooperative process, the condition to transit from a state to an other one and an explicit mental state that helps the others agents to model the agent dynamically during a cooperative process of problem resolution.

Based on the speech act classification of Ballmer and Brennentuhl[3,4], we have considered the process of cooperation as a conversational process. So, as not to cause confusion, we consider the states of the conversation instead of the states of the agents in the conversation to represent the agent "state" during a conversation. This is adopted to facilitate principly the specification of the cooperation process and it also due to many others reasons.

First, representing the cooperation process using the agents states during a conversation implies to duplicate the states of the conversation for each agent involved in the conversation. this decreases the efficiency of the system. More, the representation using the state of the conversation allow us to associate to each transition (performative) one and only one state.

Second, describing the cooperation process using states of the conversation has facilitated to MASCOOF the make of such process in each agent of a developed MAS (MASCOOF uses finite states machines (FSM)).

Third, using this representation, we have kept some information implicit. For example, the agent state of conversation *claim_received* is an additional information which is not necessary to be represented for the agent because when an agent receives a message including the *claim* performative, this explains implicitly this intermediary state (the agent needs to have the information about the accomplishment of the performative rather than information concerning intermediary states).

Simultanious multi-context conversations To be as realistic as possible, we have adopted a simultanious multi-context conversations. So any agent having this model of cooperation, it is able to manage multiple conversations simultaniously with different contexts or subjects. The conversations may be either different or complementary. In the latter case, the information provided by one will be used by another conversation. In the two cases, the agents are led to coordinate their actions based on their local and global perspectives in order to make the results provided by certain conversations useful to other ones. In the case of ore gathering, our agents can simultaniously contracting and sub-contracting [6].

Interruptibility In adopting the simultanious multi-context conversations model of interaction, we have found that is necessary to make a conversation interruptible or not. Here, we are more interested in those conversations that are uninterruptible.

Our principle is simple. All conversations are interruptible only if it is explicitly mentioned that the conversation is not interruptible. In this latter case, when an agent receives a message with this mentioned it postpones all received messages that concern other conversation until the end of the uninterruptible conversation.

We also note that any conversation can be cancelled at any time by the agent who has started it. This will be useful for the agents to stop the conversations that are no longer necessary.

How cooperation and competence levels interact? As mentioned above, our agents execute protocols to participate in cooperative activity. At this time, the agents are often led to choose between several alternatives proposed by the protocol according to the stage reached by its execution. This depends significantly on the local and global perspectives of the agents. It is affected by their local knowledge (self model) and their own views of the others agents knowledges (acquaintance models).

as assumed in the begining, the agents cooperative behavior depends on a directed communication and involves in most cases, the exchange of agents' points of view concerning a particular problem.

So, to argue the situation correctly, to persuade an agent to change its position or commit towards another agent, any agent must dispose of knowledge on the agents points of view of the actual situation or problem and must have mechanisms of evaluation of arguments, concessions and commitments. These mechanisms imply an interaction between the cooperation and the competence levels.

At this stage of analysis, we are confronted by a problem of defining dynamic models of knowledge because our model of cooperation is based on a speech act model that uses in its basis the techniques of argumentation.

To cover this problem, we have provided our architecture with mechanisms of generation and evaluation of arguments using two concepts: *views* and argument structure (see figure 2). This depends on a combined approach that involves two important aspects: generation of arguments structure and generation of views.

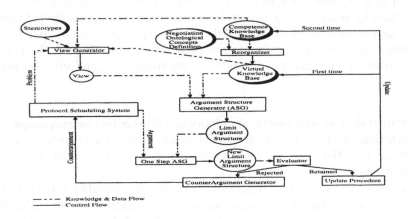

Fig. 2. A System of Arguments Generation Evaluation

For example, when an agent A proposes to another agent B to buy a car of Citroen trademark and argue this proposition using the argument that the car is a French product. Here, the associated problem P0 to this situation is which trademark of car to choose. So, to make the agent B capable to evaluate the argument of its adversory, the agent B developes an arguments structure relative to the problem P0. This structure represents the set of warrants on which the agent B can base its interpretation and evaluation of A's argument. This is the view of the agent on P0 (see figure 2).

To allow this generation of views, we have adopted the *ViewFinder*[2] framework to the case of multi-agent systems. This framework allows the generation of views corresponding to a dynamic situation based on a dynamic ascription algorithm. This algorithm combines two approaches of beliefs ascription: *ascription based on stereotypes* and *default rules of ascription based on the commonality aspect* (i.e that people have much in common, such as being human, living with other people, watching the same television programes and reading the same newspapers, etc).

At this moment, one can ask the following question: how is a view used by an agent during his argumentation process?

One alternative solution to this problem, is *progressive argumentation*[16, 17], which consists of forward reasoning. We have adopted to our problem one specific form of progressive argumentation, namely *procedural argumentation*. A brief description is given in [5]. Here the method is, by working from a state of reasoning to the next, a process which gradually constructs a stable and coherent collection of undefeated arguments. This collection is the argument structure that the agent B can use to interpret and evelute the argument of the agent A.

In the case of Veerswijk [16, 17], to generate this coherent collection, the procedural argumentation approach uses a base set of arguments as a point of departure. Although, it is said in [16] that the base set is a finite argument structure, the author has not precisely stated how the base set is formed and who does this. The formalism underlying this approach assumes only the existence of such base set with the verification of some proprieties.

So, in our case, the base set on which the final arguments structure is built, is a dynamic generated view according to the actual situation or problem. This makes the agents decisions view–directed and can help the agents to be more objective during their interaction.

2.2 The COOPLAS Language

COOPLAS allows the specification of protocols for cooperation which the user desires the agents in his system to use. The user is given via this language the means to define the global structure of the cooperation process in terms of states of conversation and transitions between those states (see Figure 3).

General Scheme of interaction behaviors We have based our work on a global scheme of interaction behaviors extracted from the linguistic work of Ballmer and Brennenstuhl classification of the speech act of the english speech activity verbs[3]. This scheme associates to each state of conversation a meaning according to the phase reached by the conversation. This depends on the temporal order that exits between the speech acts categories of the struggle model [3,4]. This model covers the semantic space of the verbal struggle. This latter starts from making a claim and overtly attacking an addressee. The competitive verbal fight (e.g. argumentation) may result in the victory of one and the defeat of the other or in a compromise. During this fight, the parties involved can employ different tactics. For example, after an agent make a claim of something from another agent, the second agent must respond to the claim either by *dissent* or by *accept* (possibles transitions). If the second agent dissents the claim then the first agent can insist on its claim by arguing its position or retreat its claim. The two agents can ask for arbitration from an institution to resolve their conflict. Here, the model used is the institutional model (not the struggle model). It consists of establishment of a behavior in an institution, especially entering the

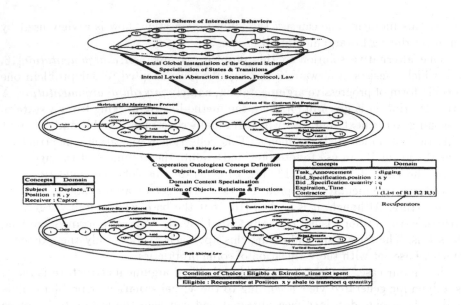

Fig. 3. Language Abstraction Model

institution and thereby adopting its norms, following its norms and rules, being persued by the upholders of the institution.

From this classification, we have proceeded to a construction of different general graphs of interaction associated to the different categories of speech act within the three linguistic models of interaction: struggle, institutional and persuasion. From our graphs, we operate a specialisation of states and transitions (speech acts or performatives) according to the meaning of the different phases of the basic linguistic models that we use and the semantic of the interaction behaviors that we want to model (e.g. the task sharing, planning, etc). For example, in the figure 4, the skeletons of two protocols are given basing on the temporal order of the speech act of the struggle model and the semantic of the task sharing to specify the needs of modelling (how many phases are necessary to model the task shiring, it is necessary to insist or not after receiving a dissent, etc). We call this specialisation *a partial global instantiation of the general scheme of interaction*.

The result of this specialisation is a protocol skeleton to which we add the definition of the ontological concepts of cooperation that the protocol manipulates. These concepts are used to define the context or the domain of the protocol in use. They serve as means to specialize the different objects, relations and functions that the cooperation process modelled by the protocol use during its execution. More details are provided in the sub–section 2.2.3.

Principle Concepts of COOPLAS At an other abstraction level, we define the principle concepts[1] of our language according to its domain of use (DAI and MAS communaties) as follows:

- **transition function**: It represents a performative (e.g. dissent, declare, argument, accept...) and its execution causes a change of state.
- **state**: It is the elementary unit (e.g proposition of a compromise, acceptation of an argument...) within a scenario or a protocol. From a state, one can choose between several transitions according to a specified condition. This later depends dynamically on the local and global perspectives of the agents.
- **scenario**: It is an alternative (e.g. postponent of the execution of a task, agent insists on the refusal of execution ...) gives to an agent and which dictate to it all possible transitions from the actual state up to the end state (it is also possible, however, to go through intermediary scenarios).
- **protocol**: It is a partial or a global instantiation of the general scheme of interaction behaviors (e.g. Contract Net, Master-Slave, ...) (see figure 3).
- **law**: It is a collection of protocols, which correspond to a particular resolution of a problem (e.g. conflicts resolution, learning, ...).

So, we see a protocol as a set of specialized states and transitions to which the user has associated a certain semantic meaning. For example, in the case of Contract Net protocol, certain meanings have been associated with the states and transitions which depend on the task sharing domain. However, within this one will find task announcement, bidding, making an award ... etc. In contrast of the principle concepts of COOPLAS, these concepts are used to characterize a certain type of cooperation which does not necessarily depend on the application domain of the Contract Net protocol. This is the case of most of protocols defined in DAI literature.

Definition of Ontological Concepts of Cooperation In order to cover most cooperative domains, COOPLAS provides the user with a definition level of ontological concepts that helps him to define the context the protocols will be used (see figure 3). COOPLAS allows the definition of three categories of cooperation concepts: objects, relations and functions.

For example, to describe a protocol of task attribution, COOPLAS allows the user to define himself the different necessary objects: a task, a task–announcement, an award, a bid, etc. This represents the definition of the specific context necessary to the execution of the protocol.

The relation is a predicate that qualifies an object or a set of objects defined in the protocol. For example, in the Contract Net protocol, a potential contracting agent can be eligible or not to the attribution of a certain task. So, we say that the eligibility condition qualifies the object *contracting-agent*.

In COOPLAS, a function associates a value to a set of object. For example, in the case of making decision based systems, the use of a particular protocol

---

[1] The concepts are those of the language itself as designed for an user, not those of the cooperation or the domain.

assumes the possibility of measurment of the degree of satisfaction of an agent towards a decision. This can be defined as a function that allows the agents to calculate their own satisfaction degree during protocol execution.

To allow such definitions, we have introduced in our language COOPLAS three definition operators. These operators facilitate the definition of new concepts of cooperation to be used in a particular protocol. So, each definition has a content that represents a set of terms. Generally, there are three parts to consider in a definition:

- Information about the categories of the concept. If the concept is a relation or a function, one must add also the information concerning their arguments.
- The axiom associated to the definiton.
- The formula.

For example, in the following definition:

(**defobject** task = (**listof** name type procedure))

defobject indicates that *"task"* is an object (category of the concept) and the term *"(listof name type procedure)"* is the formula. The equality between the term "task" and the formula represent the axiom.

In the case of the Contract Net protocol, it is necessary to introduce the notion of eligibility of an agent that we formulate as a relation whose definition is as follows:

(**defrelation** eligible (= contractor–specification.Funct funct) (= contractor–specification.Area area))

In the case of ore gathering application, the term *funct* will have as value *transporter* and the term *area* for example, the coordinates of the explored domain (e.g. latitude = 12 North, longitude = 17 West).

Here is an example that introduce the use of the function operator of definition. In the concurrent decisions system CIMES, designed for production management [1], when a group of agents is in a conflict situation concerning decisions at a certain level, they must make concessions to solve the conflict. In order to identify the best global decision, they must evaluate the quality of their own decisions relative to their own criteria. In order to do this, a common measurement of an agents' degree of satisfaction for a compromise at a level L of the conflict-resolution process it was defined . This rate of satisfaction associated with an agent A's decision D at level L can be described as a function in COOPLAS as follows:

(**deffunction** SR(D, A, L) = (/ (- 1 (- RK(PD(D)) 1)) length(List(A, L))))

Where the relation PD(D) is the decision-making policy used to make the decision D, the function RK(PD(D)) is its rank in A's decision-making policy list and the object List(A, L) indicates the list of A's decision-making policies at the level L.

3 MASCOOF

3.1 Architecture

In the COPROM modelling approch, the architecture of an agent is conceptually layered and control–directed (see figure 4). It allows, by means of its components, agents to perform their cooperative behaviors under a high–level of control mechanisms. These behaviors are defined by protocols held in the agents libraries (see figure 4). The important components are the following:

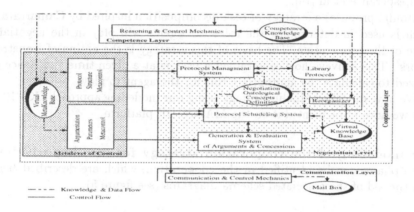

Fig. 4. MASCOOF agent architecture

– *protocol management system* This system represents the interface between a data structure, which is a protocols library, and an human agent (user or designer) during the protocols specification. It also plays the role of interface between the protocols library and the protocol scheduling system during the protocols exceexecution. This role of interfacing consists of putting at the disposal of the agent the modification and consultation mechanisms that helps him to use, modify and consult itself, the protocols of its library.
– *protocol scheduling system* From its specification, a protocol is executed by the protocol scheduling system. At each execution step and according to the used protocol to cooperate, the agent should make a choice between several alternatives to respond to a received message. This choice is based on a reasoning phase and the interpretation of the received message. This depends on the stage reached by the cooperation process and the virtual[2] knowledge of the agent.

---
[2] The virtual knowledge represent an image of the agent domain knowledge from a point of view of the cooperation. These are interpreted as beliefs, intensions and goals of the agent.

3.2 Experience with MASCOOF

In this section we describe our efforts at implementing a system to overcome the problem of meeting scheduling within a group organisation.

A system is envisaged where each user is represented by a secretary agent who is responsible for the efficient management of the users agenda. When the user wishes to organise a meeting between some of the group, he will create an organiser agent, who will be responsible for ensuring that this meeting is scheduled. When an initial time is not found satisfactory, negotiation must take place to search for a common free time amongst the agents. The cooperative behaviour to be followed by the agents will be based on the work of Moulin [13] and Lesperance et al [14].

Moulin proposes a strategy of task decomposition inspired by Camarrata [7], which is used in determining the roles the agents will play in the negotiation phase of the cooperation. The basis of this strategy is the notion of 'constraint factors'. This conveys how constrained a user is at a given time and hence can be used to calculate the appropriate role for the agent to play.

We have modelled Moulin strategy using our modelling approach COPROM, then we have implemented it on the MASCOOF platform.

Our modelling of the cooperation strategy for meeting scheduling
Three phases can be identified in the cooperation, which are described below, with the aid of the associated schema diagrams (see figure 5).

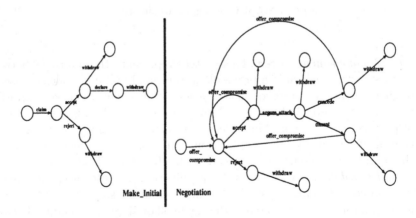

Fig. 5. Meeting Scheduling Diagrams

Phase 1 : Initial claim. The organiser agent upon given the parameters of the meeting (date, time etc) , will contact all indicated participants to ascertain their interest in the meeting. Each secretary will then ask their users if they are interested, in the case where the answer is yes, the secretary will reply with an accept and a constraint factor, calculated as the sum of the weightings of the meetings for the period proposed. Each meeting is given a weighting as follows.

- it is possible that the meeting can be moved (weighting 1).
- important meeting which cannot be rearranged (weighting 2).

If the agent rejects he will take no more part in the cooperation and withdraw.

If all the agents who accept are free for the proposed time (i.e. the total of the constraint factors collected is zero) then the meeting is arranged and the cooperation is finished.

Otherwise the organiser agent calculates the role for the negotiation stage as follows:

The agent having the highest constraint factor, and therefore the least places to offer as a compromise – reducing the search space, is given the role of MC (Most Constrained) and will coordinate the negotiation. In order of decreasing constraint factor, all remaining agents are given the roles MC2, MC3 etc., until the agent will the smallest constraint factor is given the role 'LC' (Least Constrained).

This phase of the cooperation ends when the organiser informs all the agents of their roles (declare), who then acknowledge with a withdraw from the conversation.

Phase 2 : Negotiation phase. In this phase of the cooperation process, the MC coordinates begins by compiling a list of all possible compromise spaces to offer the agents. This includes all the free spaces and also the spaces on his agenda which can be moved, having the duration of the meeting.

The first free space is then offered to the first MC (MC2) on the list (offer_compromise). This agent will check his agenda to see what is pending for that time. If there is a meeting with a weighting 2 on his agenda he will send a 'reject' directly back to the MC who will then look for the next free space on his agenda. The MC after receiving his refusal will propagate the offer to the next MC on the list.

If on the other hand the agent is free, or the period contains only meetings with a weighting of 1, he will accept and send back the constraint factor for this period which is calculated as the total of the weights for the period proposed.

The offer of the compromise is propagated down the list, and if the total of the constraint factors collected is zero then all the agents are free for the proposed time and the organiser is informed that a time has been found (FINAL PHASE).

On the other hand if the average constraint is not null, the MC will request that all the agents remove the meeting scheduled for the proposed time. An agent will 'concede' to this request if the meetings in the suggested time have a weighting 1, and if the requestor is the organiser of the given meetings. If one agent rejects (dissent) then the MC will offer the next compromise space to the second MC and the above process of propagating the offer down the MC list is carried out again.

If all agents have conceded, this space is added to a list of spaces where the agents are not completely free, but which can be used when the negotiation is finished (if necessary) to choose a space where the least amount of meeting re-arrangement is needed.

After all of the free spaces have been offered the MC begins to offer the spaces which contain meeting with a weighting 1 on his agenda. This step is carried out in the same way as the previous step.

Final Phase. The MC will inform the organiser agent if the meeting has been arranged or not. The organiser will either accept this or send back a refusal to the MC. If the meeting is acceptable he will inform his agent secretary to add the meeting to the agenda. The MC also informs the secretaries to add the meeting to their agenda. In the case of meetings that have to be moved, the secretaries will start another cooperative conversation with the agents involved.

If the organiser has the refused, the MC will check to see if there are any compromise spaces left on his agenda and start the negotiation phase over again. If there are no compromises left he will inform the organiser who will request a change of parameters for the meeting from the user.

Description of protocols in COOPLAS Here, we present the description of one of the used protocols by the agent to cooperate during the problem resolution of the meeting scheduling. The protocol that we describe here, is associated to the *negociation phase* of the strategy of cooperation used to overcome the problem of the meeting scheduling (see the Appendix).

4 Conclusion

We have presented a modelling approach of cooperation behaviors, which has led us to the implementation of the platform MASCOOF. In this approach, we define an agent model which is composed of three levels: communication, cooperation and competence. Here, we have principly presented the cooperation level and its interaction with the competence level without considering the communication issues.

The cooperation process of an agent is defined as a conversational process that represents the state of conversation and the transitions between these states. These transitions and states are described by the language COOPLAS. This language is based on a general scheme of interaction behaviors extracted from the linguistic work of Ballmer and Brennenstuhl. This scheme represents a skeleton for the protocols which can be enhanced by the developer using COOPLAS.

Three categories of basic concepts (objects, relations and functions) are introduced and allow to define the contextual use of the specified protocols.

In our approach, the cooperation process may contain argumentative situations that can also be described in protocols using COOPLAS. At a low level, this has led us to define argumentation mechanisms to allow the generation and the evaluation of arguments. These mechanisms shows the interaction that exists between the cooperation and the competence levels.

Finally, the meeting scheduling problem has allowed as to test the efficiency of our approach and also proves the power of COOPLAS to describe more complex protocols.

Acknowledgements

The authors would like to thank Lisa HOGG (DAI-Unit, EED-Queen Mary and Westfield College, UK) for its help to implement and evaluate with us the meeting scheduling application.

Appendix

Here is the description of the Negotiation protocol in COOPLAS. Note that some of the definitions are omited due to the lack of space.

```
(DEFOBJECT subject = string )
(DEFOBJECT constraint_info = float )
(DEFOBJECT meeting_arranged = integer )
(DEFOBJECT interrupt = 0 )
(DEFOBJECT datte = integer )
(DEFOBJECT start = float )
(DEFOBJECT end = float )
(DEFOBJECT organiser = string )
(DEFOBJECT people = (SETOFALL #A (AND (agent #A) (INTERESTED #A))))
(DEFOBJECT parameters = (LISTOF datte start end))
(DEFOBJECT slot = (LISTOF parameters weight))
(DEFOBJECT slot_agent = (LISTOF slot agent))
(DEFOBJECT proposed_parameters = parameters)
(DEFOBJECT free_slot_set =(SETOFALL #X (AND (slot #X)(EQ #X.weight 1))
(DEFRELATION more_compromises (EXIST #Y (AND (MEMBER #Y free_slot_set)
                                 (slot #Y))))
(DEFRELATION received_reject (EXIT #Z (AND (MEMBER #Z people)
            (EQ #Z slot_agent.agent) (EQ slot_agent.slot.weigth 2)
            (EQ slot_agent.parameters parameters))))
( DEFOBJECT TotFofC = integer )


VERSION 21/07/1995
LAW Negotiate_meeting {
PROTOCOL Negotiation {
  FUNCT offer_compromise
  CONTENT (subject; parameters; organiser; reason; weight ; people)
  STATE suggest_free                            /*  106 */
  SCENARIO suggestion_made
  [        IF (OR (EQ weight 1) (EQ weight 0))
       SCENARIO accept_compromise
```

```
        [FUNCT accept CONTENT (subject ; constraint_info )
STATE accept_comp                    /*   108  */
SCENARIO all_agreed
[
IF (NOT received_reject)
SCENARIO FofC_not_null
[
IF (NOTEQ TotFofC 0)
FUNCT argum_attack CONTENT (subject ; parameters )
        STATE ask_to_remove      /*  110*/
SCENARIO will_remove_meetings
[
IF ( NOT ( EXISTS weight 2 ) )
FUNCT concede CONTENT ( subject ) STATE will_remove
SCENARIO end_of_negotiation
[ IF ( OR (EQ TotFofC 0 ) ( NOT more_compromises))
  FUNCT withdraw CONTENT (subject; meeting_arranged; parameters)
  STATE endstate
  ELSE FUNCT offer_compromise  CONTENT (subject; parameters)
        STATE suggest_free
]  ELSE FUNCT dissent CONTENT (subject) STATE reject_comp
        SCENARIO end_of_negotiation
        [ IF ( NOT more_compromises )
  FUNCT withdraw CONTENT (subject; meeting_arranged; parameters)
  STATE endstate
  ELSE  FUNCT offer_compromise CONTENT (subject; parameters)
STATE suggest_free
] ] ELSE  FUNCT withdraw
  CONTENT (subject; meeting_arranged; parameters)
  STATE endstate
]  ELSE FUNCT reject CONTENT (subject)STATE pc_reject ]
]  ELSE SCENARIO reject_compromise
[ FUNCT reject CONTENT (subject) STATE reject_comp
      SCENARIO rejection_sc
      [ IF (NOT more_compromises)
    FUNCT withdraw
    CONTENT ( subject ; meeting_arranged ; parameters )
    STATE endstate
ELSE FUNCT offer_compromise CONTENT(subject; parameters)
    STATE suggest_free
]]]}}
```

References

1. AYEL J., *Concurrent Decisions in Production Management*, Integrated Computer-Aided Engineering Journal, 1(3) 229–240, 1994.

2. Ballim A., *ViewFinder: A Framework for Representing, Ascribing and Maintaining Nested Beliefs of Interacting Agents*, PhD Dissertation of the University of Sciences of Geneve, Thesis N-2560, Geneve, 1992.

3. Ballmer T, Brennenstuhl W., *Speech Act Classification: Study in lexical analysis of english speech activity verbs*, Springer–Verlag, berlin, 1981.

4. Belakhdar O., *Interaction Protocol Modelling and Specification in Multiagent Systems*, Second National Young Researchers Meetting on Artificial Intelligence, Marseille, France, 1994.

5. Belakhdar O., AYEL J., *Cooperation Protocols Specification Language: an Implementation based on KQML*, Third International Francophon Conference on DAI and MAS, pages 27-39, Chambery, France, Mar 1995.

6. Belakhdar O., AYEL J., *COOPLAS: Cooperation Protocols Specification Language*, Fisrt International Workshop on Decentralized Intelligent and MultiAgent Systems, pages 33-41, Krakow, Poland, Nov 1995.

7. Cammarata S., and al, *Strategies Of Coperation in Distributed Problem Solving*, Proceedings of the Eight International Joint Conference on AI, Karlsruhe, Vol 2, pages 767-770, August 1983.

8. Conry S. E., Mayer R. A., Lesser V. R., *Multistage negotiation in Distributed Planning*, Reading in DAI, Morgan Kaufman Publishers, San Mateo, pages 367-384, California, 1988.

9. Crokill D., and Lesser V., *The use of meta-level control for coordination in distributed problem solving network*, In proceeding of the Eighth IJCAI, pages 748-756, Karlsruhe, Germany, Aug 1983.

10. Durfee E., and Lesser V., *Partial global planning: A coordination framework for distributed hypothesis formation*, IEEE Transactions on Computers, C-36(11): 1275–1291, Nov 1987.

11. Finin T., and al, *Specification of KQML Agents-Communication Language*, Technical Report, The DARPA Knowledge Sharing Initiative External Interface Working Group.

12. Goss S., and al G., *Harvesting by a group of robots*, Proceeding of ECAL 91, eds., Varela, P. Bourgine, MIT Press, 1991.

13. Lesperance Y., and al, *Foundation of a logic approach for agents programing (traslated from french)*, The Third International Francophone Conference on DAI and MAS, pages 3-15, Chambery,France, Mar 1995.

14. Moulin B., *Scenarios based method to design reactive multiagent systems (traslated from french)*, The Third International Francophone Conference on DAI and MAS, pages 177-186, Chambery,France, Mar 1995.

15. Smith R. G., *Contract Net Protocol: High-Level Communication and Control in Distributed Problem-solving*, Reading in DAI, Morgan Kaufman Publishers, San Mateo, California, 1988.

16. Vreeswijk G. A. W., *Abstract Argumentation Systems: Preliminary Report*, Proceedings of the First World Conference on the Fundamental of Artificial Intelligence, Paris, pages 501-510, 1991.

17. Vreeswijk G. A. W., *Nonmonotonocity and Partiality in Defeasible Argumentation*, in Nonmonotonic Reasoning and Parial Semantics, ed W. van der Hoek, J.-J.Ch. Mayer, Y.H. Tan, C. Witteveen, Prentice Hall, pages 157-180, 1992.

Analyzing the Social Behavior of Contract Net Protocol

Cheng Gu[1] and Toru Ishida[1]

Department of Information Science, Kyoto University
Kyoto 606-01, JAPAN
{ko | ishida}@kuis.kyoto-u.ac.jp

Abstract. Contract Net Protocol (CNP) assigns subtasks to agents which are involved in multiagent problem solving. Although the logical aspects of the negotiation protocol have been analyzed, the social behavior of protocol dynamics remain unclear.

This paper introduces a quantitative analysis of protocol dynamics, an essential for constructing continuous realtime applications. We perform an application independent simulation to analyze the social behavior of CNP. We obtain the following results: contractor utilization rate (contractor utility) increases together with the system load while the manager utilization rate (manager utility) decreases; when the number of agents increases, the contractor utility rises while the manager utility does not change; the uniformity of agents causes the concentration of "bids" and "awards," and thus decreases the manager and the contractor utility.

Our simulation results are used to analyze the social behavior of Enterprise, a famous CNP application, and point out the inherent problem of Enterprise.

1 Introduction

Contract Net Protocol (CNP) [12] is a well known protocol for assigning subtasks to agents involved in multiagent problem solving. Agents negotiate with each other in order to improve the efficiency of the whole network. The literature contains results for various CNP application: the load distributed system Enterprise [8], the transportation control system TRACONET [10], and so on.

Two kinds of agent, *manager* and *contractor*, exist in CNP. Managers provide tasks to contractors which undertake them as follows: first, when a task arrives at the network, the manager responsible for it will announce it to all contractors within the network; second, each contractor will select from the announced tasks, the one that best matches its own standards, and bids for it; finally, the manager chooses what it believes to be the most appropriate bid, and awards the task to that agent. There may exist multiple managers and contractors in the network simultaneously; a manager can make multiple announcements simultaneously while a contractor can bid for only one task at a time.

CNP is based on a human activity metaphor. The most significant feature of the CNP is that both managers and contractors "award" or "bid" according to their own standards. This mechanism is called *mutual selection*. However, since CNP imitates the human contract process, the dynamic properties of its computing mechanism have not been investigated until quite recently. Lesser reformulated the negotiation protocol in terms of a distributed search problem [7], showing that CNP is essentially an AND/OR search undertaken by managers and contractors cooperatively. From the same standpoint, Conry *at al.* [2] showed how the multistage negotiation protocol works in an AND/OR tree search problem. Yokoo *et al.* [13] showed that such a protocol can be formulated as a distributed constraint satisfaction problem.

Our study extends these ideas, but unlike previous research that mainly focused on the logical aspects of the negotiation protocols, our main interest is analyzing its social behavior in a continuous realtime domain involving the subjects of communication network management (see [6] and [9]), distributed meeting scheduling [11], and heterogeneous knowledge databases [1].

We demonstrate the dynamic properties of CNP using a simulation based on queuing theory to provide answers to the following questions.

1. The basic behavior:
   How do the utilization rates of the managers (manager utility) and of the contractors (contractor utility) change when the system load on the whole network varies?
2. The effect of the number of agents:
   What happens to the managers and contractors when the number of agents changes?
3. The effect of the uniformity of agents:
   What happens to the managers and contractors if the agents are homogeneous or heterogeneous?

Our purpose is to quantitatively investigate the various effects of the mutual selection mechanism on managers' and contractors' utilities.

2 Modeling Contract Net Protocol

2.1 Agent Model

In order to evaluate CNP behavior quantitatively, we established the following model. Our evaluation results are general because this model is not based on any particular application. The message flows of a manager and a contractor are depicted in Figure 1. Managers' and contractors' basic actions are as follows.

1. Announcing:
   When a task arrives, the manager responsible for it will immediately broadcast it as an "announcement" with a bidding deadline to all contractors. The period between the moment of the announcement and the bidding deadline is called as the *bidding period*.

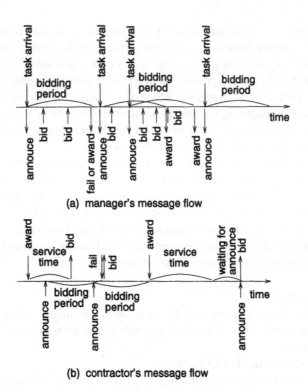

Fig. 1. Message flows for a manager and a contractor

2. Bidding:
   Each contractor will respond with a "bid" message as soon as it finishes a job, but if there is no task currently announced, it will wait for the next one, responding with a "bid" message immediately.

3. Awarding:
   When the task's bidding deadline is reached, the manager responsible will "award" it to the best "bidder." If there are no bids for this task when the deadline comes, the task is abandoned. The contractors which fail to get an "award" message will instead get a "fail" message from the manager, and they will make bids for subsequent tasks when announced.

Each manager uses evaluation function f to evaluate the bids made by the "bidders." Each contractor uses evaluation function g to evaluate the announced tasks making a "bid." We use f_i to denote the manager i's evaluation function and g_j to denote the contractor j's evaluation function. Also we use B_j to denote the attributes of bids issued by contractor j, and T_i to denote the attributes of the tasks offered by manager i. Thus, $f_i(B_j)$ represents manager i's evaluation of bids from contractor j, and $g_j(T_i)$ represents contractor j's evaluation of tasks issued by manager i. Let M_i be the maximum value of the evaluation function of manager i, also let C_j be the maximum value of the evaluation function of contractor j; i.e.,

$$M_i = \max_j \{f_i(B_j)\}$$

$$C_j = \max_i \{g_j(T_i)\}$$

Manager i will select a bidder (contractor) that achieves M_i, and contractor j will select a task that achieves C_j.

In the rest of this paper, we define the *manager utility* as

$$\frac{1}{n}\sum_{i=1}^{n}\{\frac{1}{m}\sum_{j=1}^{m}f_i(B_j)\}$$

wherein m is the number of the contracts awarded by manager i, and n is the number of managers. Also we define the *contractor utility* as

$$\frac{1}{n}\sum_{j=1}^{n}\{\frac{1}{m}\sum_{i=1}^{m}g_j(T_i)\}$$

wherein m is the number of tasks awarded to contractor j, and n is the number of contractors.

2.2 Social Model

The social model consists of the following items:

1. Number of agents:
   We let the number of managers equal the number of contractors. In order to investigate the effect of varying the number of agents, we evaluated two cases: 20 and 100 managers and contractors. Each agent is assigned a unique ID number.

2. Uniformity of agents:
   We set the value of the attribute of a task to be the ID number of the manager responsible for it, i.e., $T_i = i$ ($i \in$ *manager*). Also we set the attribute of a bid to be the ID number of the contractor submitting it, i.e., $B_j = j$ ($j \in$ *contractor*). That means both managers and contractors may select desirable partners. The evaluation function of each agent is generated as follows: first, we produced a random integer list containing the natural numbers from 1 to 100; we suppose that the w-th number in the list is the value for its companion agent w; in the heterogeneous agent setup, different evaluation lists are made for different agents; i.e., $f_{i_1}(B_j) \neq f_{i_2}(B_j)$, $g_{j_1}(T_i) \neq g_{j_2}(T_i)$ (when $i_1 \neq i_2$, $j_1 \neq j_2$); on the other hand, when agents are homogeneous, the evaluation lists for all agents are the same for a certain companion agent; i.e., $f_{i_1}(B_j) = f_{i_2}(B_j)$, $g_{j_1}(T_i) = g_{j_2}(T_i)$.

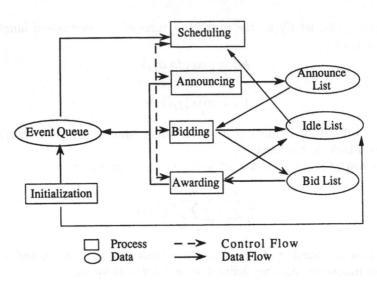

Fig. 2. Simulation structure

3. Distribution of arrival and service time:
   The arrival time of the task to each manager follows a Poisson distribution. The mean task arrival time ranged from 0.1 to 10 time units. The service time of the task was set at one time unit on average and was given an exponential distribution. The bidding period for each task was held constant at 0.1 time units.

Figure 2 shows the structure of the simulation which proceeded in an event-driven manner. The control part (scheduling process) schedules the event processes for announcing, bidding, awarding, etc. Each event refers to, or modifies, the data stored in the announce list, the bid list, the idle list (the list of contractors waiting for tasks), and the event queue. The simulation was executed for 10,000 time units. In order to compare the utilities of the heterogeneous and homogeneous agents, we also conducted experiments using combinations of both kinds of agent.

3   Social Behavior of CNP

3.1   Basic Behavior

In CNP, when the system load is low, i.e., the number of tasks issued for bidding is small, managers receive "bid" messages from many contractors as soon as each task is announced. As a result, the manager has a wide selection of bidders to choose from, and the manager utility increases. On the other hand, if the system

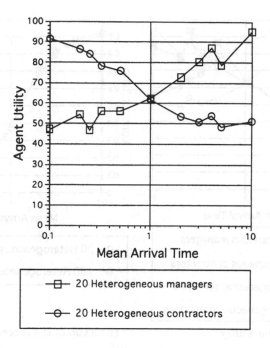

Fig. 3. Basic behavior

load is high, the number of contractors dealing with tasks will increase, and "bid" messages correspondingly decrease. As a result, the manager's selection of bidders shrinks and the manager utility decreases.

From the contractors' viewpoint, their freedom of selection is restricted at low system loads, and contractor utility decreases. When the system load is high, more tasks are broadcast allowing the contractors more freedom in selecting from the broadcast tasks at will. As a result, contractor utility increases. Obviously, high system loads favor the contractors while low loads favor the managers.

Figure 3 illustrates the relationship discussed in the preceding paragraph. The horizontal axis shows the mean task arrival time; the system load increases as the mean arrival time decreases, and vice versa. The vertical axis plots manager utility and contractor utility. Managers and contractors are assumed to be heterogeneous and there are 20 of each. From Figure 3, we learn the following properties:

- Contractor utility increases with the system load while manager utility decreases. This is because when the system load increases, the manager will lose the initiative and be forced into unilateral selection.
- In contrast, the contractors benefit as the system load increases, due to the increase in selection choice. This leads to an increase in contractor utility.

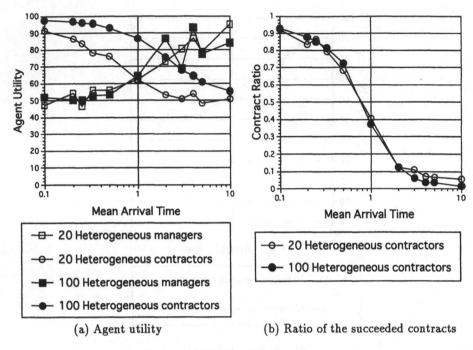

(a) Agent utility (b) Ratio of the succeeded contracts

Fig. 4. Effect of the number of agents

3.2 Effect of the Number of Agents

Figure 4(a) shows that when the number of managers and contractors increases, contractor utility increases while manager utility does not change. The reason is as follows:

- When the number of agents increases, the number of tasks that the contractor can select from also increases. Therefore, contractor utility increases. Even though one manager will have more contractors to negotiate with, the number of managers with competing tasks also increases so that fewer bids are received. As a result, for each manager, the number of bids does not change. Thus, the manager utility remains unchanged.

Furthermore, we measured the ratio of successful bids to all tasks issued. This was done because even if the utility of the successful contracts of contractors had been improved, we did not know *whether the effect of the number of agents is truly favorable for the contractor when the number of successful contracts decreases*. From Figure 4(b), however, we know the following:

- When the system load is high, a change in the number of agents has no effect on the ratio of successful bids. On the other hand, as the system load decreases, the ratio of successful bids decreases. This is because at low system

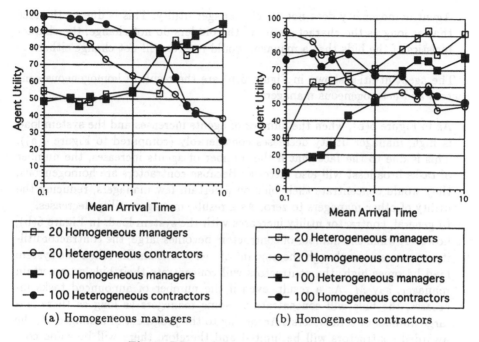

(a) Homogeneous managers (b) Homogeneous contractors

Fig. 5. Effect of the uniformity of agents

loads the corresponding increase in the number of agents per bid makes it difficult for a contractor to get an "award" even if it can issue a lot of bids because it is not busy.

Using the results just described, the following can be said in terms of contractor utility. When the system load is high enough and the number of agents increases, the ratio of successful bids does not decrease while the contracts' utility increases. In contrast, when the system load is low, although contractors' utility improves, the ratio of successful bids decreases. *Therefore, an increase in the number of agents is favorable to the contractor only if the system load is high.*

3.3 Effect of Agent Uniformity

We investigated the effect of agent homogeneity on manager and contractor utility. Figure 5(a) plots agent utility for homogeneous managers and heterogeneous contractors.

- As the system load decreases contractor utility decreases considerably (compare to Figure 4(a)). This is due to the fact that as the system load decreases the number of contractors waiting for bids increases, and there is a tendency to concentrate the awards by homogeneous managers to a certain contractor so that the utility of some contractors decreases to zero. As a result, contractor utility decreases.

– Agent homogeneity does not affect manager utility. This is due to the fact that as long as the characteristics of the bidders do not change, the characteristics of the bids that a manager would receive will not change either.

The agent utilities shown in Figure 5(b) are the result of homogeneous contractors and heterogeneous managers.

– As in Figure 5(b), when the number of agents increases and the system load is high, manager utility decreases considerably (compared to Figure 4(a)). This is due to the fact that if the number of agents increases, the number of tasks broadcast will also increase. Because contractors are homogeneous, they would concentrate their bids on a certain few managers, reducing the utility of other managers to zero. As a result, manager utility decreases.
– In general, contractor utility increases with the system load. In Figure 5(b), however, when the number of contractors becomes large, the contractor utility increases even though the amount of increase is small. When the system load becomes high, the contractors will concentrate their bids on a certain manager, say M. As a result, even if the number of announced tasks increases, the bids will concentrate on some managers as long as there is a large number of contractors[1]. According to the judgment of manager M, the awarded contractors will be limited and therefore there will be some contractors which will never be awarded a task. As a result, contractor utility decreases.

4 Social Behavior of Application Systems

In this section, we introduce Enterprise, a well known CNP application, and analyze it in terms of the results described in Section 3. Enterprise is a computer network load distributed system that uses a reformed CNP protocol called the DSP (Distributed Scheduling Protocol) for dynamically assigning tasks to the processors.

The DSP acts as follows: a manager announces a task with a certain priority; a contractor selects the task with the highest priority. As a strategy for deciding the priority P_i of the task i, the DSP uses the SPTF (Shortest Processing Time First) strategy based on the estimated processing time so as to improve system response time. The contractor j provides its estimated completion time when it responds with a "bid." The estimated completion time largely depends on the processor's speed. Managers select the bid with the shortest estimated completion time.

Among the methods of distributing tasks within a computer network, the following two methods are well known: (1) source(manager)-initiative, and (2) server(contractor)-initiative. In the former, managers decide which contractor

---

[1] In our current simulation, task mean service time is one time unit and the bidding period is 0.1 time units, so that when the number of contractors is larger than 10 the bids overlap.

should service a task, and in the latter each contractor decides which task to service from the set of tasks awarded to it. Eager *et al.* [5] reported that the source-initiative approach outperforms the server-initiative approach when the system load is light to moderate, and the server-initiative approach is preferable at high system loads. Experience with Enterprise shows: *as the system load increases, the initiative is transferred from the manager to the contractor, and as a result, the efficiency of the whole network remains high.*

Our simulation results depicted in Figure 3 can account for this as follows:

- When the system load is low, the manager, who holds the initiative, selects the contractor with the shortest estimated completion time, which quickens the response time. When the system load becomes high, the number of busy contractors will increase and fewer bids are made. As a result, contractors will get many tasks from managers, meaning the initiative shifts to the contractor and the task with the highest priority will be selected by the contractor. That shortens the response time.

In Enterprise, managers and contractors are both homogeneous in the following sense. Each manager selects the bidder which has the shortest completion time T_j. This means the value of the evaluation function $f_i(T_j)$, in which T_j is the attribute of the contractor j, doesn't depend on the manager, i.e., $f_{i_1}(T_j) = f_{i_2}(T_j)$, for all i_1, i_2. The attribute of a bid (i.e., the estimated completion time) mainly depends on processor speed. The same thing can be said about contractors – all contractors will select the task with the highest priority P_i so the value of the evaluation function $g_j(P_i)$ doesn't depend on the contractor, i.e., $g_{j_1}(P_i) = g_{j_2}(P_i)$ for all j_1, j_2.

Our analysis results (shown in Figures 5(a) and 5(b)) indicate that the following problem, which has not been pointed out, is inherent in Enterprise:

- When the number of agents increases, the awards concentrate on some specific processors. As a result, agent utility decreases, i.e., the tasks will concentrate on the fastest processors. If the application is running on a Local Area Network (LAN), the drop in agent utility is not a serious problem. However, when each computer is located at a different company, the drop in company utility cannot be accepted. If Enterprise is used on such a network, dissatisfaction among the companies might occur.

Our analysis of Enterprise shows the necessity of quantitatively analyzing the social behavior of mutual selection protocols.

5 Conclusion

We have analyzed the social behavior of CNP based on queuing theory. The main conclusions are as follows:

1. The basic behavior:
   As the system load increases, manager utility decreases while contractor utility increases.

2. The effect of the number of agents:
   As the number of agents increases, contractor utility increases. When the system load is low, however, the number of contractors not receiving an "award" increases. On the other hand, because the number of bids that a manager will receive does not increase, manager utility does not change.
3. The effect of agent uniformity:
   If either managers or contractors are homogeneous, awards and bids respectively will tend to concentrate, causing the utility of the heterogeneous agent to decrease. When all contractors are homogeneous, however, contractor utility does not increase even if the system load increases.

This work aims at clarifying the social behavior of CNP and its applications. As a future work, we will apply the same technique to the multistage negotiation protocol [2], the unified negotiation protocol [14], and the hierarchical negotiation protocol [4] to quantitatively evaluate their dynamics in artificial agent societies.

References

1. A. Aiba, K. Yokota, and H. Tsuda, "Heterogeneous Distributed Cooperative Problem Solving System Helios and Its Cooperation Mechanisms," *FGCS'94 Workshop on Heterogeneous Cooperative Knowledge-Bases*, 1994.
2. S. E. Conry, K. Kuwabara, V. R. Lesser, and R. A. Meyer, "Multistage Negotiation for Distributed Constraint Satisfaction," *IEEE Transactions on Systems, Man, and Cybernetics*, Vol. 21, No. 6, pp. 1462–1477, 1991.
3. R. Davis and R. G. Smith, "Negotiation as a Metaphor for Distributed Problem Solving," *Artificial Intelligence*, Vol. 20, No. 1, pp. 63-109, 1983.
4. E. H. Durfee and T. A. Montgomery, "Coordination as distributed search in hierarchical behavior space," *IEEE Transactions on System, Man, and Cybernetics*, 21(6):1363-1378, November 1991.
5. D. L. Eager, E. D. Lazowska, and J. Zahorjan, "A Comparison of Receiver-Initiated and Sender-Initiated Adaptive Load Sharing," *Performance Evaluation*, Vol. 6, pp. 53-68, 1986.
6. K. Kuwabara and T. Ishida, "Equilibratory Approach to Distributed Resource Allocation: Toward Coordinated Balancing," *Artificial Sociality; MAAMAW'92*, Lecture Notes in Artificial Intelligence, Springer-Verlag, 1994.
7. V. R. Lesser, "An Overview of DAI: Viewing Distributed AI as Distributed Search," *Journal of Japanese Society for Artificial Intelligence*, Vol. 5, No. 4, pp. 392 - 400, 1990.
8. T. W. Malone, R. E. Fikes, K. R. Grant and M. T. Howard, "Enterprise: A Market-like Task Scheduler for Distributed Computing Environments," *The Ecology of Computation*, North-Holland, pp. 177-205, 1988.
9. Y. Nishibe, K. Kuwabara, T. Suda and T. Ishida, "Distributed Channel Allocation in ATM Networks," *IEEE GLOBECOM'93*, pp. 417-423, 1993.
10. T. Sandholm, "An Implementation of the Contract Net Protocol Based on Marginal Cost Calculations," *AAAI-93*, pp.256-262, 1993.
11. S. Sen and E. H. Durfee, "A Formal Study of Distributed Meeting Scheduling: Preliminary Results", *Conference on Organizational Computing Systems*, pp. 55-68, November 1991.

12. R. G. Smith, "The Contract Net Protocol: High-Level Communication and Control in a Distributed Problem Solver," *IEEE Transactions on Computers*, Vol. 29, No. 12, pp. 1104-1113, 1980.

13. M. Yokoo, E. H. Durfee, T. Ishida and K. Kuwabara, "Distributed Constraint Satisfaction for Formalizing Distributed Problem Solving," *12th International Conference on Distributed Computing Systems (ICDCS-92)*, pp. 614-621, 1992.

14. G. Zlotkin and J. S. Rosenschein, "Cooperation and Conflict Resolution via Negotiation Among Autonomous Agents in Noncooperative Domains," *IEEE Transactions on Systems, Man, and Cybernetics*, Vol. 21, No. 6, pp. 1317-1324, 1991.

Effects of Different Interaction Attitudes on a Multi-Agent System Performance

Amedeo Cesta[1], Maria Miceli[1], and Paola Rizzo[2]

[1] IP-CNR, National Research Council of Italy, Viale Marx 15, I-00137 Rome, Italy
{*amedeo, maria*}@*pscs2.irmkant.rm.cnr.it*
[2] Center of Cognitive Science, Università di Torino, Via Lagrange 3, I-10123, Torino, Italy
paola@pscs2.irmkant.rm.cnr.it

Abstract. This paper explores the respective advantages of different interaction attitudes of simple agents in a common simulated environment. The attitudes (solitary, parasite, selfish, and social) have been defined along the two dimensions of self-sufficiency and help-giving. A number of experiments have investigated (a) in what degree the performance of a social system would be impaired by the presence of different kinds of exploiter; (b) which degree of self-sufficient attitude would be more advantageous. Two results are presented and discussed: the robustness of the "social" interaction attitude (both giving and seeking help), that allows to tolerate the exploiters without risking dangerous consequences for the entire social system; and the importance of the self-sufficient attitude, compared with a total dependence on or exploitation of others.

1 Introduction

Recently the problem of synthesizing and analyzing societies of autonomous agents has attracted an increasing amount of studies. While most of the classical AI works were centered on a single agent perspective, new application scenarios (e.g., the widespread diffusion of computer networks, the decrease of costs of certain classes of robots) have stimulated the investigation of multi-agent scenarios. The problem of coordination and co-evolution in the same environment has become central both in (Distributed) AI [4, 12] and robotics [7].

Our work mainly concerns social behavior in multi-agent systems. In some previous works, a theory of social interaction has been developed based on agents' power relationships and reciprocal dependence in a given social setting (see for example [2]). More recently attention has been focussed on the study of help, which we view as an interesting and rich case study for examining the reasons for cooperative behavior in multi-agent worlds. In particular we have performed a theoretical analysis of both *help-seeking* [3, 8] and *help-giving* [11] grounded on the application of *dependence theory* [2].

In those works we resort to complex reasoning abilities useful for the agent to take into account and profit from the presence of others in a given environment. In the current work we shift to a rather different perspective, and consider some basic-level questions about agents' help-giving and help-seeking interactions, such as: what happens if agents, instead of performing computationally heavy reasoning about others, just resort to a fixed behavior? and how do different fixed behaviors influence the performance of a multi-agent system in a given situation?

This work reports on a number of explorations we have performed in this direction. We have built up a multi-agent environment in which quite simple agents behave, performing a repetitive task (looking for food). The agents' welfare (represented by their amount of internal energy) is related to their success in the accomplishment of the task. When their energy goes above a given upper threshold they may or may not give help if requested. Considering the two dimensions of the help-giving attitude and the self-sufficient (or, in a complementary way, the help-seeking) attitude, we have designed a number of fixed characters (solitary, parasite, selfish, social) to be inserted in an experimental setting. Two of the characters show quite "extreme" attitudes: the *solitary* that neither ask nor give help but just find food for themselves, and the *parasite* that only ask and wait for others' help. The other two characters are more "balanced": the *selfish* that ask for help only if they are in danger, otherwise they find food, but never give help, and the *social* that, under given conditions, are able to either ask for help, find food or give help.

By "fixed" or "rigid" attitudes we mean that the agent behavior is stable during its life (according to the character it is endowed with) and does not vary according to the outcomes of past or future interactions with others. From this standpoint we have performed a number of experiments aimed at understanding the significance of different characters for the collective welfare. In the experiments the number of agents that survive after a given number of simulation cycles is taken as a measure for the system's performance. In particular we investigate how robust is the social behavior —that can be considered as cooperative in this setting— when both cooperative and non cooperative agents (like parasite and selfish) are put together. Furthermore, by comparing selfish, solitary and parasite agents, we explore which degree of self-sufficiency produces the best results.

The rigid behavior that characterizes our agents distinguishes the set of experiments we have performed from other works. In particular, classical game-theoretical works on strategic behavior (e.g. [1]) take an individualistic perspective, and allow the agent's choice to be influenced by its previous interactions. Our work takes a more classical DAI view because it considers the performance of the multi-agent system as a whole and tries to understand how robust is a system which includes agents that come to interact with each other with different fixed strategies. An independent research [13], though sharing some aspects of our work, includes agents that may contextually modify their interaction strategies.

The paper is organized as follows: Section 2 introduces the features of the experimental environment describing the agent architecture and defining the different characters. Section 3 presents the questions we addressed in the experiments and the related results. In Section 4 some conclusions are drawn from our findings.

2 A Controlled Artificial Setting

Our simulated environment metaphorically represents a multi-agent system in which some agents, behaving in a common world with limited shared resources, can pursue different and autonomous goals, and find themselves in dependence relations with one another.

The environment is a two-dimensional grid where some food is randomly located; this world is populated by simple agents that need to look for food and eat in order to survive, and that can interact with one another. The dependence relationships among agents consist in the differences among their "power" (energy), which continuously changes as a side-effect of their actions.

The simulated environment is interfaced with the MICE testbed [9], a public domain software for simulating two-dimensional worlds in which agents can interact. Its task is to modify the world as a consequence of the agents' actions, and to facilitate the gathering of different experimental data. MICE is able to produce the effects of an agent's movement, or the consequences of its taking an object. Time, environment characteristics, events, and agents' actions, are treated as discrete units. The testbed allows the user to build a preferred agent architecture, while giving support for the background structures for simulation and experimentation.

2.1 Agent Architecture

The agent architecture is quite simply composed of a visual sensor, a goal generator, a planning module, and a set of effectors that are here quickly described.

- *Sensor.* The sensor lets the agent perceive both the pieces of food and the other agents within a limited area. Such area is measured in terms of grid units, and consists in a square of side $2n + 1$ around the agent, where n is a given sensorial range.

- *Goal Generator.* The goal generator chooses a goal to pursue on the basis of the sensorial information and of the agent's internal state; the latter is related to the energy level, which ranges with integer values from 0 to 100. Agents die when their energy goes below 0. The energy has two intermediate thresholds that play a role in the switch of the agent's internal state, as shown in Figure 1.

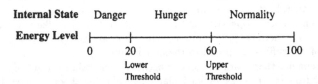

Fig. 1. Relationship between Energy Level and Internal States

- *Planner.* The planner selects a plan suitable to pursue the agent's goal, and controls its execution. At present, the planning module limits itself to choose a plan from a set of canned ones indexed by goals. Each plan is composed of a sequence of actions; f.i., the plan for giving help to a needy agent requires to look for food, choose a piece of food, go toward it, take it, go to the recipient, and give the food to the recipient.
- *Effectors.* The effectors execute elementary actions: moving (from one grid location to another at a time), taking, giving, and eating (one piece of food at a time), choosing a piece of food among a set of perceived ones, and signalling a needy state to the other agents (by changing one's own appearance). Each action affects the agent's internal state by lowering the energetic level in a specified amount, except for the action of eating which increases it by an amount equal to the food energetic value. Actions have either a procedural implementation or a direct translation in terms of MICE commands.

2.2 Agents' Behavior and Interaction Attitudes

As already mentioned, we are interested in exploring the effect of different interaction attitudes upon the agents' survival; such attitudes are generated by embedding different associations between the symbolic internal states (the set *Danger, Hunger, Normal*), and the agent's goals. The built-in characteristics of our agents make the helping behavior possible without resorting to a sophisticated cognitive system. The relationships among types of agent, internal states, and goals are summarized in Table 1.

Four types of agent are defined:

- "Solitary", that just ignore one another, so that there is no interaction among them; their goal is always to individually find food, regardless of their internal state.
- "Parasites" that, regardless of the internal state, always stay still, having the only goal of looking for help and eating the food received by other agents; this means that if parasites are not given help they will definitely die.
- "Selfish" that, depending on their internal state, either ask for help (when in danger) or autonomously look for food (when hungry or in the normal state). The only social behavior showed by both the selfish and the parasites is help-seeking.
- "Social", that may have different goals according to their different internal states; more precisely, in case of danger their goal generator activates the goal of looking for help;

when hungry, their goal is to find food; and finally, in case of normal state, if there are any visible help-seekers, the goal of giving help is activated; otherwise, they go on looking for food. In other words, at different times of a simulation the same social agent could either look for help or find food or give help (if help-seekers are seen), depending on the variations of its energy level.

Type of Agent	Internal State	Goal
Solitary	*any*	Find Food
Parasite	*any*	Look for Help
Selfish	Danger	Look for Help
	Hunger, Normal	Find Food
Social	Danger	Look for Help
	Hunger	Find Food
	Normal	*(if help-seekers are seen:)* Give Help *(if no help-seekers are seen:)* Find Food

Table 1. Relationships among Types of Agent, Internal States, and Goals

The characters of the different agents[3] can be placed along the two dimensions of the self-sufficient attitude and the helping attitude as shown in Table 2. It is interesting to notice that the leftmost upper vertex of the table is left empty: in fact, there cannot exist an agent with a help-giving attitude without at least a minimal self-sufficient attitude, in that it would be impossible for it to help without being able to autonomously get some food.

Self-Sufficient Attitude

		null	*med.*	*max.*
Helping	*yes*		Social	Altruist
Attitude	*no*	Parasite	Selfish	Solitary

Table 2. Relationships between Agent Characters, Self-Sufficient Attitude, and Helping Attitude

2.3 Experimental Conditions

The experimental conditions of our simulations can be summarized as follows. The world is a 15 x 15 grid which contains 60 food units and 30 agents, all randomly located. The food units keep constant until the end of the simulation by randomly reappearing on the grid each time one or more agents eat some food. The initial energy of each agent is set to 50; when they move, agents waste 2 units of energy per time unit, while for staying still they waste 1 unit of energy per time unit. The sensorial range is 3 (i.e. agents can perceive things within a 7 x 7 square around themselves). They choose to help the nearest recipient, and to eat the nearest piece of food. Each simulation lasts 500 iterations, and data are collected every 50 iterations (for a total amount of 10 temporal samples).

---

[3] In the current experiments, we are not interested in the altruist character (placed in the righmost upper vertex of the table) that always gives and never asks for help.

3 Questions and Related Results

In a previous exploratory work [11] we aimed at testing the effect of the helping behavior on the overall performance of the social system, in terms of the agents' survival. We wanted to compare a system where agents help each other when in need with a system where agents neither give nor receive help, and actually ignore each other. Here we first present those results, and then enrich that piece of experimentation by making comparisons among new kinds of agent.

3.1 Solitary vs. Social

We supposed that *the helping behavior would increase the probability of survival of the entire system.* In other words, agents with an extreme self-sufficient attitude, that try to find food just for themselves and never ask for help, would be outperformed by agents helping each other when in need. That is why we realized a set of preliminary simulations by varying the type of agent: solitary vs. social. Each simulation has been performed with a homogeneous group of agents (either 100% of solitary or 100% of social agents).

The results in Figure 2 (and in all the subsequent ones) concern the percentages of alive agents after 500 time steps, plotted against the food energetic values; each point in the figure represents the mean value across 10 simulations.

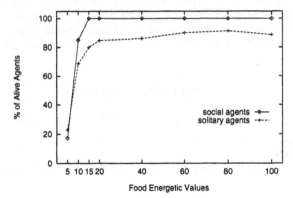

Fig. 2. Comparison between Solitary and Social

Results show that the social condition increases (in a statistically significant way[4]) the percentages of survived agents compared with the non social condition, for every food energetic value but the lowest one.

The advantage of the social over the solitary agents seems to depend on two reasons:

(a) Firstly, it is evident that the helping acts performed by normal agents in favor of the needy ones increase the probability of survival of the latter. And since each agent can become a needy one in given circumstances, the helping behavior turns into a powerful strategy for increasing the probability of survival of the helper itself (thus showing the well-known advantages of "reciprocal altruism" [14]), and ultimately of the entire social system.

---

[4] All results have been submitted to the analysis of variance, with a level of probability of 5%.

(b) Secondly, in case of danger, needy agents do not move until they die or receive some food from another agent, thus decreasing the number of agents competing over the food resources. In other words, the degree of competition and, as a consequence, the probability of failure in finding the food, is lower among the social agents than among the solitary.

3.2 Some New Questions

On the grounds of the previous findings, we have addressed two kinds of question.

Firstly, one could wonder what is the destiny of a social system where social agents (helping each other) come to interact with exploiters, that ask for help without ever giving it. Would the global performance of the system be impaired (in terms of percentages of survived agents) by the presence of the exploiting ones? Or would the social agents be able to "tolerate" such exploitations without great danger both for the entire system and for themselves? Finally, one could also wonder which kind of exploiters would be more dangerous: the parasites, that always ask for help without doing anything of their own, or the selfish, that ask for help just when in danger, but otherwise autonomously compete for the food resources?

Secondly, as it can be easily observed, the two groups of exploiters differ from each other in their degree of self-sufficient attitude: the parasites are totally dependent on others, while the selfish combine help-seeking with a certain degree of self-sufficient attitude (in that they autonomously look for food when not in danger). Going back to the solitary, they show a maximum degree of self-sufficient attitude, in that they never resort to others' help, even when in danger. Now, one might wonder which degree of self-sufficient attitude is more advantageous, in terms of the percentages of survived agents of each type.

Let us start with the first kind of questions, and look at the comparisons between social agents and exploiters, either parasites or selfish. Then, we will consider the comparisons between the exploiters (either parasites or selfish) and the solitary.

3.3 Social with Parasites

Our primary interest was to explore *how the coexistence of parasites and social agents in the same environment would affect the performance of the entire system, and to see how much the performance of social agents would be impaired by such coexistence.* We expected some decrease both in the global percentages of survived agents, and in the percentages of survived social agents, in comparison with the results obtained with the social agents by themselves (shown in Figure 2). However we had no specific hypothesis as to the extent of such a decrease. The simulations have been done putting 15 parasites and 15 social agents in the same environment (with the same parameters as in the previous experiments). Results are shown in Figure 3.

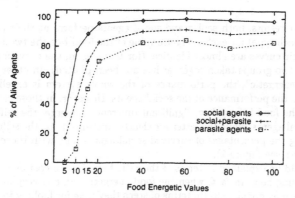

Fig. 3. Comparison between Parasite and Social

As one can see, the system as a whole performs pretty well (curve in the middle), in spite of the presence of the parasites. The same holds for the group of social agents. If compared with the social agents by themselves (Figure 2), we can observe that the present group stabilizes around 100% of survival when the food energetic value is 20 (rather than 15). But apart from this minor difference, their interaction with the parasites does not seem to affect their survival. As for the parasites, though in great danger when the food value is very low (5 to 10), they generally take advantage of the help they receive and are able to survive relatively well (if we consider that, if left alone, they are destined to die).

3.4 Social with Selfish

We wanted to see whether similar results would be obtained with another kind of exploiters. So, we explored *how the coexistence of selfish and social agents would affect the performance of the entire system, and that of the social agents*. On the one hand, in fact, the selfish (that do not ask for help all the time) can be considered as less "disturbing" than the parasites. On the other hand, however, they might be more dangerous than the parasites because, by actively looking for food when not in danger, they compete with the social agents over the available resources.

Again, the simulations have been done putting 15 selfish and 15 social agents in the same environment. Results are shown in Figure 4.

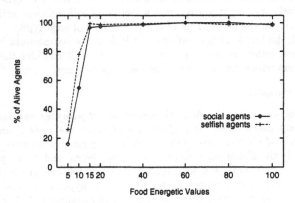

Fig. 4. Comparison between Selfish and Social

According to our results, both selfish and social agents perform at their best (100% of survived agents of each type) for each energetic value of the food but the two lowest ones (5 and 10), so that their curves are almost identical (for this reason, the curve for the average performance of the two groups taken together has not been plotted). In other words, when the food is quite "energetic", the performance of the whole system is excellent, and the selfish do not impair the performance of the social agents. However, in those cases where the energetic value of the food is very low, significant differences emerge: the selfish definitely outperform the social agents, while the latter are clearly "disturbed" by the selfish (as results also from comparing the percentages of survived social agents here with those of the social agents by themselves; see Figure 2).

Such results could be explained in terms of the ratio between the cost of giving help and the benefit of receiving help. In fact, when the food energetic value is very low, the energy that help-givers waste by giving help (in terms of steps they take for looking for food, taking it, going to the recipient, etc.) is not easily restored by the food received from others or got autonomously. That is why the selfish outperform the social agents under these conditions: when giving help is particularly costly, they are a serious disturbance for the social agents, while at the same time they survive much better by taking advantage of the latter's help.

Moreover it has to be noticed that in our environment there is a sort of "ceiling effect", in that the performance of the system, measured as the percentages of survived agents, has of course a maximum value of 100%; this means that one could not observe the possible advantage of an interaction strategy over another when both produce a 100% survival (because, in terms of survival, it is impossible to do better). In another environment, where the agents' performance would be measured differently (f.i. in terms of accumulated resources without any limitation), it could be interesting to see whether the selfish would outperform the social agents independent of the food energetic value.

3.5   Solitary vs. Parasites vs. Selfish

Going back to our question about self-sufficiency, by comparing solitary, parasites and selfish with each other, we aimed at assessing *which degree of self-sufficient attitude is more advantageous*, in terms of percentages of survived agents of each type. Of course, both parasites and selfish, being help-seekers, should be put in condition to find help, that is they should be seen in interaction with potential help-givers, such as our social agents. Otherwise, their strategy would automatically reveal itself as disadvantageous, if compared with that of the solitary. The parasites, if left alone, are destined to die. The selfish too, if left alone, are at a disadvantage in comparison with the solitary because, when in danger, they stop and uselessly ask for help, while the solitary still go on looking for food, thus increasing the likelihood to eat and survive.

Therefore, the parasites and the selfish considered for the comparison with the solitary are those helped by social agents in the previous simulations; i.e. in Figure 5 we compare the parasites helped by social agents (see Figure 3), and the selfish helped by social agents (see Figure 4), with the solitary by themselves (see Figure 2).

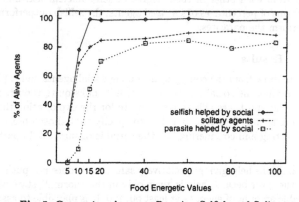

Fig. 5. Comparison between Parasite, Selfish and Solitary

Parasites vs. Solitary. One might assume that asking and waiting for help (where help is likely), without wasting one's own resources in an active search of food, is always better than a self-sufficient attitude, typical of the solitary agents. In other words, an exploiting help-seeker, that never gives help and always asks for it (independent of its actual state of need), might survive more than a self-sufficient agent, that never resorts to others for help. This might be particularly likely in an environment (such as ours) where (a) the help-giving is constrained just by the internal state of the help-giver, that is by its possibility to give help, and not by the actual need of the seeker and (b) there is no sanction against exploitation.

However, results show that the parasite condition significantly decreases the percentage of survived agents compared with the solitary condition. As shown in Figure 5, there is a significant difference between solitary and parasites for every food energetic value but the highest ones (of course, the higher the food energetic value, the more likely is any type of agent to survive, in spite of the possible disfunctionality of its behavior). In other words, the parasites survive less than the solitary, in spite of the latter's continuous employment of energy and level of competition over the food.

This implies that a certain degree of self-sufficient attitude is a basic condition for survival. Parasites, that score zero in self-sufficient attitude, do not compensate for this with others' help at least for the following reasons: (a) others, however benevolent, cannot help all the time; they should first "help themselves", look for their own food, and be in condition to help; (b) while parasites wait for help, they lose energy, though slowly; so, their strategy does not prevent them from dying, if help does not come, or comes too late.

Selfish vs. Solitary. The previous results show that an extreme help-seeking attitude is less advantageous than an extreme self-sufficient attitude. But, what about a "moderate" help-seeking, or, which is the same, a moderate self-sufficient attitude?

Results show that the selfish condition significantly increases the percentages of survived agents compared with the solitary condition, for every food energetic value but the two lowest ones (see Figure 5). In other words, the selfish, that both actively look for food and ask for help when in danger, survive more than the solitary, that do not resort to anybody and, when in danger, behave and live "dangerously", still moving and looking for food. This implies that help-seeking combined with autonomous search for food is the "winning" strategy.

In sum, as shown in Figure 5, the three kinds of agent that share a "zero" in helping attitude and differ from each other in their degree of self-sufficient attitude (see Table 2) rank as follows in terms of percentages of survived agents: the selfish outperform the solitary, that in turn outperform the parasites.

3.6 Summary of Results

A conclusion one can draw from the comparisons among social agents and exploiters (either selfish or parasite) is that the social interaction attitude looks quite robust. Social agents, through their mutual support, are able to compensate for the exploitation they suffer from the non-reciprocating agents. However, it is fair to specify that those observations hold in the given artificial setting and considering just the variable of survival. In particular we can observe that:

(a) In the given conditions help-giving is relatively safe, i. e., it does not put in great danger the survival of the giver because help is given only in the "normal" state when the agent has a considerable amount of energy - at least 60/100. It is plausible to assume that help given in more risky conditions would be more disturbing for the social agents.

(b) As already observed, though social and selfish do not show considerable differences in terms of survival, chances are that differences exist in terms of accumulation of resources, which is not allowed in our current setting.

As for the comparisons among solitary, selfish and parasites, it can be concluded that a "moderate" self-sufficient attitude, that is, self-sufficiency combined with help-seeking (selfish), is more advantageous than an extreme self-sufficient attitude (solitary). Conversely, the latter is still more advantageous than a complete dependence on others (parasites), in that others' help can not compensate for a total lack of self-sufficiency.

4 Conclusions

In this work, our primary concern has been to explore the relative advantageousness of different interaction attitudes of simple agents placed in a common environment. The metaphor chosen to test the strength or robustness of such attitudes is survival, both of the entire social system and of the various sub-groups of agents.

Unlike other works (e.g. [1, 5, 6, 10]), that look at the interaction among various "strategies" in conditions where agents are sensible to each other's behavior, and adapt their own strategy to those shown by their interactants, our agents' behavior is fixed: each kind of agent behaves according to its built-in attitudes, independent of the rewards or punishments it receives from others. In addition, we are not concerned with how such kinds of agent (and their interaction attitudes) evolve across generations.

What we would like to stress is that, even under such conditions, one could find interesting results and provide stimulating suggestions. In particular, a major conclusion one can draw is that the well-known advantage of cooperation (or, in our terms, of mutual help) can be shown and tested in very simple and rigid social systems, where agents neither show any ability to modulate their behavior in accordance with that of others, nor are able to predict and calculate the outcomes of their strategies.

A general suggestion one might give to agent designers is that setting up a multi-agent system of agents with "social" attitudes, even rigid and simple like ours, appears quite useful. Such agents that both seek and give help maintain a high level of performance. The social attitude allows to tolerate some (in our experiments, no less than 50% of the population!) non-reciprocating and exploiting help-seekers without risking dangerous consequences for the entire social system.

As for the advantage of help-seeking for the help-seekers themselves, another major conclusion we can draw is that total dependence and extreme exploitation are not very rewarding. To perform at one's best and actually profit from exploitation, an agent should be endowed with a certain degree of self-sufficient attitude. Pure parasitism does not pay very much. With respect to a radical choice between pure parasitism (to depend just on others for one's survival) and pure self-sufficiency (to depend just on oneself), the latter option is the most rewarding.

Acknowledgments

We are grateful to Cristiano Castelfranchi for his insightful comments and suggestions on a previous version of this paper. This research is partially supported by Esprit III BRWG project No.8319 "A Common Formal Model of Cooperating Intelligent Agents (ModelAge)", and by IP-CNR – Division of Artificial Intelligence, Cognitive Modeling and Interaction.

References

1. Axelrod, R., *The Evolution of Cooperation*. London, Penguin, 1984.
2. Castelfranchi, C., Miceli, M., and Cesta, A., Dependence Relations among Autonomous Agents. In Werner and Demazeau (eds.), *Decentralized Artificial Intelligence 3. Proceedings of the 3rd European Conference on Modelling Autonomous Agents in a Multi-Agent World* (pages 215-227) Amsterdam, Elsevier, 1992.
3. Cesta, A., and Miceli, M., In Search of Help: Strategic Social Knowledge and Plans. In *Proceedings of the 12th International Workshop on Distributed Artificial Intelligence* (pages 35-49), Hidden Valley, PA, 1993.

4. Durfee, E., *Coordination of Distributed Problem Solvers*. Dordrecht, Kluwer, 1988.
5. Glance, N.S., and Huberman, B.A., The Outbreak of Co-operation. *Journal of Mathematical Sociology* (pages 281-302), 17, 1993.
6. Lindgren, K., and Nordahl, M.G., Cooperation and Community Structure in Artificial Ecosystems. *Artificial Life* (pages 15-37), 1, 1994.
7. Mataric, M.J., Issues and Approaches in the Design of Collective Autonomous Systems. *Robotics and Autonomous Systems*, to appear.
8. Miceli, M., and Cesta, A., Strategic Social Planning: Looking for Willingness in Multi-Agent Domains. In *Proceedings of the Fifteeenth Annual Meeting of the Cognitive Science Society* (pages 741-746), Boulder, CO, 1993.
9. Montgomery, T. A., and Durfee, E. H., Using MICE to Study Intelligent Dynamic Coordination. In *Proceedings of the IEEE Conference on Tools for Artificial Intelligence*, IEEE Computer Society Press, 1990.
10. Novak, M.A., May, R.M., and Sigmund, K., The Arithmetic of Mutual Help. *Scientific American* (pages 50-55) , 272, 1995.
11. Rizzo, P., Cesta, A., and Miceli, M., On Helping Behavior in Cooperative Environments. In *Proceedings of the International Workshop on the Design of Cooperative Systems (COOP-95)* (pages 96-108), Juan-les-Pins, France, January 1995.
12. Rosenschein, J.S., and Zlotkin, G., *Rules of Encounters. Designing Conventions for Automated Negotiation among Computers*. Cambridge, MA, MIT Press, 1994.
13. Sekaran, M., and Sen, A., To Help or Not to Help. In *Proceedings of the Seventeenth Annual Conference of the Cognitive Science Society* (pages 736-741), Pittsburgh, PA, July 1995.
14. Trivers, R. L., The Evolution of Reciprocal Altruism. *Quarterly Review of Biology* (pages 35-57), 46, 1971.

Bacterial Evolution Algorithm for Rapid Adaptation

Chisato Numaoka

Sony Computer Science Laboratory Inc. Takanawa Muse Building
3-14-13 Higashi-gotanda, Shinagawa-ku
Tokyo 141, Japan
chisato@csl.sony.co.jp
TEL: +81-3-5448-4380   FAX: +81-3-5448-4273

Abstract. In this paper, we propose a Bacterial Evolution Algorithm (BEA), inspired by the mechanism of bacteria rapidly adapting themselves to an ever-changing environment. In this paper, we call adaptive agents *bacteroids*. Bacteroids have their own fitness function that reflects the rates of energy replenishment and collision avoidance. The characteristic of this algorithm is that a selection of bacteroids is made by their environment with their death as a trigger of the selection. This selection is, in general, done irrespective of the bacteroids own fitness function. Even if they have a higher fitness value at a given moment, they will die when they are exposed to a sudden severe environmental condition. If some bacteroids die, the strongest adjacent bacteroids will take over their bodies by inserting their chromosomes, which should be most adaptive in that local area. Mutation is applied at the moment of this takeover to give the bacteroids a chance at evolution. The BEA is appropriate in an environment where many agents like bacteroids are working together in one place with many chances of interaction.

1 Introduction

Evolution, in general, is a repeating process of increase of variation and natural selection of species. The increase of variation of species involves complex chemical reactions carried out on the genotypes (genes) of creatures. Natural selection works especially on the phenotypes of creatures with sex. This is a Darwinian view of the evolutionary process that is applicable to eukaryotes: insects and animals including human beings.

Historically, creatures seem to have evolved their own ways of mixture or recombination of their genes, i.e., sex, in order to increase variation of genotypes within a narrow enough range that the mixture or recombination does not generally contribute to the creation of strange creatures. As a result, the Darwinian evolution process proceeds quite slowly by repeating slight gene modifications (e.g. [1]).

Observing the world of bacteria tells us that they use different evolution strategy from that of eukaryotes such as animals. Bacteria are prokaryotes, that are characterized by the absence of a nuclear membrane and by DNA that is not organized into chromosomes. They are by nature endowed with a sort of "natural" genetic engineering that has been in use for billions of years. According to [3]:

> ... Over the past fifty years or so, scientists have observed that prokaryotes routinely and rapidly transfer different bits of genetic material to other individuals. Each bacterium at any given time has the use of accessory genes, visiting from sometimes very different strains, which perform functions that its own DNA may not cover. Some of the genetic bits are recombined with the cell's native genes; others are passed on again. Some visiting genetic bits can readily move into the genetic apparatus of eukaryotic cells (such as our own) as well.

> ... The speed of recombination over that of mutation is superior: it could take eukaryotic organisms a million years to adjust to a change on a worldwide scale that bacteria can accommodate in a few years.

As Lynn Margulis and Dorion Sagan describe it, bacteria are creatures equipped with a mechanism for adapting to ever-changing environments. This suggests that the same kind of mechanism could be used for for adaptive agents. If adaptive agents had such a mechanism, then a team of such adaptive agents would be quite stable and capable of maintaining a complex group metabolism.

In this paper, we propose an algorithm for adaptive agents. This algorithm is inspired by the adaptive mechanism of bacteria and is called the *Bacterial Evolution Algorithm* (BEA). This paper is organized as follows: in Section 2, we explain how our algorithm works; in Section 3, we give an example of an agent working environment involving an energy replenishment task and demonstrate the results of experiments using this example; in Section 4, we address the Bacterial Evolution Algorithm by comparing with other evolutionary algorithm from some aspects and discuss the features of this algorithm and the contribution of these features to behavior adaptation for a collection of agents; and finally, in Section 5, we conclude this paper.

2 The Bacterial Evolution Algorithm (BEA)

2.1 Components

Bacteroids *Bacteroids* are defined as simple bacteria-like adaptive agents. Henceforth, we will use the word bacteroids instead of adaptive agents in this paper. Here is a summary of the characteristics of bacteroid necessary to understand the BEA introduced later in this section.

- They are assumed to have a physical body. This body is like a snail's shell and is reusable.

- They have a single "chromosome," explained below.

- They have a certain amount of energy. As long as they have enough energy (that is, are not hungry), they wander. When they are hungry, they go to an energy base to replenish their energy.

- They have a fitness function that calculates a degree of adaptability at any place in their world.

- They have an ability to know whether the energy of adjacent bacteroids has decreased below a tolerable level and, if they find such a bacteroid, insert their chromosomes into the bacteroid.

Chromosomes Chromosomes are basically strings coding some parameters (genes), characterizing the behavior pattern of bacteroids, and control bits, which suppress or activate the emergence of the parameters. The interaction between a parameter and a bit corresponds to an interaction between non-allelic genes called *epistasis* in genetics. The basic structure of chromosomes is depicted in Figure 1.

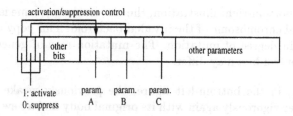

Fig. 1. Chromosome as a string: a specific bit controls activation/suppression of the function related to its corresponding gene.

2.2 The Algorithm

Figure 2 illustrates the life cycle of a bacteroid with four scenes explaining the Bacterial Evolution Algorithm.

Step 1 The top-left figure illustrates the situation where four healthy bacteroids are inserting a copy of their chromosomes to a weakened bacteroid at the center. If a bacteroid is weak and there are no healthy bacteroids adjacent, the weakened bacteroid stops moving.

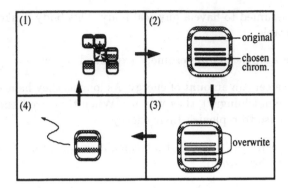

Fig. 2. Life cycle of a bacteroid: The bacteroids move through four cyclic phases: (1) the insertion of chromosomes from other bacteroids to a weakened one, (2) selection of one chromosome inside the invaded bacteroid, (3) replacement of that chromosome, and (4) reactivation.

Step 2 The top-right figure depicts the internals of the invaded bacteroid. The invaded bacteroid has five chromosomes inside the body at this moment. The top one is the original and the others are inserted chromosomes. In this step, only one chromosome is chosen, using certain criteria.

Step 3 In the bottom-right illustration, the chosen chromosome is being copied onto the original chromosome of the invaded bacteroid. This copy operation will involve a certain degree of mutation. The mutation rate of genes and that of their related control bits may differ.

Step 4 Finally, in the bottom-left figure, the previously weakened bacteroid begins to wander vigorously again with its original body and a new chromosome.

3 Experiments

In this section, we take a problem called the Blind Hunger Dilemma, proposed in [4]. By viewing how bacteroids overcome this problem and adapt to their environment, we will understand the benefits of adaptive agents (bacteroids) in multi-agent problems over agents with fixed behavior.

3.1 The Blind Hunger Dilemma: A Experimental Subject

Suppose that many bacteroids are living on an island or some place isolated by fences. The shape of the island is a 15 × 15 lattice. In this island, there is only a single energy supply base, in the middle of the island, equipped with 8 docks. The base has the capacity to supply energy to 8 bacteroids simultaneously. This energy base produces a potential field by emitting a smell, producing a sound, or using a light.

The routine activity of these bacteroids is quite simple. They can move one step to either of 8 adjacent places [1] if the place chosen is not already occupied by another bacteroid. When the bacteroids have sufficient energy, they simply wander around the island. Each bacteroid must choose one direction from the 8 for the next move based on information gathered by its sensors [2]. When the bacteroids feel hungry, they approach the energy base drawn by the potential field created by the base. When replenished, they initially move away from the energy base as if they are repelled by it. They then return to wandering.

However, if many bacteroids need to be replenished at the same time, this will cause a problem, which we term "the Blind Hunger Dilemma " [4]. One reason why we invented the BEA is to make the bacteroids themselves solve the problem in an evolutionary fashion.

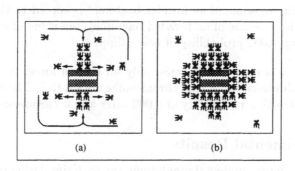

Fig. 3. Energy Replenishment: (a) a collection of bacteroids behaving in a well-trained manner. (b) a collection of bacteroids behaving fully selfishly: the situation of the Blind Hunger Dilemma.

3.2 Basic Experimental Conditions

Experiments were carried out using a Monte-Carlo simulation. In each simulation, we assumed the following conditions:

- Fitness function is defined as follows: Fitness = $\mathcal{R}$ #Replenishment - $\mathcal{C}$ <#Collisions> where #x means the number of x and <y> means a mean

---

[1] This is not always true. If a bacteroid is in one corner of the square island, of course, the choice is limited to 3 directions.

[2] I do not explain the details of bacteroids' sensing ability because of the space limitations. I recommend that interested readers read [5]. Roughly speaking, they recognize the strength of the potential field of the energy base at any point. In addition, they have a capacity to sense local information through interaction with their adjacent bacteroids: inward pressure, attractive force, and viscous force.

value of y. We consider only collisions between two bacteroids.

- Bacteroids potentially have the ability to sense three types of forces: inward force, attractive force, and viscous force. After taking into account these sensations, they choose a direction to move. Although the equations for calculating these three types of force are not listed, each equation has a coefficient: A_P for inward force, A_A for attractive force, and A_V for viscous.

- A chromosome is on 18-bit string, composed of two genes, α and β, and two control bits. $\alpha = A_A/A_P$ and $\beta = A_V/A_P$. Both α and β are 8-bit integers. Coefficient A_P was always set to 3000.0. As explained in Section 2, the two other bits control whether or not the bacteroid has an ability for sensing attractive and viscous forces. If these bits are 1, the corresponding abilities emerge.

- When a chromosome of an invader bacteroid is copied to the field of the original chromosome of an invaded bacteroid, the value of each bit in the genes has a 0.002 probability of being flipped.

- All bacteroids can initially sense only an inward force. Namely, both of the two additional bits in the chromosome are set to 0. These two bits can be flipped with a probability of 0.002 after a new chromosome is chosen.

3.3   Experimental Results

We carried out a large number of simulations and each simulation ran for 300,000 time steps. In this section, we will see a typical example of the gradual adaptation of a collection of bacteroids for each of two experiments: homogeneous bacteroids and heterogeneous bacteroids.

Experiment 1: Homogeneous bacteroids   I this simulation, two control bits are assumed to always be 1. This indicates that every bacteroids has all sensing abilities: inward pressure, attractive force, and viscous force. As we know from Figure 4 (a), the value is largely fluctuating but is stable around 0.3 as an average, although, as Figure 4 (b) demonstrates, the mean values of two parameters continue to search a proper value in their search spaces without showing any obvious direction of modification of their values.

Experiment 2: Heterogeneous bacteroids   In this simulation, four types of bacteroids can appear: BOTH, ONLY-ALPHA, ONLY-BETA, and NEITHER. BOTH can sense all three forces, ONLY-ALPHA cannot sense the viscous force, ONLY-BETA cannot sense the attractive force, and NEITHER can sense only the inward pressure. According to Figure 5 (a), bacteroids of ONLY-ALPHA

145

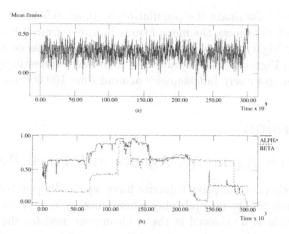

Fig. 4. Evolution of bacteroids: (a) Time vs. mean fitness. (b) Time vs. mean value of two parameters α and β.

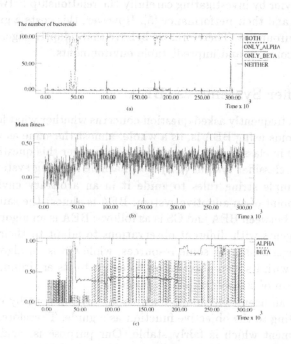

Fig. 5. Co-evolution of four types of bacteroids: (a) Time vs. the number of bacteroids of each type. (b) Time vs. mean fitness. (c) Time vs. mean value of two parameters α and β.

type have come to dominate the population at time 50,000. At this same moment, as Figure 5 (b) shows, the mean fitness improves from 0.1 to 0.3, although the value is also highly fluctuating. Furthermore, in accordance with this dominance, as seen in Figure 5 (x), the value of α increases. Interestingly, this increase does not happen gradually but stepwise around time 100,000 and 200,000.

4 Discussion

4.1 Adaptive Agents vs. Agents with Fixed Behavior

As many researchers on adaptive behavior have repeatedly pointed out, adaptive agents bring their ability into full play when working in very complex and unpredictable worlds as we showed in the environment used for the Blind Hunger Dilemma. If the working environment of the agents is not so complex, is completely predictable, and is carefully programmed, agents with fixed behavior work well. They can achieve a very high level of performance from the beginning. In fact, we have proved that we can develop an effective group of agents with fixed behavior by investigating carefully the relationship between the properties of agents and their performance [5]. However, this costs a great deal even for a simple environment. Therefore, we believe that adaptive agents are needed for working in complex and unpredictable environments.

4.2 Classifier Systems vs. BEA

One of the most frequently asked question concerns whether what happens in the world of bacteroids using BEA is, as a whole, almost the same as what happens to an individual in classifier systems. We always answer this question as follows: First of all, "A classifier system (CS) is a machine learning system that learns syntactically simple string rules to guide it in an arbitrary environment' [2]. From the viewpoint of an adaptive system, BEA is almost the same as CS. The main difference between BEA and CS is as follows: BEA is an algorithm allowing many simple agents with different observations to adapt to their environment as a group of agents sharing some resources, while CS is an algorithm for one complex agent with its own observation to adapt to its environment, normally given by the form of a stable objective function.

With a CS, an agent will adapt itself to an environment by using a fitness function according to the objective function as a guide. Therefore, it works well in the environment which is fairly stable. Our purpose is, again, to give an algorithm for agents living in an environment for which it is very difficult to define one stable objective function, or in which the objective function is always changing and varies due to the location in which agents find themselves at any moment.

For our purpose, CSs lack an important feature, namely, selection by their environment. The BEA provides this feature by their death and by assuming an environment where many agents are working together in one place. As a result, the BEA gives us one possible solution for many agents to live together, adapting quickly to a very complex and variable world.

4.3 Conservative Adaptation vs. Rapid Adaptation

In general, eukaryotes adapt to their environment slowly, in a conservative manner. This is because cells including a nucleus are protected against invasions by any other creatures by a cell membrane, their DNA are further kept inside a distinct membrane-bound nucleus, and the DNA has chemically stable structure, which consists of two long chains of nucleotides twisted into a double helix and joined by hydrogen bonds between the complementary bases adenine and thymine or cytosine and guanine, and because eukaryotes use a very complex self-replication mechanism, which is accompanied with meiosis during which genetic materials between homologous chromosomes are exchanged.

On the other hand, as quoted Lynn Margulis and Dorion Sagan's description, bacteria can rapidly transfer their materials between two individuals. It is sure that this is possible because bacteria do not have nuclear membrane and DNA and, instead, have a very simple genetic structure. Because of this, bacteria can adapt themselves rapidly to their environment. On the other hand, they are not able to evolve in a direction that increases the complexity of their structure beyond a level that they have. They may have to be quite simple. If we need individuals that have a very complex structure and metabolism, we may have to abandon the use of the BEA. The BEA may be applicable only to a rapid evolution of a group of very simple organisms as far as what we have learned from the life of bacteria is concerned.

In fact, the above statements must be true for the BEA. To go beyond these limitations, we have to learn more about evolutionary dynamics. Take the example of symbiotic evolution that Lynn Margulis assumes. We experimented with an evolutionary dynamics of heterogeneous bacteroids within the framework of the BEA. The motivation of this experiment was to investigate effects of a sudden creation of new species by making a tight endosymbiotic relation between two different creatures. An example of endosymbiosis can be seen between mitochondria and the ancestors of the current eukaryotic cell. This example suggests that, by establishing this relation, creatures can have functions that they could not developed rapidly by themselves only.

Of course, our experiment in this paper may be too simple. Nevertheless, this experiment indicates a possibility that, by having a collection of many kinds of creatures and by giving them a mechanism to create a kind of metabolic relation among some creatures, they can develop and improve themselves as they adapt to their environment. We are now studying more about this type of symbiotic evolution (See [6]). In a sense, the BEA is a research instrument we can use for investigation of symbiotic evolution before going far toward the study.

5 Conclusion

In this paper, we proposed an algorithm suitable for an adaptation of a team of agents, *bacteroids*, working in an ever-changing environment. We also showed one typical example of adaptation for a group of bacteroids using the BEA in an experimental environment.

The primary benefit of BEA is that it is a very simple algorithm that takes into account the complexity of the real world both in time and in space. In an environment where many agents are moving, a complex and unpredictable situation is produced. A the agents interact with each other at a very high rate, the speed of distribution of information is also very high.

Bacteria in our world live in a situation in which they adapt themselves to the environment quickly. Of course, our method is not the same as that which bacteria use in the real world. Nevertheless, bacteroids using BEA are gradually able to adapt to their environment and increase their mean fitness level. This result is achieved by the simple mechanism of replacing worse chromosomes with better chromosomes. This mechanism is, we believe, essentially similar to that used by bacteria, although the bacterial mechanism is much more complex.

References

1. Douglas J. Futuyma. *Evolutionary Biology (2nd ed.)*. Sinauer Associates, Inc., 1986.

2. David E. Goldberg. *Genertic Algorithm – in Search, Optimization & Machine Learning*. Addison Wesley, 1989.

3. Lynn Margulis and Dorion Sagan. *Microcosmos*. A Touchstone Book, 1986.

4. Chisato Numaoka. Blind Hunger Dilemma: An Emergent Collective Behavior from Conflicts. In *Proceedings of From Perception to Action Conference*. IEEE Computer Society Press, September 1994.

5. Chisato Numaoka. Introducing Blind Hunger Dilemma: Agents' Properties and Performance. In *Proceedings of the First International Conference on Multiagent Systems (ICMAS'95)*. AAAI Press, June 1995.

6. Chisato Numaoka. Symbiosis and Co-evolution in Animats. In *Proceedings of the Third European Conference on Artificial Life (ECAL'95)*. The Springer-Verlag, June 1995.

Distributed Interaction with Computon

Toru Ohira[1] and Ryusuke Sawatari[2] and Mario Tokoro[1,2]

[1] Sony Computer Science Laboratory
3-14-13 Higashi-gotanda,
Tokyo 141, Japan
(ohira, mario)@csl.sony.co.jp
Tel:+81-3-5448-4380, Fax:+81-3-5448-4273
[2] Department of Computer Science
Keio University,
3-14-1 Hiyoshi, Yokohama 223, Japan
(sawatari, mario)@mt.cs.keio.ac.jp

Abstract. One of the major challenges of distributed artificial intelligence is to obtain useful and effective emergent behaviors of agents in the system based on the local decision–making of each agent. The effectiveness of the system as a whole is as much dependent on the form of interactions between agents as on the capabilities or strategies of each one. The focus and main theme of this paper is to put forth the idea of distributed interactions through an elementary medium. In this conceptual picture, the interaction between agents is distributed over the collective behavior of a basic unit or "particle", which we call "computon". The key feature of distributed interaction is the distribution of contents of information among objects or computational agents. This model allows each agent to make a decision on its behavior based on simple all-local transactions for a possibly effective emergent collective behavior. In order to evaluate and examine the feasibility and possibility of distributed interactions, We consider two examples of distributed interaction models with computons. The first example is a conceptual discussion of a "Quantized" Computational Field Model. In this model, computon is introduced as a "fundamental particle" of the computational field. Interaction of objects and computational field is envisioned as an interaction between objects via exchanges of computons. To gain more quantitative insight into distributed interactions, we constructed a model using computons to address the problem of load balancing. A dynamic load balancing model applied to a ring of processors was investigated using simulations. When compared with a load balancing model without computons, the load was found to be distributed better over a model ring of processors. Through these examples, we infer and discuss general advantages and problems of distributed interactions among distributed agents or computational resources.

1 Introduction

One of the major goals of distributed artificial intelligence is to obtain, through interactions between agents, effective and useful emergent decisions or computations fromm relatively simple actions by each agent in a given environment (e.g. [5, 13, 14, 15, 26]). Research toward this goal faces the difficult challenge of designing each agent's actions and interactions with others in an ever changing environment to obtain a desired macroscopic computation or action.

These issues and challenges in distributed artificial intelligence are becoming increasingly shared by distributed computations in large–scale networks. We would like to overcome the disadvantages of the large–scale network, such as the cost and delays in communications and the associated difficulty with coherent computation using distributed resources, and obtain an effective emergent computational method or model[3, 4, 6, 8].

The main focus and theme of this paper is the notion of "distributed interactions" among distributed autonomous agents or computational resources in a large-scale network. Distributed interaction is a form of interaction between agents, where the information contents are distributed over basic units or "particles". In other words, the distributed interaction information each agent receives is not represented by a single packet, but is expressed by some collective behaviors or characteristics of a basic unit.

The concept of "computon" has recently been proposed [12] as a basic unit of distributed interaction for the Computational Field Model (CFM) suggested by Tokoro[16, 17, 18, 19, 20]. The CFM has been formulated using an analogy between a computation in a distributed environment with an interaction of mass in a gravitational field in physics. The conceptual framework is developed to facilitate distributed interactions using computons in the CFM: distribution of the control information itself in the network through local transactions. With the distributed interactions using computons, we seek to design a system in which semi–global information of the system (field) is constructed through all–local simple transaction of computons by objects or computational agents. The object or computational agents, in return, interact with this field locally to make its behavioral decisions such as migrations.

There are a couple of advantages of distributed interactions with a simple basic unit like computon. First, since the information is collectively represented by computons, the lack of a few computons during communications does not affect the transmission of information. In other words, some degree of fault tolerance of interaction can be achieved. When combined with an appropriate encoding scheme, this collective representation by computons can also lead to security of communication. The disadvantages are the increase of overhead and complexity of interactions. Each agent needs to have schemes with which to analyze computons collectively to obtain the information. As will be seen in the following application to the dynamic load balancing problem, however, the transactions of computons can be naturally separated from the main computation of agents and executed in parallel.

The design principle of distributed interactions is, hence, to keep computons of simple nature with a suitable all–local transaction scheme so that the advantages of distributed interaction are put forward without too much increase in overhead. In order to address these issues seeking design principles for distributed interactions leading to an effective emergent structure, we will consider two examples of models with distributed interactions in the following. The first is a conceptual account of computons for the CFM, the second example is a more concrete application to the dynamic load balancing problem.

2 Computational Field Model

In this chapter, we give an conceptual account of the computational field model and computons. The model is based on concurrent objects[1, 24] and an open distributed environment. Objects are modular units which contain a set of procedures and local storage. The computation is modeled as their message passing among themselves. The notion of concurrent objects is an extension of the concept of the object in order to model the computation in an open distributed computational environment[7, 22, 23, 25]. An open distributed environment is a computational environment where services, processing capacity and connection topology of computing elements change from time to time. It is a multi-user environment which supports various computational tasks to be processed in parallel and in real time. It is a homogeneous environment in the sense that any mobile user can be provided with the same environment regardless of accessing location. A concurrent object possesses a virtual processor in addition to its local storage and set of procedures. This incorporation of a processor in an object enables us to eliminate the concept of the locus of execution from the object-oriented computing. This notion of the concurrent object is thus more suited for the open distributed environment. The central issue of a computational model using the concurrent object in an open distributed environment is the way in which objects can migrate or distribute themselves so that the existing resources are utilized efficiently. The CFM provides a theoretical framework to deal with this issue. Just as the gravitational field is created by masses in the system, we model the computational field being created by concurrent objects. Then, the computation in the open distributed environment is envisioned as interactions of concurrent objects with the computational field. The distribution of objects is achieved by the balance of two forces: gravitational forces between objects which depend on frequency and size of information change for communication between objects, and repulsive forces which depend on object size. The gravitational force tries to minimize the communication costs between closely related objects, while the repulsive force tries to avoid a concentration of computation at one local point. When an object is introduced, it interacts with the computational field and is affected by these forces as a result of the interaction. The result is a migration of all the objects to a new location so that the entire system and the computational field reaches a new equilibrium.

Computons are introduced by considering "quantization" of the computational field so that they serve as a basic particle to form computational fields (Quantized Computational Field Model (QCFM)) . The conceptual framework is developed to facilitate distributed interactions using computons in the CFM: a distribution of the control information itself in the network through local transactions. With the distributed interactions using computons, we seek to design a system in which semi–global information of the system (field) is constructed through all–local simple transaction of computons by objects or computational agents. The object or computational agents, in return, interact with this field locally to make its behavioral decisions such as migrations.

There are a couple of motivations in taking the step to the QCFM from the CFM. In the CFM, the interaction of the field and the objects is locally evaluated, however, the construction algorithm of the field itself is yet to be developed. If we are to push a simple analogy of the computational field with the classical field, this construction of the field is a non–local operation using information on the entire (or approximate surrounding area) distribution of the objects. What we aim at with computons in the QCFM is to further bring in the principle of locality to the creation of the field as well as to its interaction with objects. We would like to design the QCFM so that the field, which has a correspondence with some aspects of collective behavior of computons in the environment, can be created by all–local operations. Another motivating factor is that comparing to continuous analog fields, discrete units like computons can be more naturally implemented in the actual digital environment.

Here, let us consider a computational environment in which many concurrent objects with motion are present. The computons must collectively carry the following information for the objects in a field:

(1) Location and motion

(2) Size (or computational load)

(3) Relations (communication load) between objects

A variety of designs can be considered for computons. A guiding principle, however, is to keep individual computons as simple as possible for efficiency of local computations as well as to minimize the load for the network of the computational field. We propose here one example of computon design.

Objects with higher load emit less computons indicating their computational load. If there are particular relations among objects, they are noted on computons from the objects involved. For example, one can design objects which require a high communication load to send computons of the same binary "color" code. In addition, we can have each computon carry a time stamp of its emission from an object. Provided we design the frequency of emission of computons so that it is high enough compared to the motions of objects involved, objects which receive computons can estimate the position and motion of other objects.

In this design, computons can carry the above mentioned three pieces of information collectively, when objects are equipped with the simple ability to analyze incoming computons. The effectiveness of the system depends very much on how these pieces of information can be utilized by each object in deciding its action. As in the CFM, a design of this part of the algorithm, particularly that incorporating actual message exchanges between objects, is yet to be worked out for the QCFM. An example of implementation using concurrent objects is also left for the future.

3 Applications of Computons to Load Balancing Problems

The conceptual model of the QCFM with computons presented in the previous section has flexibility in its design and its efficiency depends on how it is implemented. However, it is desirable for us to have some ideas on general characteristics of the distributed interaction models with computons based on more quantitative observations. For this purpose, we change our focus from the QCFM to the application of a model with computons for the problem of load balancing.

3.1 Model

We explicitly consider a particular computon model for the load balancing of interconnected processors (Figure 1). Here, communication between the objects is assumed not to be present. The major point of difference in this model from the QCFM, reflecting this lack of communication between objects or processes, is that the distribution of processes is achieved by computons coming out of processors rather than out of processes.

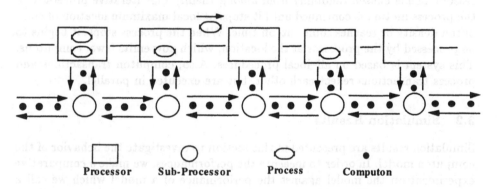

Fig. 1. Schematic view of the load balancing system model with computons.

We take a one–dimensional ring network of processors. Each processor has a main part which does the actual processing of a task and an associated part (sub–processor) which performs transactions of computons. At a given time, the main part sends out a number of computons, which is a function of its load. For simplicity, we take that number to decrease linearly with the load of the main part (i.e., the processor with more computational capability sends out more computons). Computon transactions are done by the sub–processors. Each sub–processor sends the computons it has equally to the two neighbors and to its processor. (Hence, it sends out one third (or approximately one third when not divisible) to each of them.) The computons sent to its processor are absorbed.(This absorption of computons is necessary so that the total number of computons is bounded and the system operates near equilibrium.) The number of computons a sub–processor retains is now the sum of those from its processor and its neighboring sub–processors. In this manner computons are distributed reflecting the load information of the main parts of the processors (Figure 2).

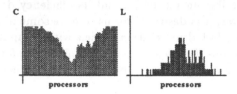

Fig. 2. Densities of computons, C, and the corresponding load of processors, L, with the model on the ring.

When a new process is introduced into the system at some point on the network, it compares the number of computons on the neighboring sub–processors including its own. Then, the process is moved to the processor with the greatest number of computons on its sub–processor. (If there is more than one such processors, one is chosen randomly from among them.) This iterative procedure of the process motion is continued until it stops at local maximum location of computon density or reaches some cut–off time. When the process stops, it begins to be processed by the processor at the location, which now emits fewer computons. This system is based on all–local procedures. Also, computon transactions and process transactions reflect each other, but are executed in parallel.

3.2 Simulation Results

Simulation results are presented in this section to investigate the behavior of the computon model. In order to measure the performances, we make a comparative experiment on the model against the performance of a model which we call a "diffusion model". The diffusion model is also a model of load balancing based on all–local procedures. It differs from the computon model in that it does not utilize sub–processors or computons and the process moves simply by comparing the computational capabilities of its neighboring processors, including itself, to the best capable processor. In other words, it directly compares the capability of neighboring processors, rather than the number of computons on the neighboring sub–processors. The quantities which are focused in the experiments to measure the performances of these two models are as follows:

1. Number of busy processors. The more processors that are busy, the better the loads are distributed over a network.
2. Time a process takes to reach and stop at a processor after its introduction to a network. This will be called "stopping time". The shorter the stopping time, the quicker a process starts being processed after its introduction to a network.

3. Standard deviation of computational capabilities of processors being busy. This will be termed "deviation". A smaller deviation means the load is distributed evenly over the busy processors.

The number of processors on the network is kept fixed as $N = 80$ and we investigate the behaviors of the model with respect to the measure of performance described above. The basic time unit of the system is set to be the time for the transaction and update of computons by sub–processors. We define this basic time unit as 1.

The variables of the system relating to the process and computons are the following:

S: the number of computons emitted by a processor without any process.

U: the number of computons each process consumes, i.e., a processor which emits U less computons per process on it (Weight of the process.)

L: the time for each process to be processed (Lifetime of the process).

We will perform a series of experiments varying these parameters to explore characteristics of computon models. All our experiments in the following are comparative experiments between the computon model and the diffusion model.

Number of Busy Processors The number of busy processors in the network is investigated here as we vary the conditions of the system. The first experiment is to drop the series of processes from a single point on the network. We set $S = 160$, $U = 20$ and $L = 4000$, and drop the processes one by one with the interval of $\tau = 100$. Each movement of a process to the neighboring process is assumed to take the unit time. The physical assumption behind this parameter setting is that the transaction cost in time for computons and processes is not much compared to the lifetime of the processes.

Figure 3 (a) shows the number of busy processors as a function of time. It is clearly seen that the computon method can distribute the processes to roughly twice as many processors as the diffusion method. We vary the ways to introduce the processes into the network. Figure 3 (b) shows the same plot when we increased the introduction points to 2 places on the network. The results when we doubled the time interval ($\tau = 200$) between processes to be introduced to the network are shown in Figure 3 (c). These results show that the computon method can distribute the process better over the network resources than the diffusive process under different process introduction conditions.

Our attention is now turned to the question of the effect of the nature of the processes to be introduced. Figure 4 shows the result of simulations when we increased the lifetime of the process from $L = 1000$ to $L = 4000$; the results of changing the weights of the processes ($U = 5$ and $U = 20$) are shown in Figure 5. Again, the findings show that the computon method can use more processors than the diffusion method. We note also that the ratio of busy processors for the

Fig. 3. Number of busy processors, X, as a function of time with the computon method (solid line) and the diffusion method (dashed line). The parameters are $S = 160$, $U = 20$, and $L = 4000$. The processes are introduced into the network in the following ways: (a) From a single point on the network at every $\tau = 100$, (b) From two points on the network at every $\tau = 100$, (c) From a single point on the network at every $\tau = 200$ (half-frequency).

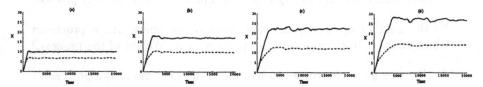

Fig. 4. Number of busy processors, X, as a function of time as we change the lifetime of the processes with the computon method (solid line) and the diffusion method (dashed line). The parameters are $S = 160$, and $U = 20$, and the processes are introduced into the network from a single point at every $\tau = 100$. The lifetime of the processes is (a) $L = 1000$, (b) $L = 2000$, (c) $L = 3000$, and (d) $L = 4000$.

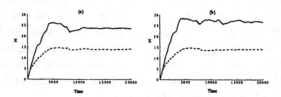

Fig. 5. Number of busy processors, X, as a function of time as we change the weights of the processes with the computon method (solid line) and the diffusion method (dashed line). The parameters are $S = 160$, and $L = 4000$ and the processes are introduced into the network from a single point at every $\tau = 100$. The weight of the processes is (a) $U = 5$ and (b) $U = 20$.

computon method over the diffusion method improves as the lifetime and the weights get larger. This implies that the advantage of the computon method is more notable for the processes of longer lifetime and more weight.

Finally, we consider the network with inhomogeneous computation capabilities. We compare the number of busy processors on a homogeneous network (Figure 6 (a)) and on an inhomogeneous network on which every 10th processor is "weak" with about 60% capability (Figure 6 (b)). The results indicate that more processors are employed with these changes in the network environment.

In summary with respect to the number of busy processors we observed that the computon method generally performed better than the diffusion model. The improvement of the distribution is particularly notable when the processes introduced onto the networks are of longer lifetime and "heavier" in weight.

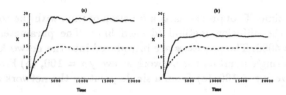

Fig. 6. Number of busy processors, X, as a function of time as we change the conditions of the processor in the network with the computon method (solid line) and the diffusion method (dashed line). The parameters are $U = 20$, and $L = 4000$ and the processes are introduced into the network from a single point at every $\tau = 100$. The computational capabilities of processors are (a) homogeneous with $S = 160$ for all processors, and (b) inhomogeneous with $S = 160$ for most processors, but $S = 100$ (weaker) for every 10th processor in the ring.

Stopping Times In this section, we address the issue of "stopping time" of the process. This is the average time a process takes before it reaches a processor and begins to be processed. The shorter the "stopping time", the more efficient the system is. We expect that the computon method will perform less efficiently with this measure as it takes more time on average to distribute the process to more processors. We see in the following with our simulation results that this is the case. (The sets of data are taken with the same simulation runs as in the previous section.)

Figure 7 shows the effect on the stopping time by the change in the way of introducing the processors into the network. (The system parameters are the same as in Figure 3.) It shows the stopping time is longer with the computon method than the diffusion method. Similar results are obtained when we change the lifetime and weights of the processes (Figures 8 and 9), and when we change the network environment to have inhomogeneous computational capabilities (Figure 10).

These results show that stopping time performance is in a reciprocal relation to the number of busy processors using the two methods. The computon method can distribute over more processors with sacrifice of the stopping time for each process introduced. When we compare, for example, Figures 4 and 8, we note that roughly 50% to 95% better distribution by the computon method is at the expense of 40% to 80% loss in stopping time over the diffusion method. We note that, in terms of these ratios, the gain for the better distribution is slightly more than the loss in stopping time with the computon method. It is, however, roughly reciprocal.

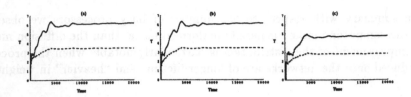

Fig. 7. Stopping time, T, of processes as a function of time with the computon method (solid line) and the diffusion method (dashed line). The parameters are $S = 160$, $U = 20$, and $L = 4000$. The processes are introduced into the network in the following ways: (a) From a single point on the network at every $\tau = 100$, (b) From two points on the network at every $\tau = 100$, (c) From a single point on the network at every $\tau = 200$ (half-frequency).

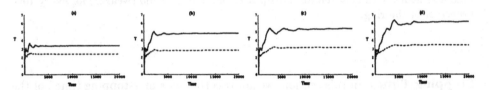

Fig. 8. Stopping time, T, of processes as a function of time as we change the lifetime of the processes with the computon method (solid line) and the diffusion method (dashed line). The parameters are $S = 160$, and $U = 20$, and the processes are introduced into the network from a single point at every $\tau = 100$. The lifetime of the processes is (a) $L = 1000$,(b) $L = 2000$, (c) $L = 3000$, and (d) $L = 4000$.

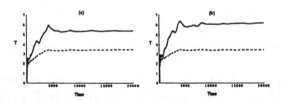

Fig. 9. Stopping time, T, of processes as a function of time as we change the weights of the processes with the computon method (solid line) and the diffusion method (dashed line). The parameters are $S = 160$, and $L = 4000$ and the processes are introduced into the network from a single point at every $\tau = 100$. The weight of the processes is (a) $U = 5$ and (b) $U = 20$.

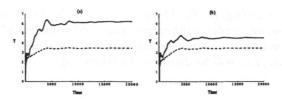

Fig. 10. Stopping time, T, of processes as a function of time as we change the conditions of the processor in the network with the computon method (solid line) and the diffusion method (dashed line). The parameters are $U = 20$ and $L = 4000$, and the processes are introduced into the network from a single point at every $\tau = 100$. The computational capabilities of processors are (a) homogeneous with $S = 160$ for all processors, and (b) inhomogeneous with $S = 160$ for most processors, but $S = 100$ (weaker) for every 10th processor in the ring.

Deviation We now look at the "deviation" which is the measure of how evenly processes are distributed over the busy processors. More precisely, we define the deviation as follows. We measure the computational capabilities of a processor at a certain time by the number of computons it emits. With an even distribution of processes, then, the number of computons emitted by each processor is roughly the same over the network. The deviation is defined as the standard deviation of the number of computons which a processor gives out to its sub–processor. The more even distribution is indicated by the smaller value of the deviation.

The same set of simulations is performed with varying parameters. The results show that the computon method consistently performs better with respect to the deviations.(The details and figures for these results will be shown elsewhere[10].)

3.3 Summary

Here, we briefly summarize and discuss the result of simulation experiment of the computon model for dynamic load balancing. We found that this model can distribute processes to more processors and more evenly over the network than the diffusion model. The stopping time for the processes are, however, longer for the computon model. From these results, we qualitatively infer that computons can collectively carry some amount of global information of the load even though that information is formed by local procedure only. This characteristic of transmission of some amount of global information by local procedures could be developed into construction of an effective structure from the distributed interactions.

The load balancing performance of the model here depends on the balance of the trade–off between use of more processors and stopping times. It is expected to be effective in a situation as that under our experimental conditions where the processes are computationally large compared to the extra cost of computon transactions. There are previously proposed algorithms for load balancing solely with local operations (e.g. [2, 9]). The distribution of load information itself over computons causes our model to differ from these ohter models. More quantitative comparison as well as simulation experiments on 2–dimensional networks is in progress, however, and will be discussed in future[10].

4 Discussion

We have proposed and examined a concept of distributed interactions among distributed agents or computational resources. The basic unit of interactions is called a computon and their collective behaviors represent information content of communication. Even though such collective representation of interactions is more costly in local transactions, the possibility of constructing an effective emergent computation as a system is demonstrated by its application to the dynamic load balancing problem. Also, as conceptually presented in the framework of the CFM, the same set of computons can possibly carry different information by looking at different characteristics of their collective behaviors. In other words, an agent or object, with appropriate multiple analyzing schemes, can extract different information which is useful to it at a particular time by looking at the different aspects of the same sets of computons, such as densities,frequencies and so on. This notion of collectively transmitting multiple information for efficient communication could be developed into one of useful features of collective interactions together with fault tolerance and security. This development is left for future research together with the following three issues.

The first is how the model can be designed so that more information of the entire system can be available locally. Some of this was achieved in our experiment which showed smoothing out of some local minima and distribution to more processors. However, we still lack a well-defined design principle to implement this concept of delivering information for the entire system by purely local transaction. The second point is what kind of structure of information is useful for efficient computation. We can view the model with computons as two interactive diffusive systems, one for processes or objects, and the other for computons. The interaction here can possibly contain some time delays , and, even though it is microscopically intricate, analytical concepts such as "Delayed Random Walks"[11] could be used to describe the macroscopic structure and behavior of a model with computons. Construction of a useful information structure is a common problem in the design of a distributed computational system. Whether a model with computons can find its own direction to resolve this problem is currently under investigation. The third point is the issue of whether we can design a model in terms of object–oriented operating systems[23] or languages[21]; this appears to be a natural place to bring in the concept of computons. Further research on these three issues is required to show the efficacy of models with computons.

References

1. Agha, G., Wegner, P., and Yonezawa, A., eds: Research Directions in Concurrent-Object Oriented Programming, MIT Press, Cambridge, 1993.
2. Chowdhury, S.: The Greedy Load Sharing Algorithm. Journal of Parallel and Distributed Computing, Vol.9, 1990.
3. Dickman, P. W.: Effective Load Balancing in a Distributed Object-support Operating System. In the Proceedings of Second International Workshop on Object Orientation in Operating Systems, pp.147–153, 1992.
4. Fox, G. C.: The user of physics concepts in computation, In Computation: The Micro and The Macro View. (Huberman, B.A. ed.), World-Scientific, 1992.
5. Georgeff, M. P.: Communication and Interaction in Multi–Agent Planning. In the Proceedings of AAAI-83, 1983.
6. Gruber, O., Amsaleg, L.: Object grouping in EOS. In the Proceedings of the International Workshop on Distributed Object Management. pp.184–201, 1992.
7. Hewitt, C. E.: A Universal, Modular Actor Formalism for Artificial Intelligence, In the Proceedings of International Joint Conference on Artificial Intelligence, 1973.
8. Huberman, B.A., ed.: The Ecology of Computation, North-Holland, 1988.
9. Lin, F.C.H. and Keller, R.M.: The Gradient Model Load Balancing Method. IEEE Trans. Softw. Eng., Vol. SE-13, No. 1, 1987.
10. Ohira, T., Sawatari, R., and Tokoro, M.: (submitted).
11. Ohira, T. and Milton, J. G.: Delayed Random Walks. Physical Review E, Vol. 52, No. 3, 3277, 1995. Also Available as Sony Computer Science Laboratory Technical Report TR-94-026, November, 1994.
12. Ohira, T. and Tokoro M.: Computational Field Model with Computon. Sony Computer Science Laboratory Technical Report TR-95-016, August, 1995.
13. Osawa, E. and Tokoro, M.: Collaborative Plan Construction for Multiagent Mutual Planning. In the Proceedings of the 3rd European Workshop on Modeling Autonomous Agents in a Multi–Agent World, (MAAMAW-91), 1991.
14. Raverdy, P. and Folliot, B.: Presentation of the Execution Territory: a Two Level Load Balancing Mechanism. In the Proceedings of European Research Seminar on Advances in Distributed Systems, Alpes d'Huuez, France, April, 1995.
15. Rosenshein, J. S. and Genesereth, M. R.: Deals Among Rational Agents. In the Proceedings of IJCAI-85, pp.91-99, 1985.
16. Tokoro, M.: Computational Field Model: Toward a New Computational Model / Methodology for Open Distributed Environment, In the Proceedings of Workshop on OS for the 90s and Beyond, July, 1991 Kaiserslautern, Germany. Also Available as Sony Computer Science Laboratory Technical Report TR-90-006, June, 1990.
17. Tokoro, M.: Toward Computing Systems for the 2000's, Cairo, September 1990. Also Available as Sony Computer Science Laboratory Technical Report TR-91-005, December, 1991.
18. Tokoro, M. and Honda, K.: The Computational Field Model for Open Distributed Environments, In Concurrency: Theory, Language, and Architecture, Lecture Notes in Computer Science, No. 491, Springer Verlag, 1991.
19. Tokoro, M.: The Society of Objects, Addendum to OOPSLA'93 Proceedings (Invited Talk). Also Available as Sony Computer Science Laboratory Technical Report TR-93-018, December, 1993.

20. Uehara, M. and Tokoro, M.: An Adaptive Load Balancing Method in the Computational Field Model,Proc. of ECOOP/OOPSLA '90 Workshop on Object Based Concurrent Programming, Oct. 1990.
21. Watari, S., Honda, Y., and Tokoro, M.: Morphe: A Constraint-Based Object-Oriented Language Supporting Situated Knowledge, Proceedings of International Conference on Fifth Generation Computer Systems, 1992. Also Available as Sony Computer Science Laboratory Technical Report TR-94-026, November, 1994.
22. Yokote, Y. and Tokoro, M.: The Design and Implementation of ConcurrentSmallTalk, Proceedings of OOPSLA'86, 1986. Also Available as Sony Computer Science Laboratory Technical Report TR-94-026, November, 1994.
23. Yokote, Y.: The Apertos Reflective Operating System: The Concept and its Implementation, Proceedings of OOPSLA'92, 1992. Also Available as Sony Computer Science Laboratory Technical Report TR-94-026, November, 1994.
24. Yonezawa, A. and Tokoro, M. eds: Object Oriented Programming, MIT Press, Cambridge, 1987.
25. Yonezawa, A., eds.: ABCL An Object-Oriented Concurrent Systems, MIT Press, Cambridge, 1990.
26. Zlotkin, G. and Rosenschein, J. S.: Negotiation and Task Sharing Among Autonomous Agents in Cooperative Domains. In the Proceedings of IJCAI-89, pp.912-917, 1989.

SIGMA: Application of Multi-Agent Systems to Cartographic Generalization

Christof BAEIJS *   Yves DEMAZEAU **   Luis ALVARES

Université de Grenoble   Université de Grenoble   Inst. de Informatica
LEIBNIZ-IMAG-INPG   LEIBNIZ-IMAG-CNRS   U.F.R.G.S.
46, Avenue Félix Viallet   46, Avenue Félix Viallet   Caixa Postal 15064
38031 Grenoble Cedex   38031 Grenoble Cedex   91501-907 Porto Alegre
FRANCE   FRANCE   BRASIL

Christof.Baeijs@imag.fr   Yves.Demazeau@imag.fr   alvares@inf.ufrgs.br

Abstract. In this article we present the approach and the model used in
the SIGMA (SemI automated Generalization using Multi-Agent systems)
project, which is being developed in collaboration with the COGIT group
of IGN (the French National Geographic Institute) and the LAMA group
of the IGA laboratory (the Alpine Geographic Institute).
The proposed approach to cartographic generalization is based on the
PACO paradigm, as it has been introduced by Dr. Yves Demazeau, and
is thus situated within the framework of Reactive Multi-Agent Systems.
It extends the paradigm by including the notion of types of agents and
organizational information between agents. In this article we briefly discuss the main principles of Reactive Multi-Agent Systems, Cartographic
Generalization and our experimental framework. We afterwards discuss
the model as it has been developed for the SIGMA system, following its
decomposition in Environment, Agents, Interactions and Organizational
aspects. Before concluding, we take a look at the dynamics of the system
and the first results of the protype of this semi-automated cartographic
generalization process.

1   Introduction

In this article we present the approach and the model used in the SIGMA (SemI
automated Generalization using Multi-Agent systems) project, which is being
developed in collaboration with the COGIT group of IGN (the French National
Geographic Institute) and the LAMA group of the IGA laboratory (the Alpine
Geographic Institute). This project consists of trying to partially automatize
the generalization process in cartography, meaning the readible visualization of

* Doctoral Research Funded by the European Commission, DGXII, through HCM
  Bursary no. ERBCHBICT930672
** Research Fellow of the CNRS

a subset of preordered agents from a geographical database. In Cartographic Generalization the goal of the generalization process is to create a readable and useful cartographic map from a geographical database. We therefore have to take the graphical constraints into account. This encloses the symbolization which will be used (the legend of the map) and the resolution of the cartographic support (resolution of a printed map, resolution of the computer display,...). A typical example consists of the visualization of 180 features of 15 different types from a geographical database containing 1000 features of 75 different types. As the generalization process is often presented as a holistic process, which means that one may not generalize an object independently from its context, Reactive Multi-Agent Systems seem well suited and adapted to solve such a type of spatial problem.

Our approach is situated within the framework of Reactive Multi-Agent Systems, and we are using an extension of the PACO (COordination PAtterns) model, as it has been introduced by Demazeau [Demazeau90b] [Demazeau93].

In the following sections, we are briefly reminding the basic principles of Reactive Multi-Agent Systems, Cartographic Generalization and the experimental framework of the SIGMA system. After this, we are detailing the model used in the system, its dynamics and the first results obtained.

2 Reactive Multi-Agent Systems

In Distributed Artificial Intelligence (DAI) and Multi-Agent Systems (MAS), agents need to cooperate in order to acheive their local goals and the goals of the community as a whole because no one individually has sufficient competence, resources or information to solve the entire problem alone [Jennings93].

Following the emergent functionality approach, Reactive Multi-Agent Systems offer the possibility to find an acceptable solution within a resonable time and complexity range. Even though the found solution offers no guarantee about the optimality, the search for a possible and acceptable solution is predominant to the search for the optimal solution [Ferber91] [Demazeau93]. Within this framework, interaction structures are often classified as physics-based interactions. Reactive agents do not encompass deliberate control, nor explicit reasoning. Physics-based models like electrostatic forces permit to express simple interactions with attraction and repulsion, and such models are widely used to model the interactions between reactive agents. This kind of interactions is implemented by communicating through the environment, using it as a shared resource.

In Reactive Multi-Agent Systems, an acceptable solution can be seen as an equilibrium state of the society of autonomous agents, and the detection of this equilibrium state can only be observed from an external point of view, for example by an external observer. The conceiver therefore needs to translate locally within the agents the global problem which has to be solved, assuring the capacity of an agent to detect a local equilibrium state, although no agent by itself has the complete knowledge of the problem to be solved, nor the abilities to detect a global equilibrium state at the society level. This implies that the problem solving process using Reactive MAS is adaptive and that a minor change in the environment, or workspace of the agents, results in an immediate renewed activation of the search for a global equilibrium state.

3 Cartographic Generalization

3.1 Geographical Information Systems and Generalization

A generalization process may be defined as the transformation of information - geographical information in our case - which corresponds to a certain representation level, in generalized information at a higher representation level which is more abstract/schematic.

We may distinguish two types of generalization:

- *Generalization of Data.* In this case, one transforms a set of data with respect to a certain specification of the contents ("data scheme") and a certain resolution, into a new data set which corresponds to a new couple (data scheme and resolution). We thus obtain a generalized dataset.
- *Cartographic Generalization.* In this case, the goal of the generalization process is to create a cartographic map. We therefore have to take the graphical constraints into account. This encloses the symbolization which will be used (the legend of the map), the resolution of the cartographic support (resolution of a printed map, resolution of the computer display,...) and the point of view (or *focalisation*) of the user which determines what kind of map he wants to obtain (hydrography, military, a road map,...).

In the optimal case, the generalization process starts with a data set the content of which is close to the map we want to obtain [Ruas93]. Otherwise we necessarily have to perform the two phases mentioned above: generalization of data and afterwards the cartographic generalization process [Müller93] [Ruas94].

3.2 Generalization and DAI

The generalization process is often presented as a *holistic process* [Müller91], which means that one may not generalize an object independently from its context. This aspect is difficult to take into account in a pure procedural approach. At the actual stage, research following a procedural approach is limited to the generalization of objects out of their context. This approach is called *Intrinsic Generalization* [Ruas93]. In order to overcome this problem, researchers are interested in applying the techniques found in Artificial Intelligence: essentially knowledge-based systems ([Beard91], [Müller91], [Kipeläinen93]) and neural networks ([Müller93]). The application of these techniques have led to the construction of costly systems (from a computational point of view), mostly limited to generalize locally a small set geographical objects (displacements, simplification of lines,...) and automatic name placement of horizontal toponymes.

As we want to generalize a large data set in a reasonable time, taking into account the holistic aspect of the generalization process, Reactive Multi-Agent Systems seem well suited to tackle this kind of spatial problem.

4 Experimental Framework

The aim of the SIGMA system is to generate clearly readible cartographic maps given the point of view of the end-user of the system. This means that the user will express the type of map he wants to obtain (e.g. roadmap, hydrographical map, military map,...) and that the system will generate a cartographic map emphasizing the most important geographical classes while taking the various display constraints into account. Performing this type of operation with a "classical" generalization system (which is rule- or knowledge-based) is very time-consuming and computationaly expensive.

Within the SIGMA framework, the geographical objects are stored in an object-oriented database which is taken as input for the system. Such an object may represent a punctual, linear or areal feature in the real world. Punctual objects are represented by a single node, linear objects by an initial node, a final node and intermediate points, and areal objects are specified by one or several linear objects. These geographical objects are internally translated to so called *geographical entities*, corresponding to nodes or intermediate points, and are used as data carriers in the system.

Within the SIGMA project, two experimental frameworks have been defined:

- A first experiment is concerned with the realisation of a new equilibrium state after the system has been submitted to external actions (displacement of objects,...). This means that we are studying the convergence of the system, and in particular the modelling of the agents, of the possible interactions and of the organization of the society; we then study how the system converges through the effect of the interactions between the agents and through the effect of the generalization operators given the point of view (translating the interest of the user).
- A second experiment is concerned with the conception of the legend (the specifications of the map) and the organizational structure of the different geographical classes given the aim of the map (i.e. the point of view).

In this paper we are focussing on the first application, meaning on the search of the system towards a new convergence and equilibrium state.

5 The Agent Model

The Multi-Agent System model used for the SIGMA system is based on an extension of the PACO (COordination PAtterns) paradigm for reactive multi-agent systems as it is described in [Demazeau90b] [Demazeau93]. It extends the paradigm by introducing symbolic information in this framework, meaning the notion of types of agents and related organizational information between types.

5.1 The PACO Paradigm

In this section we are briefly reminding the basic principles of the PACO (COordination PAtterns) paradigm [Demazeau93]; instead of considering the search for a solution of a given problem as the minimisation of some kind of energy function, PACO proposes to conceive the search for this solution as a coevolution of a possibly organized finite set of interacting agents (each of them representing a partial solution - cf. communication -), that also interact with their environment (the data of the problem, i.e. the objects - cf. perception -). The behaviour of an agent is characterized by the predefined combination of a set of independant elementary interactions. Each type of interaction is associated with the capacity of an agent to perceive another agent or object in its environment. The interactions are modeled as forces which constrain the agents to move in the environment. The interest of an agent to interact at a given point in time with another agent or object (which is translated in an explicit control of its perception and communication scopes) leads to the execution of an elementary action (if the agent's action scopes authorizes this action): an interaction with the environment (motion) or an interaction with another agent. A partial solution is then obtained when an agent has reached a stable position in the environment. A global solution is reached as soon as an external observer detects the convergence towards an equilibrium state, meaning a stable position of every agent.

5.2 Geographical Entities

The main difference with the initial PACO model, is that we have introduced in the SIGMA system agents that may have different roles although they have the same internal homogeneous structure. Having agents with different roles offers us the possiblity to introduce in our Multi-Agent System the explicit notion of organizations of agents, for studying the impact of organizational structures on the behaviour of the agents (local effect) and on the convergence of the system (global effect).

In our approach, a geographical entity belongs to one and only one geographical object and thus represents an initial node, a final node or an intermediate point. This means that one geographical object is represented by a collection of geographical entities. We can then define a class of geographical entities as the collection of entities that represent the same type of geographical object.

The focalisation plays a major role in the problem solving process, and is translated in *pre-orders* of the system:

- the global pre-order (or *objective pre-order*): this pre-order translates the focalisation of the user, and leads to a classification of the classes of the geographical entities. This classification offers the possibility to construct the organizational structure of the system and to give a mass to the geographical entities which will be used to calculate the interaction forces. *As soon as the mass of the geographical entities becomes big enough, and thus its power in the organizational structure, we may call these geographical entities agents.*

An entity thus becomes an agent as soon as he is not only submitted to forces emitted by other agents, but is also exerting forces on other agents or entities.

- the local pre-order (or *subjective pre-order*): in order to solve local conflicts, each class has such a pre-order which is in fact a binary relationship with all the other classes, showing if this class is more or less important than another one.

These pre-orders are defined in advance by the user in the first experimental framework, while they should be constructed automatically within the second.

In our model we also introduced the notion of *groups*. These groups are collections of agents that have common geographical or topological properties:

- *objective groups*: these groups are regrouping agents which are located at the same position in the environment (and thus on the map), these groups are formed automatically by the system and are maintained throughout the entire problem solving process.
- *subjective groups*: are collections of agents which are constrained by a common topology (e.g. aligned buildings, remarkable topological features in the real world,...). These groups are formed by the user through the graphical interface, and have to maintain their topology even under the effects of the different interactions.

These groups may therefore be considered as local organizations within a set of agents.

5.3   The Environment

The environment, denoted E, initially groups the raw non-generalized data, and serves as *World of Reference*. The system will work with a copy of this world of reference, called the *Active World*. At any moment, the environment is equal to the collection of all the entities; the value of the position $p = (x, y)$, denoted $E(p)$, then gives acces to the data of the agents who occupy the position (x, y) in the environment.

5.4   The Agent Model

Let's consider N agents indexed by i and addressed through their position p_i, their perceptional filter FP_i, and their relational (i.e. communicational) filter FR_i [Ferrand94], which permit to obtain the following scopes: the perception scope PS_i, the class scope CS_i, object scope OS_i, proximity scope $ProS_i$ and the group scope GS_i and their corresponding action scopes.

In order to illustrate the different aspects of the model we are using a simplified data set as shown in Figure 1.

Similarily to the PACO model, the agents in the SIGMA system use a set of scopes to determine their interactions and control their behaviour. They are defined for each agent in the following way:

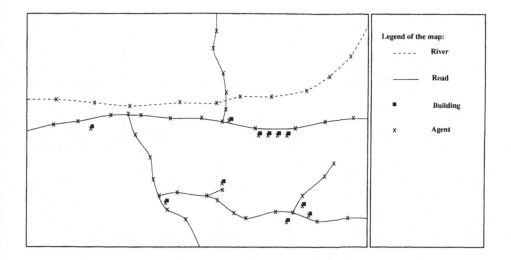

Fig. 1. Simplified illustration of a dataset

- The *Perception Scope* PS_i: this scope corresponds to the set of agents an agent is able to perceive in the environment. This set corresponds to all the agents (of any type) that are situated within a disk with radius δ (see figure 2(a)).

- The *Class Scope* CS_i: containing all the agents (or geographical entities) that belong to the same geographical class (see figure 2(b)); at the same time a corresponding and identical action scope CAS_i is attached to the agent that will be used for changing dynamically the current legend (cf. section on interactions).

- The *Object Scope* OS_i: groups all the agents that are part of the same geographical object (see figure 2(c)); an identical action scope OAS_i will be used to calculate the proportional following (cf. section on interactions).

- The *Proximity Scope* $ProS_i$: this scope contains all the agents the distance of which is close to the resolution the user defined, and is a disk with radius α (see figure 2(d)); the corresponding action scope $ProAS_i$ is used to perform the interactions based on repulsion forces (cf. section on interactions).

- The *Group Scope* GS_i: constituting the agents that are in the same groups (objective or subjective); an identical action scope GAS_i will be used to maintain the groups and to calculate the unconditional following (cf. section on interactions).

Apart from these scopes, the agent model possesses some additional attributes (like its position, an identifier,...) due to the implementational aspects of the system.

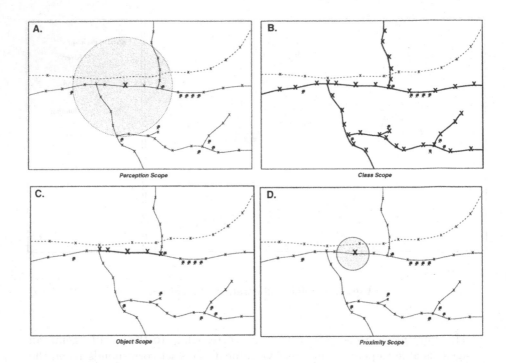

Fig. 2. Illustration of the different scopes: Perception Scope (A), Class Scope (B), Object Scope (C) and the Proximity Scope (D)

5.5 Interactions

The interactions in the system are based on the physics-based approach of electrostatical forces, and are thus expressed in terms of attraction and repulsion, resulting in a displacement of the agent in the environment.

The first interaction (the repulsion force) can be seen as *constructive*, meaning that it is helping to obtain a solution, while the other interactions can be seen as *conservative*, meaning that they are limiting the impact of the first one in order to avoid displacements which are too abrupt.

- Repulsion force between agents. This interaction takes the proximity scope $ProS_i$ as input and has the associated action scope $ProAS_i$ as targeted output scope. This means that an agent will try to push every other agent outside of this disk in order to increase his visibility, and thus the space he occupies in the environment. The magnitude of this force is depending on the resolution, the respective masses of the agents, their distance and the size of their current symbols. An illustration of this force is given in Figure 3.
- Unconditional following. This interaction aims to maintain the objective or subjective groups. This means that the agents or entities belonging to the

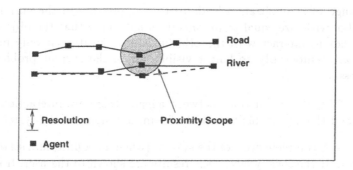

Fig. 3. Repulsion Force between agents

same group are submitted to the same forces as the one who occupies the highest authority within this local organizational structure.

– Proportional following. In order to avoid that the deformation of an object is too local due to the repulsion force to which one agent is submitted, a fraction of this force is spread among the other agents that are belonging to the same geographical object. This interaction takes OS_i as input scope, OAS_i as output scope and is proportional to the repulsion force considered, and the distance between the pair of agents and is limited to the nodes of the objects (see Figure 4).

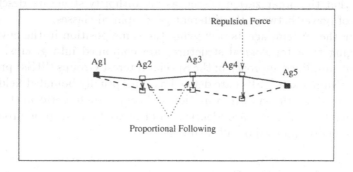

Fig. 4. Proportional Following between agents

– Change of symbolization. When an agent detects that a conflict cannot be solved locally (i.e. he detects an oscillation in his movements), he asks for a change of the current symbol used for this class (taking a smaller symbol than the current one) in order to occupy a smaller space in the environment and thus enlarging the free space in which he can be displaced. In the case a change of symbolization leads to the suppression of the current symbol (symbol with size equal to 0), this does not imply that the objects stop to exist nor to interact with the other agents or entities, it only means that they are temporarily no longer visible within the current problem solving process.

Apart from the interactions between agents, there are interactions between the user and the agents due to aspect of semi-autonomy of the system:

- After each complete cycle of the system (when an equilibrium state has been reached at the society level), the results are shown to the user. If the legend which is used at that stage does not correspond to his actual needs the user may provoke a change of the symbolization of the different geographical classes.
- At the same time he may create or destroy subjective groups in order to maintain or break topological structures by pointing the implied agents through the graphical interface. By doing so, the user intervenes directly in the organizational structures of the groups.
- In order to guide the problem solving process, and thus the generalization process, the user may displace some agents to avoid that the system is not striving towards an acceptable local solution.

5.6 Organizations

The major aspect of the organizational knowledge is translated into the pre-order, and corresponds to the organizational model proposed in [Meehan80], meaning that the organization is seen as an authority structure describing the relations of power between the different geographical classes.

Within the system, agents occupying the same position in the environment, or belonging to a topological structure, are combined into groups. This is a similar but simplified approach of the Special Interest Groups (SIGs) proposed by Numaoka [Numaoka92]. SIGs are defined as conceptually bounded fields through which agents share the same information and cooperate to perform the same job. All the members of a SIG are identical, and restrictions such as group specific rules are equally imposed on all members.

6 Dynamics of the System

Similar to the PACO approach, the behaviour of the agents in SIGMA system is based on a three step problem solving cycle:

- Local perception and communication
  - Tune the sensitivity with the environment (perception)
  - Perceive: calculation of PS_i
  - Tune the sensitivity with the other agents (communication)
  - Communicate: construction of CS_i, OS_i, GS_i and $ProS_i$

– Local processing
  - Compute the interactions with the other agents: repulsion forces, proportional following, unconditional following (maintenance of groups) and change of symbolization.
  - Compute the interactions with the environment: attraction to the initial position.
  - Combine the forces exerted on the agent
– Local action
  - Tune the sensivity by acting on the action scopes
  - Act: perform displacement and possible change of symbolization

7 Obtained Results

The actual prototype of the system runs on a single SUN-Sparc computer, has been implemeted in C++ and uses InterViews 3.1 as user interface support.

We present here the first results we have obtained using the SIGMA system. They are still far from optimal and the processing method has to be slightly revised in order to reach a better solution in terms of quality and computational cost. Despite of this, the results can be considered as promising and encouraging. The first experimental results are obtained within a short time (approximately 3 minutes - compared to approximately 100 man-hours to produce the same map manually), and are quite acceptable from a geographic point of view (both compared to a manually obtained map and to the appreciation of a human expert), although some local problems still remain unsolved.

The actual dataset used as testbed within the system, is *"Les Matelles"*, a small village in the neighborhood of Montpellier in southern France. A small subset of the initial data set (cf. World of Reference) is shown in Figure 5. The grid printed as background of the map is formed with squares which are 50 by 50 pixels wide, representing data from the topographic database (BDTopo) of IGN and at a scale of 1:15000 and thus squares representing approximately 360 square meters with a fault-tolerance of 1 meter. Which gives us for the complete village a zone of 1500 by 700 meters to generalize.

Although we are using a simplified set of geographical objects (about 300 objects are present on the map), the SIGMA system translates them into approximately 1800 geographical entities used for producing the generalized map. The type of objects present are: roads (higways, primary and secondary roads), rivers (primary and secondary), walking tracks, buildings, altitude lines, vegetation and other unclassified objects. The goal is in this case to create a map which stresses in order of importance: highways, primary and secondary roads, and hydrographical aspects. This is translated into the corresponding pre-order, meaning that we attach the highest degree of importance to roads and rivers, an intermediate one to altitude lines and vegetation, and the smallest one to buildings and the unclassified objects.

Figure 6 shows the results of the same zone as in Figure 5 after one computation cycle of the program, using a resolution of 5 pixels and a radius for

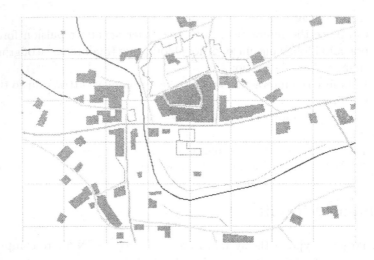

Fig. 5. Subset of the initial data of Les Matelles

the Perception Scope equal to 20 pixels. Within this example and taking into account the defined pre-order, about 1000 of the 1800 geographical entities raise to the status of agents.

Comparing the center of the village before and after one phase of the generalization process (see Figure 7), shows that although the Multi-Agent System did not yet reach a global equilibrium state, the system is striving towards an acceptable solution.

8 Conclusion

In this article we have presented an application of Reactive Multi-Agent Systems in the domain of Geographical Information Systems, and more precisely to perform Cartographic Generalization.

The agent model we are using within the SIGMA system is extending the PACO paradigm by explicitly introducing organizational concepts in the system, and by handling a multitude of agents having different roles in the problem solving process. The introduction of these notions offers us the possibility to test different organizational models [Baeijs95a] [Baeijs95b] and to study their impact on the convergence of the problem solving process.

The SIGMA system, as it has been described above, is currently in a prototyping stage, producing its first results. These results are promising and encouraging enough to continue the work in the same direction.

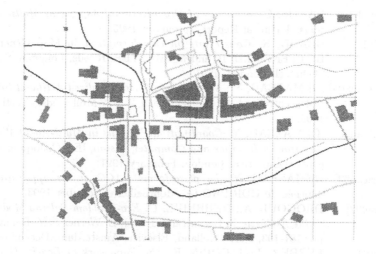

Fig. 6. Subset of the results after one stage

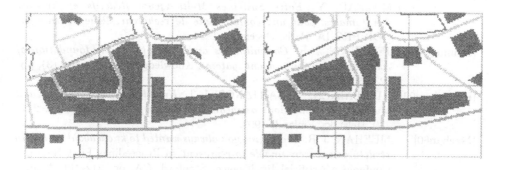

Fig. 7. The center of the village before (left) and after (right)

9 Acknowledgements

The authors would like to thank Dr. Jean-Philippe Lagrange and Anne Ruas of the COGIT group of IGN for the numerous discussions during the construction of the SIGMA model, as well as Prof. Pierre Dumolard of the LAMA laboratory for his constructive remarks.

References

[Baeijs95a]   BAEIJS, C.; DEMAZEAU, Y. *Les Organisations dans les Systèmes Multi-Agents*, 4ème Journée du GDR-PRC IA, Toulouse, December 1995.

[Baeijs95b]   BAEIJS, C. *A Survey of Organizational Aspects in Multi-Agent Systems*, Technical Report, *to appear*, 1995.

[Beard91]   BEARD, K. *Constraints on rule formation*, in Map Generalization, BUTTENFIELD, B. and MCMASTER, R. eds, Longman Scientific & Technical, London, 1991.

[Demazeau90a]   DEMAZEAU, Y.; MULLER, JP. *Decentralized Artificial Intelligence*, in Decentralized AI, Y. Demazeau & J-P. Müller eds., North-Holland, 1990.

[Demazeau90b]   DEMAZEAU, Y. *Coordination Patterns in Multi-Agent Worlds: Application to Robotics and Computer Vision*, IEE Colloqium on Intelligent Agents, IEE, London, February 1991.

[Demazeau93]   DEMAZEAU, Y. *La plate-forme PACO et ses applications*, 2ème Journée du GDR-PRC IA, Montpellier, December 1993.

[Drogoul92]   DROGOUL, A.; DUBREUIL, C. *Eco-Problem-Solving Model: Results of the N-Puzzle*, in Decentralized AI 3, E. Werner & Y. Demazeau eds., pp. 181-193, North-Holland, Elsevier, Amsterdam, December 1992.

[Ferber91]   FERBER, J.; JACOPIN, E. *The framework of Eco-Problem Solving*, in Decentralized AI 2, Y. Demazeau & J-P. Müller eds., pp. 283-295, North-Holland, Elsevier, Amsterdam, August 1992.

[Ferrand94]   FERRAND, N.; LABBI, A.; GIACOMETTI, A.; AMY, B.; DEMAZEAU, Y. *Entre Systèmes Multi-Agents Réactifs et Réseaux d'Automates: pour une communauté de recherche*, 3ème Journée du GDR-PRC IA, Paris, December 1994.

[Jennings93]   JENNINGS, N.R. *Commitments and conventions: the foundation of coordination in multi-agent syatems*, Knowledge Eng. Revue 8 (3), pp. 223-250, 1993.

[Kipeläinen93]   KIPELAINEN, T.; SARJAKOSKI, T. *Knowledge-based methods and multiple representations as means of on-line generalisation*, pp. 211-220, Helsinki, Finland, 1993.

[Meehan80]   MEEHAN, J. R. *Everything you always wanted to know about authority structures but were unable to represent*, in Proceedings First National Conference Artificial Intelligence, Stanford, CA, pp. 212-214, August 1980.

[Müller91]   MULLER, JC. *Building knowledge tanks for rule based generalization*, International Cartographic Conference, Bournemouth, pp. 257-265, 1991.

[Müller93]   MULLER, JC.; WEIBEL, R.; LAGRANGE, JP.; SALGE, F. *Generalization: State of the Art and Issues*, Position-Paper - ESF GISDATA Workshop on Generalization, Compiègne, December 1993.

[Numaoka92]   NUMAOKA, C. *Conversation for organizational activity*, , in Decentralized AI 3, E. Werner & Y. Demazeau eds., pp. 189-198, North-Holland, Elsevier, Amsterdam, December 1992.

[Ruas93]   RUAS, A.; LAGRANGE, JP.; BENDER, L. *Survey on Generalization*, IGN rapport DT 93-0538, 1993.

[Ruas94]   RUAS, A.; LAGRANGE, JP. *Modélisation pour la généralisation*, EGIS'94, Paris, 1994.

A Decision-Theoretic Model
for Cooperative Transportation Scheduling*

Klaus Fischer**, Jörg P. Müller

German Research Center for Artificial Intelligence (DFKI GmbH),
Stuhlsatzenhausweg 3, D-66123 Saarbrücken

Abstract. In this paper we analyse the domain of transportation scheduling in shipping companies from the perspective of decision theory.
After giving a brief description of the application and the simulation
system MARS based on the multiagent paradigm, the transportation domain is characterised according to [11]. The paper comes up with the
result that it is useful to split up the class of task-oriented domains into
two subclasses: *cooperative* and *competitive* task-oriented domains. The
paper shows that properties like subadditivity only hold only for very
specific subproblems in the transportation domain. We prove that lying
may be beneficial in the transportation domain. We argue that, based on
this result, it is highly desirable to have negotiation strategies for agents
in the transportation domain which are robust against lying. The last
section describes such a negotiation strategy.

1 Introduction

Over the past few years, the scheduling of transportation orders has been established as an important application area for multiagent systems technology both
from an academic and from a practical perspective (see [10] [8] [9] [5]). It offers interesting complexity properties, an inherent distribution of knowledge and
control, natural possibilities to study coordination and cooperation, and finally,
there is a considerable economic interest in obtaining good solutions for these
kinds of problems[1].

The MARS (**M**odeling a Multi-**A**gent Scenario for **S**hipping Companies) system [4] [5] constitutes a multi-agent approach to these problems: a scenario of
transportation companies is described. The companies have to carry out transportation orders which arrive asynchronously and dynamically. For this purpose,
they have a set of trucks at their disposal. Trucks are agents that maintain local
plans. Interaction between a company and its trucks is implemented by contractnet–like auction protocols [4].

---

* The work presented in this paper has been supported by the German Ministry of
  Research and Technology under grant ITW9104
** email: kuf@dfki.uni-sb.de, phone: ++49 681 302 5328, fax: ++49 681 3025341
[1] For a comprehensive overview of related work in the areas of Operations research
  and AI, see [5].

This paper provides a decision-theoretic analysis of the domain. It investigates in how far the results achieved by Rosenschein and Zlotkin [7] can be applied to the transportation domain. We come up with the result that it is useful to divide the class of task-oriented domains into two subclasses: cooperative and competitive task-oriented domains. The transportation domain provides examples for both categories of task-oriented domains. The cooperative setting characterises the situation within one shipping company where the main problem is to optimally allocate orders to a set of trucks, which is a complex scheduling problem. Results from an analysis of this setting have been published in [5]. The focus of this paper is on the competitive setting, which describes the situation in negotiation processes among shipping companies. Furthermore, we show that properties like subadditivity hold only in very specific subdomains of the transportation domain. The fact that the results of Zlotkin and Rosenschein only partially map to the transportation domain enforces us to prove separately certain properties of the domain: In Section 4, we show that lying may be beneficial also in the transportation domain. These results justify the need for negotiation strategies for the transportation domain which do not give agents an incentive to lie. We present preliminary work on a negotiation strategy that fulfils these requirements.

2 The Transportation Domain

The domain of application of the MARS system is the planning and scheduling of transportation orders which is done in everyday life by human dispatchers in transportation companies. Many of the problems which must be solved in this area, such as the Travelling Salesman and related scheduling problems, are known to be NP-hard. Moreover, not only since *just-in-time* production has come up, planning must be performed under a high degree of uncertainty and incompleteness, and it is highly dynamic. In reality these problems are far from being solved.

Cooperation and coordination seem to be two very important processes that may help to overcome the problems sketched above. Indeed, they are of increasing importance even in the highly competitive transportation business of today. Using the MARS system, several patterns of cooperation such as the announcement of unbooked legs, order brokering, and different strategies for information exchanges have been experimentally evaluated [3].

Corresponding to the physical entities in the domain, there are two basic types of agents in MARS: *transportation companies* and *trucks*. Companies can communicate with their trucks and among each other. The user may dynamically dedicate transportation orders to specific companies. Looking upon trucks as agents allows us to delegate problem-solving skills to them (such as route-planning and local plan optimisation). The *shipping company* agent has to allocate orders to its trucks, while trying to satisfy the constraints provided by the user as well as local optimality criteria (costs). A company also may decide to cooperate with another company instead of having an order executed by its own trucks. Each *truck* agent is associated with a particular shipping company from which it receives orders of the form "**Load amount a_1 of good g_1 at location l_1 and transport it to location l_2 while satisfying time constraints $\{c_{t_1}, \ldots, c_{t_k}\}$**". More formally the setting can be described as follows:

$\mathcal{S} = \{S_1, \ldots, S_l\}, l \in \mathbb{N}$: is the set of shipping company agents.

$\mathcal{L}^2 = \{\mathcal{L}_{S_1}, \ldots, \mathcal{L}_{S_l}\} = \{\{L_1^{S_1}, \ldots, L_{m_1}^{S_1}\}, \ldots, \{L_1^{S_l}, \ldots, L_{m_1}^{S_l}\}\}, m_i \in \mathbb{N}$: is the set of truck agents, where the set $\mathcal{L}_{S_i}$ specifies the truck agents of shipping company S_i. All trucks have the same abilities and each of them has the same limited capacity. Trucks must return to their shipping companies home base after they have executed a set of orders, i.e., they plan round trips.

$\mathcal{O} = \{o_1, \ldots, o_n\}, n \in \mathbb{N}$: is a set of orders. Each order is specified by a tuple $(a, g, l_1, l_2, c_{t_1}, \ldots, c_{t_k})$ where a: amount, g: type of good, l_1: source, l_2: destination, and $c_{t_1}, \ldots, c_{t_k}$: time constraints. The orders may be announced to individual shipping companies dynamically at arbitrary points in time.

3 Characterisation of the Domain

3.1 Definition and Basic Properties

Tasks (i.e., orders) are the main focus of the problem solving and negotiation process in the transportation domain; therefore it is intuitive to classify it as a task-oriented domain:

Definition 1. A *Task-Oriented Domain* (TOD) is a tuple $\Omega = < \mathcal{T}, \mathcal{A}, c >$ where:

1. $\mathcal{T}$ is the set of all possible tasks;
2. $\mathcal{A} = \{A_1, A_2, \ldots, A_n\}$ is an ordered list of agents. Agents can be referred to by their index $1 \leq i \leq n$ or by their name A_i;
3. c is a cost function $c : 2^{\mathcal{T}} \rightarrow \mathbb{R}^+$. For each finite subset $\mathcal{X} \subseteq \mathcal{T}, c_A(\mathcal{X})$ is the cost of executing all tasks in $\mathcal{X}$ by a single agent A. c is monotonic, i.e., for any two finite subsets $\mathcal{X} \subseteq \mathcal{Y} \subseteq \mathcal{T}, c(\mathcal{X}) \leq c(\mathcal{Y})$;
4. $c(\emptyset) = 0$.

Note that the transportation domain matches the definition of a TOD only if no time constraints are specified for the orders.[3]. If orders are time-constrained,

---

[2] To avoid name clashes, we use $\mathcal{L}$ for the set of trucks, derived from the British word *lorry*.

[3] At a first glance, it may seem that capacity constraints also might blow Definition 1. However, this is only true if the size of orders exceeds the capacity of a single truck, and if it is not possible to split orders. As we assume that all trucks have the same capacity, such an order would exceed the capacity of the multiagent system as a whole, leading to an unrealistic setting. In the MARS system, e.g., orders can be split.

the cost function in Definition 1 has to be modified to $c : 2^{\mathcal{T}} \to I\!R^+ \cup \{\infty\}$; the semantics of $+, <, \ldots$ has to be adopted accordingly.

Rational agents in TODs defined according to Definition 1 will always try to avoid executing tasks because saving costs increases their utility. However, an important feature of the transportation domain is that a shipping company is paid for each task it performs (see [9]). For this reason, we introduce the notion of a price for TODs. As we will see below, this notion allows an important further classification of TODs. One could argue that Rosenschein and Zlotkin introduce the notion of price (worth) in worth-oriented domains (WOD), which is in fact a super-class of the task-oriented domains. However, in WOD, worth is assigned to goal states rather than to single tasks, which is less desirable for modelling the transportation domain realistically. To be able to assign a price to individual tasks and thus, to give the agents an incentive to execute tasks, we extend Definition 1 by a price function p:

Definition 2. Let $\Omega = < \mathcal{T}, \mathcal{A}, c >$ be a TOD. A price function for Ω is a function $p : 2^{\mathcal{T}} \to I\!R^+$. For each finite subset $\mathcal{X} \subseteq \mathcal{T}$ holds:

$$p(\mathcal{X}) = \begin{cases} \sum_{t \in \mathcal{X}} \hat{p}(t) & \text{if } \mathcal{X} \neq \emptyset \\ 0 & \text{otherwise} \end{cases}$$

where $\hat{p}(t)$ is the price to be paid to an agent for executing task t. Throughout this paper, we will write $\Omega = < \mathcal{T}, \mathcal{A}, c, p >$ for a TOD Ω with price function p.

Agents in the TODs defined according to Definition 2 have a desire to execute tasks (in our application domain: transportation orders), because doing so will increase their utility. The real trick for the agents is to execute tasks at minimal costs. The payoff an agent obtains for performing any given subset of tasks $\mathcal{X} \subseteq \mathcal{T}$ is defined by:

$$tpo(\mathcal{X}) = p(\mathcal{X}) - c(\mathcal{X}).$$

Rosenschein and Zlotkin characterise TODs by specifying several attributes they can have, the weakest of which is *subadditivity*. We refine the definition for our purposes.

Definition 3 Subadditivity. Let $\Omega = < \mathcal{T}, \mathcal{A}, c, p >$ be a TOD. Ω is called:

1. *locally subadditive* if for all finite sets of tasks $\mathcal{X}, \mathcal{Y} \subseteq \mathcal{T}$ and each agent $A \in \mathcal{A}$, we have: $c_A(\mathcal{X} \cup \mathcal{Y}) \leq c_A(\mathcal{X}) + c_A(\mathcal{Y})$.
2. *globally subadditive* if for all finite sets of tasks $\mathcal{X}, \mathcal{Y} \subseteq \mathcal{T}$ and for all agents $A, B, C \in \mathcal{A}$, we have: $c_A(\mathcal{X} \cup \mathcal{Y}) \leq c_B(\mathcal{X}) + c_C(\mathcal{Y})$.

For the price function we require that $p(\mathcal{X} \cup \mathcal{Y}) = p(\mathcal{X}) + p(\mathcal{Y})$. The following useful property can be shown to hold for the transportation domain.

Theorem 4. *If no time constraints are allowed for the transportation orders, the transportation domain is a locally subadditive TOD.*

Proof Idea: The key observation is that an agent can benefit from joining two round trips into a single round trip. Note that this assertion remains true even if capacity constraints are considered. However, in this case the probability decreases that an agent really benefits from joining two round trips. □

Unfortunately, as stated by Theorem 5, there is no global subadditivity:

Theorem 5. *Even if the specification of transportation orders does not contain time constraints, the transportation domain is not a globally subadditive TOD.*

Proof Idea: It is easy to construct an example in which two trucks located in two geographically distinct locations can execute two sets of orders at less costs than any of them could do on its own. □

If transportation orders are allowed to have time constraints, things look even worse; in this case, we even do not have local subadditivity:

Theorem 6. *If time constraints are specified for a set of transportation orders $\mathcal{X} \subseteq \mathcal{T}$, the transportation domain is not locally subadditive, even if we assume that $c(\mathcal{X}) \neq \infty$.*

Proof: Because this result is less obvious than the previous one we give the proof via a more detailed example shown in Figure 1. In the example, four orders are

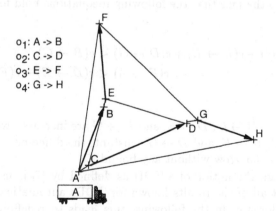

o_1: A -> B
o_2: C -> D
o_3: E -> F
o_4: G -> H

Fig. 1. If time constraints are specified, the transportation domain is not locally subadditive

specified. The due date (dda) of an order is the latest point in time the truck is allowed to finish the order. Let t_{cur} denote the current time. The four orders are given by:

o_1: $\quad A \to B, \quad dda_{o_1} = t_{cur} + \text{time-needed}(A \to B)$
o_2: $\quad C \to D, \quad dda_{o_2} = t_{cur} + \text{time-needed}(A \to B \to C \to D)$
o_3: $\quad E \to F, \quad dda_{o_3} = t_{cur} + \text{time-needed}(A \to B \to C \to D \to E \to F)$
o_4: $\quad G \to H, \quad dda_{o_4} > t_{cur} + \text{time-needed}(A \to B \to C \to E \to F \to G \to H)$

The orders do not exceed the capacity of one truck and no further time constraints are specified for the orders. This means that the trucks do not have to worry about being early in a specific city. All they have to take care of is not to be late. Therefore, the best routes for two trucks starting in city A are:

$$A \to B \to E \to F \to A \text{ and } A \to C \to D \to G \to H \to A.$$

The only possible route satisfying the time constraints for one truck executing all the orders is:

$$A \to B \to C \to D \to E \to F \to G \to H \to A.$$

For these routes we have:

$$c(A \to B \to E \to F \to A) + c(A \to C \to D \to G \to H \to A)$$
$$< c(A \to B \to C \to D \to E \to F \to G \to H \to A)$$

This is due to the fact that the following inequations hold for the example:

$$c(A \to C) + c(B \to E) + c(D \to G) < c(B \to C)$$
$$c(F \to A) < c(D \to E) + c(F \to G)$$

If the distances $B \to C$, $D \to E$, and $F \to G$ are increased while keeping the distances $A \to C$, $B \to E$, and $D \to G$ constant, the difference in costs between the two solutions can grow without any bound. $\square$

Thus, although the notion of a TOD as defined by [7] is useful for guiding our analysis, not all of the results known for TODs automatically apply to the transportation domain. In the following, this leads to redefinitions of notions such as deals, encounters, and to a further refinement of the original notion of TODs.

3.2   Encounters and Deals in the Transportation Domain

A distribution of tasks among the agents is called an *encounter*. This is formalised with the following definition:

Definition 7. An *encounter* within a TOD $< \mathcal{T}, \mathcal{A}, c, p >$ is an ordered list $(E_1, E_2, \ldots, E_n)$ such that for all $k \in \{1, \ldots, n\}$, $E_k = (T_k, p_k) \in 2^{\mathcal{T}} \times \mathbb{R}$. We define two access functions to the elements of an encounter: $tasks(E_k) = T_k \subseteq \mathcal{T}$ is a finite set of tasks of A_k; $sp(E_k) = p_k \in \mathbb{R}$ is the side-payment agent A_k gets. $\sum_{i=1}^{n} sp(E_k) = 0$, i.e. agents are not allowed to take money from their savings to buy tasks.

The global order scheduling problem can be decomposed into two steps, which can be analysed separately. The first one is the distribution of orders among shipping companies. The second one is how orders can be allocated within one shipping company among its set of trucks. Therefore, in MARS encounters are defined at two layers. At the layer of the shipping companies, an encounter specifies which set of tasks is assigned to which shipping company. At the layer of the trucks in each shipping company an encounter specifies how the set of tasks that is currently assigned to a specific company is distributed among its trucks. If we assume that there are $n \in \mathbb{N}$ shipping companies, the distribution of the current task is specified by $n+1$ encounters, i.e., one within each company plus one among the companies. This allocation solves a very complex scheduling problem. In MARS, this solution is initially computed by a contract-net-like negotiation mechanism between the shipping companies and their trucks. This initial solution is further optimised using negotiation mechanisms based on the notion of **deals** [4]:

Definition 8. Let $\Omega = < \mathcal{T}, \{A_1, \ldots, A_n\}, c, p >$ be an n-agent TOD; let E be an encounter within Ω, $E = (E_1, \ldots, E_n)$. A *deal* is a redistribution of set of tasks among agents. It is an encounter $(D_1, \ldots, D_n)$ such that $tasks(D_1), \ldots, tasks(D_n) \subseteq \mathcal{T}$, and $\bigcup_{i=1}^{n} tasks(D_i) = \bigcup_{i=1}^{n} tasks(E_i)$. The semantics of such a deal is that each agent A_k commits itself to executing all tasks in $tasks(D_k)$.

Now, we can define the notion of deal payoff and the conflict deal:

Definition 9. Let $\Omega = < \mathcal{T}, \{A_1, \ldots, A_n\}, c, p >$ be a TOD; given an encounter $(E_1, \ldots, E_n)$ within Ω, we have:

1. For any deal $\delta, 1 \le k \le n$ the deal payoff for agent A_k is defined by:

$$dpo_k(\delta) = tpo(tasks(\delta_k)) - tpo(tasks(E_k)) + sp(\delta_k) - sp(E_k)$$

2. The deal $\Theta \equiv (E_1, \ldots, E_n)$ is called the conflict deal.

Side-payments are only used in negotiation processes among shipping companies. In the dynamic case, where orders are announced to the system at random points in time, the system starts with an encounter where each of the task sets in the encounter is the empty set and sp components are equal to 0. The sp components may change within negotiation processes when an agents buys an order from another agent. Their purpose is to express how much the agent has gained from the encounter.

Definition 10. For vectors $\alpha = (\alpha_1, \alpha_2, \ldots, \alpha_n)$ and $\beta = (\beta_1, \beta_2, \ldots, \beta_n)$, we say that α dominates β and write $\alpha \succ \beta$ iff $\forall k(\alpha_k \geq \beta_k)$, and $\exists l(\alpha_l > \beta_l)$. We say that α weakly dominates β and write $\alpha \succeq \beta$ iff $\forall k(\alpha_k \geq \beta_k)$.

For deals δ and δ' we define:

$$\delta \; \mathcal{R} \; \delta' \Leftrightarrow_{def} (dpo_1(\delta), \ldots, dpo_n(\delta)) \; \mathcal{R} \; (dpo_1(\delta'), \ldots, dpo_n(\delta'))$$

where $\mathcal{R} \in \{\succ, \succeq\}$. We say that δ dominates δ' **iff** $\delta \succ \delta'$ and we say δ weakly dominates δ' **iff** $\delta \succeq \delta'$. Deal δ is individual rational if $\delta \succeq \Theta$ and *Pareto optimal* if there is no other deal δ' such that $\delta' \succ \delta$. One possibility to find out if a given encounter is Pareto optimal, is to prove it using a branch and bound algorithm. However, in general this procedure is much too time-consuming. Therefore, we introduce the notion of *weak Pareto optimality*: a deal δ is *weakly Pareto optimal* if no agent is able to compute a deal δ' which dominates δ within a specified time limit. The set of all deals which are individual rational and weakly Pareto optimal form the negotiation set in negotiation processes.

Based on the notion of weak Pareto optimality, an anytime algorithm [2] for schedule optimisation can be defined. If we assume that in the transportation domain the set of tasks $\mathcal{T}$ is given by all tasks which are present at a specific point in time, the set of all possible encounters has an enormous size. Starting with some encounter $(T_1, \ldots, T_n)$ which is not weakly Pareto optimal in general, we defined negotiation strategies which will lead to weakly Pareto optimal solutions. Of course, global optimality of these solutions is not guaranteed.

3.3 Cooperative vs Competitive TODs

We are now at the point to refine the definition of a TOD, leading to two subclasses that each describe important cases of domains with different properties.

Definition 11. A TOD $\Omega = < \mathcal{T}, \mathcal{A}, c, p >$ is called:

1. a *competitive TOD* if an agent A_k only accepts a deal δ if: $dpo_k(\delta) \geq 0$
2. a *cooperative TOD* if the agents accept a deal δ if: $\sum_{i=1}^n dpo(D_i) \geq 0$

According to this definition, task allocation within one shipping company describes a cooperative TOD because trucks of one shipping company switch orders even if one of them receives a smaller payoff by the deal than it had before. In this situation, it is possible to define negotiation protocols that result in surprisingly good solutions [1]. Results from an analysis of cooperative TODs have been published in [5]. For the rest of the paper, we concentrate on the competitive setting which describes task allocation among different shipping companies.

4 The Competitive Setting

The cooperative and the competitive setting not only differ in how the payoff is split among the agents. In a competitive setting it is not very likely that agents always tell the truth. It has been shown in [11] [7] that lying in subadditive and general TODs may be beneficial. In this section, we investigate whether this is also the case in the transportation domain.

4.1 Phantom Tasks

From the previous considerations we learned that the transportation domain is on the verge between general and subadditive TODs. However, because in the TODs originally defined by Rosenschein and Zlotkin agents try to avoid the execution of tasks whereas in our case agents are eager to execute tasks, lying in the two settings has different effects.

Theorem 12. *In the transportation domain phantom lies may be beneficial.*

Proof: The proof of Theorem 12 is accomplished by providing an example: Assume that there is a shipping company S_A located in city A and a shipping company S_B located in city B (see Figure 2). For simplicity further assume that both shipping companies own one truck with a capacity of 40. Let o_1 be an order of 20 from $C \to D$ offered to S_A. The distances the trucks have to go is computed as the Euclidean distance between the locations of the cities in the pictures. Now we can distinguish the following cases:

1. If nothing else is known and both shipping companies do not have further orders to be executed, a truck of shipping company S_B would be the best to execute the order. We define

$$\Delta_{S_A} := tpo_{S_A}(o_1) = \hat{p}(o_1) - c(A \to C \to D \to A)$$

and

$$\Delta_{S_B} := tpo_{S_B}(o_1) = \hat{p}(o_1) - c(B \to C \to D \to B),$$

where Δ_{S_A} and Δ_{S_B} specify the payoff S_A and S_B receive by executing the order. We have $\Delta_{S_A} < \Delta_{S_B}$ because C is closer to B than to A. If $\Delta_{S_A} > 0$, it would not be rational for S_A to give the order to S_B without receiving a side-payment from S_B. On the other hand, in this situation it would not be rational for S_A to execute the order by itself. S_A could offer the deal $((\emptyset, +\Delta_{S_A}), (\{o_1\}, -\Delta_{S_A}))$ to S_B and it would not be rational of S_B to reject this deal because it obtains a payoff of $\Delta_{S_B} - \Delta_{S_A} > 0$ from it.

2. Assume that S_A already has an order o_2 of 20 from $A \to D$; S_B does not have any orders at all. In this case it is not rational for S_A to give the order to S_B, because

$$\Delta'_{S_A} > \Delta_{S_B}, \text{ where } \Delta'_{S_A} = \hat{p}(o_1) - c(A \to C \to D) + c(A \to D)$$

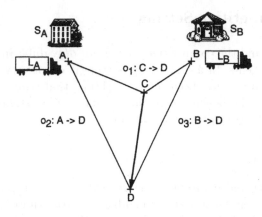

Fig. 2. Example: phantom lies may be beneficial

holds and therefore S_B is not able to pay S_A a side-payment that is higher than the payoff A could get by executing the order on its own.

Now assume that S_A does not really have an order o_2 of 20 from A to D, but there is a probability of 70 % in getting such an order. Is it still rational for S_A to execute the order o_1 on its own? With a probability of 70% S_A receives more payoff than it could get by selling the order to S_B. By computing the expected payoff [6] for both alternatives, we can infer that keeping the order would be individual rational for S_A. Therefore, in the transportation domain, phantom lies which have a fair chance to actually turn into reality, i.e., into a task that actually must be performed, can be beneficial for an agent. □

The situation described in the proof again changes if we assume that S_A has an order o_2 of 20 from A to D, and that S_B has an order o_3 of 20 from B to D. In this situation S_B is the best to execute the order o_1 but it has to pay S_A a high price for the order. Hence, S_B will earn only little money by executing o_1 because S_A was already able to execute the order at low costs.

Now assume that both companies S_A and S_B do not really have the orders o_2 and o_3, but that there is a 70 % probability to get such orders. In this case, in the beginning, S_B is the best one to execute the order. With a probability of 49 % both will get the expected order and S_A would lose payoff if it gave away the order without the assumption of getting the additional order o_2. There is a chance of 9 % that neither S_A nor S_B will get the expected additional order, and there is a chance of 42 % that only one of them will get the order. In both of the latter cases S_B might lose payoff if o_1 is transferred for the price where S_A assumed that it would have the additional order. Is it rational for S_B to buy the order? At which price should S_B buy the order?

4.2 A Negotiation Strategy for Competing Shipping Companies

To answer the above questions, one could try to compute expected utilities for sets of tasks; however, this turns out to be rather awkward because the probability of being offered a specific set of orders is not known beforehand. Therefore, we suggest a different solution to the problem. For this purpose, we return to the situation where we have truck L_A located in city A and truck L_B located in city B. There is only one order o_1 (20 units to transport form C to D) present which was received by the shipping company S_A and is currently scheduled to truck L_A. When L_A executes the order, S_A gets a payoff of Δ_{S_A}. A threshold payoff $\overline{\Delta}$ is specified which defines the amount of payoff a truck has to get to stop the shipping company from looking for partners to execute the orders currently scheduled to the truck. The situation for the shipping company agent with respect to truck L_A is now characterised by figure 3. S_A invents a phantom task o^*

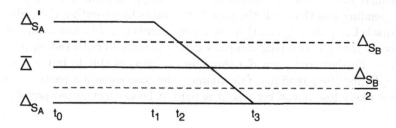

Fig. 3. A time-dependent decision function to determine the price of an order in a negotiation process.

which ideally completes order o_1 — in the example: 20 units to transport from A to D just at the time o_1 has to be executed — and which gives S_A a payoff of Δ'_{S_A}. S_A announces o_1 at time t_0 to S_B specifying the expected payoff Δ'_{S_A} as a price to be paid if the order is to be transferred. Because Δ_{S_B} is less than Δ'_{S_A}, S_B does not accept this offer.

While time passes and nothing changes significantly, i.e., no new orders arrive, at time t_1 S_A starts to believe that the probability for an order to arrive which can substitute o^* decreases linearly. Therefore, S_A continuously reduces the price Δ'_{S_A} after t_1. This continues at most until t_3 because this is the time when L_A actually has to start executing the order to meet the specified time constraints. However, at time t_2 we have $\Delta'_{S_A} = \Delta_{S_B}$ which signals that the deal is becoming attractive for S_B. It would not be individually rational for S_B to buy the order exactly at time t_2 because S_B would pass all its payoff to S_A. But from the next time on S_A reduces the price of its offer, it will be individual rational for S_B to accept the offer.

For S_B the question is now when is the right time to accept the offer. Even if we assume that S_B knows t_3, the time L_A has to start executing o_1, there could be another shipping company waiting for its chance to get o_1. For the sake of the example let us assume that

$$\Delta_{S_A} \leq \frac{\Delta_{S_B}}{2}$$

In this case the price of $\frac{\Delta_{S_B}}{2}$ seems to be fair because it exactly splits the payoff between S_A and S_B. Therefore, a general strategy a shipping company could choose to negotiate about prices for orders is, to wait until the price of the offer is less or equal to half the payoff the shipping company could get out of executing the order.

Although this is a quite robust negotiation strategy in practice, this strategy is not in a Nash-Equilibrium. The problem is that at any time a shipping company who has an advantage for executing a specific order (mostly because of its location) is able to profit from this situation if it is aware of it. More concretely, if a shipping company knows that it is able to execute an order at costs which are significantly lower than the costs of any other shipping company, it can buy this order spending less than half the payoff it obtains by executing the order. Still, if the market is quite big, i.e., there is a large number of shipping companies, the probability that one shipping company gets into such an outstanding position is quite low. Furthermore, even if a shipping company is able to buy an order without splitting the payoff in a fair manner, the corresponding partner company does not really lose payoff because it is paid at least its expected payoff.

5 Discussion

In this paper, we have provided a decision-theoretic analysis of the transportation domain. It extends the definition of a task-oriented domain given in [11] [7] by the notions of cooperative and competitive task-oriented domains. In the MARS system, which was implemented to simulate a set of distributed shipping companies in the transportation domain, we identified instances of both domain types: if we look at the agent society within one shipping company (the company and its trucks), we have a cooperative task-oriented domain. On the other hand, at the layer of the different shipping companies, there is a competitive task-oriented domain.

The development of the MARS system has currently reached the border of industrial applicability. Global communication and information technology is becoming available at reasonable prices that already medium-sized companies can afford. Having this more commercial background in mind, what is the significance and what are the implications of the results presented in this paper?

First, drawing a distinction among cooperative and competitive TODs allows us more fine-grained investigations of different patterns of interaction occurring in real-life transportation business. Second, Theorems 1 – 3 show that there are some differences between the transportation domain and the TOD defined by Rosenschein and Zlotkin. Therefore, the results from [7] could not be automatically adopted for the transportation domain, but had to be proved separately.

The third important point has been made by replacing the unrealistic notion of Pareto optimality by that of weak Pareto optimality, which takes into account the resource-boundedness of the agents. This extends the work of Rosenschein and Zlotkin towards practical applicability, as computing the negotiation set in the transportation domain actually involves solving a (dynamic) scheduling problem, which in general cannot be solved optimally[4]. The notion of weak Pareto optimality aims at the powerful heuristic scheduling algorithms used in MARS [5].

A last major implication is that as we cannot be sure that agents always tell the truth (see Theorem 4), in the transportation domain, it is important to use protocols that make telling the truth the dominant strategy [7]. Developing such protocols for practical applications is an area of future work.

References

1. A. Bachem, W. Hochstättler, and M. Malich. Simulated Trading: A New Approach For Solving Vehicle Routing Problems. Technical Report 92.125, Mathematisches Institut der Universität zu Köln, Dezember 1992.
2. M. Boddy and T. L. Dean. Deliberation scheduling for problem solving in time-constrained environments. *Artificial Intelligence*, 67:245-285, 1994.
3. K. Fischer, N. Kuhn, H. J. Müller, J. P. Müller, and M. Pischel. Sophisticated and distributed: The transportation domain. In *Proceedings of MAAMAW-93*, Neuchatel, CH, August 1993. Fifth European Workshop on Modelling Autonomous Agents in a Multi-Agent World.
4. K. Fischer, J. P. Müller, and M. Pischel. A model for cooperative transportation scheduling. In *Proceedings of the 1st International Conference on Multiagent Systems (ICMAS'95)*, San Francisco, June 1995.
5. K. Fischer, J. P. Müller, and M. Pischel. Cooperative transportation scheduling: an application domain for DAI. *Journal of Applied Artificial Intelligence. Special issue on Intelligent Agents*, 10(1), 1996.
6. P. Haddawy and S. Hanks. Utility models for goal-directed decision-theoretic planners, 1994. Submitted to *Artificial Intelligence* journal.
7. J. S. Rosenschein and G. Zlotkin. *Rules of Encounter: Designing Conventions for Automated Negotiation among Computers*. MIT Press, 1994.
8. T. W. Sandholm. An implementation of the contract net protocol based on marginal cost calculations. In *Proceedings of the Eleventh National Conference on Artificial Intelligence (AAAI-93)*, pages 256-263, 1993.
9. T. W. Sandholm and V. R. Lesser. Coalition formation among bounded rational agents. In *Proceedings of the 14th International Joint Conference on Artificial Intelligence (IJCAI-95)*, pages 662-669, 1995.
10. M.P. Wellman. A general-equilibrium approach to distributed transportation planning. In *Proceedings of AAAI-92*, pages 282-290, 1992.
11. G. Zlotkin and J. S. Rosenschein. A domain theory for task-oriented negotiation. In *Proc. of the 13th International Joint Conference on Artificial Intelligence*, volume 1, Chambéry, France, 28.8.-3.9. 1993.

---

[4] In [9], Sandholm and Lesser investigated coalition formation among bounded rational agents. However, their work focusses on self-interested agents and does not cover the case of cooperative TODs.

A Real-Time Agent Model in an Asynchronous-Object Environment

Z. GUESSOUM[*], M. DOJAT[**]

*Equipe OMC de J-F Perrot, LAFORIA-IBP, Université Paris 6, Boîte 169,
4, place de Jussieu, F-75252 PARIS

**INSERM Unité 296, Faculté de Médecine
8, avenue du Général Sarrail, 94010 CRETEIL FRANCE
e-mail: {guessoum, dojat}@laforia.ibp.fr

Abstract

To build intelligent control systems for real-life applications, we need to design software agents which combine cognitive abilities to reason about complex situations, and reactive abilities to meet hard deadlines. We propose an operational agent model which mixes AI techniques and real-time performances. Our model is based on an ATN (Augmented Transition Network) to dynamically adapt the agent's behavior to changes in the environment. Each agent uses a production system and is provided with a synchronization mechanism to avoid the possible inconsistencies of the asynchronous execution of several rule bases. Our agents communicate by message-passing and are implemented in an asynchronous-object environment. We report on the use of our agent model in intensive care patient monitoring.

Key Words

Multi-Agent, Actors, Real-Time, ATN, Production Rules, Object-Oriented Language, Artificial Ventilation.

1 Introduction

Artificial intelligence (AI) techniques are well adapted to perform tasks such as diagnosis, design and classification. To build intelligent control systems for real-life applications, AI techniques must also handle specific real-time aspects, such as resource limitations and guarantee of timely response. This leads to the emerging research area of "real-time AI" [Charpillet and Théret 1994; Garvey and Lesser 1994; Musliner et al. 1995].

Multi-Agent Systems (MASs) seem well adapted to model a variety of real applications. To be useful for real-time domains, MASs must (1) handle asynchronous events, (2) manage resource overload and time constraints and (3) ensure a control of distributed autonomous entities. We propose here an agent model which achieves these goals by integrating smoothly so-called reactive abilities (to meet hard deadlines) and cognitive abilities (to act rationally by using knowledge and to reach a fixed goal when constraints are relaxed).

1.1 Blackboards & Actors

MASs proposed in the literature rely on two approaches to achieve communication between agents: 1) the blackboard model introduced in the Hearsay-II system [Erman et al. 1980] and used in several recent systems [Hayes-Roth et al. 1992; Bussmann and Demazeau 1994; Charpillet and Boyer 1994] ; and 2) the actor model initially proposed by [Hewitt 1977] which developed into various concurrent languages [Agha 1986; Yonezawa et al. 1986; Yokote and Tokoro 1987; Ferber and Briot 1988] .

In the blackboard approach, knowledge sources use available information without knowing its origin and produce information without worrying about its destination, whereas in the actor approach, an actor communicates information directly to another actor via message-passing. As observed by [Nii et al. 1989], blackboard systems are prone to inefficiency problems, which are to be solved by parallelization, e.g. with actors. Actors may thus be considered as the basic element for building agents. Further, the combination of the actor concept and the object paradigm leads to the notion of "agent-oriented programming" [Shoham 1993], which is the framework of the present paper. We start from an environment which provides objects, classes (with inheritance), production rules, and processes.

1.2 Cognitive, Reactive and Hybrid Models

Several agent models have been proposed. Two main approaches can be distinguished: *cognitive* and *reactive* (see [Ferber 1995]). In the cognitive approach, each agent contains a symbolic model of the outside world, about which it develops plans and makes decisions in the traditional (symbolic) AI way. In the reactive approach, on the other hand, simple-minded agents react rapidly to asynchronous events without using complex reasoning.

Many researchers have suggested that neither a completely reactive nor a completely cognitive approach is suitable for building complete solutions for real-life applications. Hybrid models, such as *TouringMachines* [Ferguson 1992], *InteRRaP* [Müller and Pischel 1994] and the model presented in [Bussmann and Demazeau 1994], have been proposed to combine the advantages of both reactive and cognitive models. In these models, agents are decomposed in a set of modules which can in turn be of a reactive or cognitive nature. However, the problem with such models is that of controlling the interactions between these fundamentally different modules: reactive and cognitive modules, so to say, do not live with the same time scale, which makes it difficult to integrate the different temporal sequences.

1.3 Our Model

Our hybrid agent model relies on a first layer made up of interactive modules that can be either reactive or cognitive, and interact asynchronously and concurrently. A higher level *supervision* module controls these interactions via an ATN so as to impose a global temporal sequencing. As we shall see, this time scale is based on the firing of individual rules as its basic unit. Modules of the base layer include the *perception* module (reactive), the *reasoning* module (cognitive) and the *communication/action* module (which can be either reactive or cognitive).

In our model, each reasoning module owns a (first order, forward chaining) rule base, which represents the bulk of its cognitive abilities. Control of the reasoning process is achieved by a set of metarules (called a metabase) also owned by the module. These control metarules operate on objects that are also accessed by the supervisor's ATN, thus establishing the supervision link at the level of the individual rule firing. As opposed to the blackboard approach, where control is achieved through a separate architecture [Hayes-Roth 1985], in our model each individual agent carries its own control knowledge, represented by the metabase of its reasoning module.

As regards real-time response, our model is adequate provided a time granularity of single rule firing. This seems to be acceptable in many industrial applications [Barachini and Grenec 1993]. As our application example will demonstrate, it exhibits:

- Ability to monitor in real-time information provided by the environment and to adapt its behavior to respond in real-time to changes in the environment.

- Ability to coordinate its actions in accordance with other agents actions to avoid inconsistencies.

The purpose of this paper is to present our model and to show its use to design a real-time prototype for intensive care unit patient monitoring. Section 2 presents the main Smalltalk-based tools of our implementation: *Actalk* and *NéOpus*. Section 3 describes the collective behavior of a society of agents. Section 4 describes the individual modules of our model. In Section 5, we report on the application to patient monitoring. Finally, we discuss the advantages of our approach to design real-time MASs.

2 Technical Context

We have opted for an environment which combines object-oriented programming and production rules. We use *Smalltalk-80* as our base language. This enables our implementation to make use of various software components (alias frameworks) such as the Smalltalk Discrete Event Simulation Package (see [Guessoum 1995]) for observing the temporal behavior of the system under simulated real-time conditions (see 5.4 below). We have used *RPC-Talk* [Wolinski 1994], which provides *Smalltalk-80* with RPC (Remote Procedure Call) facilities, to put any number of machines at the service of our MASs. Our actors are built with *Actalk* [Briot 1989, Briot 1995] a generic platform for implementing various actor models in *Smalltalk-80*. *Actalk* may be seen as the foundation stone of our model. The rule bases and metabases of the reasoning modules use *NéOpus* [Pachet 1992; Pachet 1995], a first order inference engine completely embedded in *Smalltalk-80*. We have added a few features to customize these components to meet the specific needs of our model.

2.1 Actalk

Among other things, *Actalk* allows to transform ordinary Smalltalk objects into actors. Asynchronism, a basic principle of actor languages, is implemented by enqueuing the received messages into the mail box, thus dissociating message reception from its interpretation. In *Actalk*, an actor is composed of three objects:

- an instance of class `Address` represents the mail box of the actor. It defines the way messages will be queued for later interpretation;

- an instance of class `Activity` represents the internal activity of the actor. It provides autonomy to the actor. It owns a Smalltalk process which continuously removes messages from the mail box and launches their interpretation by the actor;

- an instance of class `ActiveObject` represents the behavior of the actor, i.e. the way individual messages will be interpreted.

To build an agent with *Actalk*, all one has to do is to create the three components (call them *ad*, *act* and *actObj* respectively) and put them together as an actor by sending the message *active* to *actObj*. Customizing *Actalk* therefore means defining subclasses of `Address`, `Activity` and `ActiveObject`. See 5.2 for some details on our realization.

2.2 NéOpus

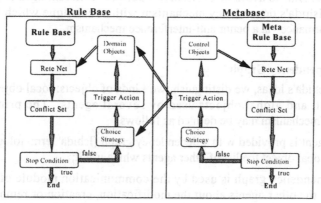

Fig. 1. Control with metarules in NéOpus.
This figure highlights the organizational similarity between domain knowledge and control knowledge. The fired metarules act on the firing strategy of rules, on the stop condition and on the objects moving in the associate rule-base net.

NéOpus realizes a neat integration of rule-based programming with *Smalltalk-80*. It uses the Rete algorithm to compile rule bases. One of its prominent features is declarative specification of control with metarules [Pachet and Perrot 1994]. Metarules are similar to rules and operate on so-called control objects. With each rule base there may be associated a metabase which controls the firing of its rules (see Fig. 1).

A number of metabases have been designed by *NéOpus* users to define standard types of control. In particular, specific metabases have been built to reason on critical situations [Dojat and Pachet 1992]. We have adapted some of them to our needs by changing a few individual metarules.

3 Relations Between Agents

We are interested in situations where an agent shares a collection of resources with other agents. Thus, agents must adapt themselves to take advantages of resources as needed, but must coordinate their actions to avoid inconsistencies. Researchers have evolved a range of approaches to coordinate a collection of autonomous entities. [Durfee et al. 1987; Gasser 1992] describe the mechanisms that improve the network coherence: organization, exchanging meta-level information, local and multi-agent planning, and explicit analysis and synchronization.

With a synchronization mechanism as proposed in [Ishida 90], each agent protects itself against conflicts or redundant actions concerning the other agents, at a cost of (1) reduced concurrency, and (2) synchronization overhead. However, if the level of dependency is low, and the granularity of actions is high, this mechanism can provide useful coordination, as observed by [Gasser 1992]. This is the case for our model. The granularity of our agents is high, each agent possesses its own rule base and the agent's rules are fired sequentially. Therefore dependency and interference between individual rules of the same agent do not have to be considered. Thus the dependency between agents is low.

There remains to avoid inconsistencies between different agents. To do so, we implement Ishida's dependency mechanism with a technique which improves its overall performance via a better anti-interference mechanism.

3.1 The Dependency Graph

Following Ishida's ideas, we distinguish two kinds of objects: local objects used by a single agent, and global objects used by several agents. The principle of the dependency mechanism may be defined as follows:

- each agent is provided with a dependency graph (Ishida' terminology) giving for each global object the list of other agents which use it;

- the dependency graph is used by the communication module of the agent to inform the other agents about the modification, creation or removal of global objects by the reasoning module. It is updated gradually when rules are triggered: if a global object is removed by rule actions, it is also automatically removed from the dependency graph and a message is sent to the other agents to update their graphs.

Inter agents conflicts resulting from access to global objects are thus avoided.

3.2 Anti-Interference Mechanism

Interference exists among two rules if there is a global object that both rules access and at least one modifies. The principle of our anti-interference mechanism may be defined as follows:

- each agent is provided with a list of those global objects that it is currently modifying (objects-in-use);

- each agent is provided with the collection of the objects-in-use lists of the other agents;
- we add two steps in the inference engine cycle:
  * *test*: before the firing of the selected rule, the agent verifies that no global object that is modified by the selected rule is also being modified by some other agent (as is apparent from its objects-in-use list collection). In this case, the global objects that are modified by the selected rule are added to its own objects-in-use list and the rule is triggered, otherwise another fireable rule is selected;
  * *updateList*: after the firing of the rule, the agent removes from its own *objects-in-use* list those global objects that were added to its in the *test* phase, i.e. the global objects that were modified by the rule.

The proposed solution presents conflicts and redundant actions. It avoids also the synchronization messages used by Ishida.

4 Our Real-Time Agent Model

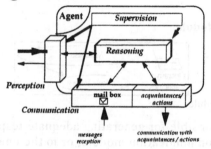

Fig. 2. Agent model

4.1 The Supervision Module

This module synchronizes the execution of concurrent actions of the other modules. It relies on two notions: *states* and *transitions*. States qualify the context as perceived by the other modules. Changes in the context are reflected as transitions between states. Now, these states and transitions naturally build up an ATN [Woods 70]. The ATN is a synthetic and deterministic representation of the agent's behavior.

Fig. 3. Main states of agent modules
Different states correspond to each module. The combination of these states defines the global agent's state.

Each transition links an input state with an output state. The various signals received by the agent's modules represent the conditions of transition and the actions of transition change the state of the various modules (activate reasoning, terminate reasoning, ...). When these conditions are verified, the transition actions are executed and the agent's state is modified.

4.2 The Perception Module

Fig. 4. The perception module

The perception module manages the interactions between the agent and its environment. It monitors sensors, translates and filters sensed data in accordance with the instructions of the reasoning or supervision modules (see Fig. 4). It may package information concerning the same phenomenon to facilitate interpretation. The data set obtained is used mainly by the reasoning module.

4.3 The Reasoning Module

Fig. 5. The reasoning module

This module is responsible for generating adequate responses to the messages transmitted by the communication module, or to the changes detected by the perception module. To do this it relies on two kinds of capacities: operative, represented by the standard behavior of the associated Smalltalk objects (procedures, alias *methods* in the Smalltalk terminology), and cognitive, embodied in a NéOpus-based asynchronous production system [Guessoum 1994]. This production system mainly comprises: (1) a rule base which includes objects describing the agent's environment and rules representing suitable operations over these objects; (2) an inference engine which includes the dependency and anti-interference mechanisms; and (3) a metabase which provides a declarative representation of the control of reasoning.

4.4 The Communication/Action Module

Fig. 6. The communication/action module

This module allows the agent to receive and to send messages asynchronously. It filters the received messages, determines their priority (LIFO, FIFO,...) and the type of treatment to give them. It owns the list of the agent's acquaintances. It sends them messages with various modes corresponding to specific protocols (*urgent, answer needed, ...*). The messages and their modes are provided by the reasoning module.

This module also effects the direct actions (modification of the environment via effectors) and indirect actions (information transmission to other agents) as directed by the reasoning module.

5 From Actalk Objects to Agents

In this section, we illustrate the implementation of our model with an application: intensive care unit patient monitoring.

5.1 Application: Artificial Ventilation Control

The system deals with patients suffering from respiratory insufficiency, assisted with mechanical ventilation. The problem is to monitor in real-time various ventilation signals (tidal volume (Vt), respiratory rate (RR) and expired-CO_2 pressure (PCO_2)), in order to diagnose the patient current state and to adapt the mechanical assistance accordingly. To perform this task, it is necessary to develop a complex temporal reasoning to diagnose the time-course of the patient's status [Dojat and Sayettat 1995]. In alarming situations such as hypoventilation or apnea the current therapy must be modified quickly (1 second). A first system, NéoGanesh, is in use at the hospital Henri Mondor (Créteil near Paris) [Dojat et al. 1995]. The extension based on a distributed architecture using our agent model, aims at increasing the system reactivity and incorporating additional distributed medical expertise.

5.2 Agents

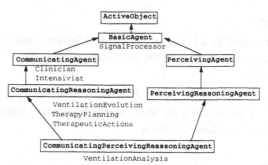

Fig. 7. Excerpt from the agents hierarchy used for artificial ventilation control application

All "intelligent" agents have the same general structure but they differ in 1) their sensor-driving layer: perception and communication/action modules; 2) their behavior: the know-how, the domain and control knowledge. Agents are complex entities and a hierarchy of agents (see Fig. 7) may be built according to several criteria, such as type of the sensor-driving structures, know-how and type of cognitive functions. BasicAgent, root of the classes describing our agent behavior, is encapsulated according to the Actalk principle to be transformed in an actor.

Note that, for example, agent *SignalProcessor* has only a simple behavior to process data acquisition. Whereas, agent *VentilationEvolution* exhibits a complex behavior to appreciate the time-course of the patient's ventilation.

Supervision Module

The supervision module represents the kernel of agent. Its main activity is to interpret its ATN. This is effected by the method `setProcess` redefined in subclass `AgentActivity` of the *Actalk* standard class `Activity`.

In Actalk , `Activity` manages and transmits the messages which are interpreted by `ActiveObject`. The method `setProcess`, which creates a process to remove continuously the messages buffered in the mail box, is redefined in `AgentActivity`. The new role of this process is to interpret the ATN. The ATN itself is defined in subclass `BasicAgent` of *Actalk*'s `ActiveObject`.

For example, the ATN of *VentilationEvolution* (see Fig. 8) gives priority to urgent messages such as alarms. In state 1, the condition "no message" leads to the action "wait" and to the persistence in state 1. The condition "an urgent message" leads to the action "read mailbox" whatever the state may be.

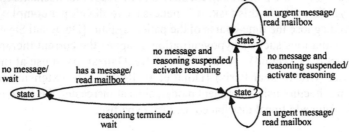

Fig. 8. *VentilationEvolution* ATN

Perception Module

It is mainly characterized by a list of sensors and an instance method which interprets the sensors data, compares them with the previous ones and transmits the new data to the reasoning module.

For example, several sensors (CO_2, RR, Vt) are connected to *SignalProcessor*. It scans the different sensors at a variable sample frequency, interprets the data and transmits the result to *VentilationAnalysis*.

Reasoning Module

To implement the anti-interference mechanism we have redefined the NéOpus inference engine cycle. The new cycle includes the two steps *test* and *updateList* (see 3.2).

The statements, that inform the Rete net of NéOpus about modifying, removing and adding of objects, have been redefined. The new statements use the dependency graph (see 3.1) to inform the agent itself and the other agents indicated by this graph.

For example, the rule base o f *VentilationEvolution* uses a global object (VentilatoryState) which is also filtered by the rules of *TherapeuticActions*. Indeed, these two agents have dependency graphs to inform each other about the modification of this object.

The metarules fire the rules which deal with alarming situations preferentially to other fireable rules. They operate on objects such as *stop condition, time* and *state*. These objects are of course referenced and modified by the ATN to etablish the supervision link at the rule level.

Communication Module

This module follows the ABCL/1 model [Yonezawa 86] as realized in Actalk by Briot.

The only technical difficulty lies with the continuation of asynchronous messages [Agha 1986] when a reply is expected by the agent. We propose to endow such messages with a process which waits for the answer (class MessageWithSenderAndReceiver, subclass of the *Actalk* standard class MessageWithSender which appears in the last version of *Actalk* [Briot 1995]).

5.3 Asynchronous Agents Management

Each agent is mapped to a process which interprets its supervisor's ATN. The execution model of all agents is closely related to the process management by *Smalltalk-80*. In the latter, a scheduler (Processor) manages processes with a simple mechanism based on priority levels. It does not stop an active process i.e. it is not preemptive. Therefore, each agent must of its own will free the processor to give a chance to other agents (sociability) by inserting the expression Processor yield.

In order to accommodate several agents and/or modules on a single processor, we must simulate parallelism. To do so we choose a process allocation strategy at two levels: supervision module level (simulation of parallelism between agents) and perception, reasoning and communication modules level (simulation of the internal parallelism of the agent).

At the supervision module level, the agent suspends its activity after each transition. A message self suspendBehavior (which includes a Processor yield) is sent at the end of each transition by the ATN interpreter.

At the reasoning module level, process control is performed after each rule firing. At the communication and the perception modules, the process control is effected after each mail box reading and at the end of the method scan.

5.4 An Example of Real-Time Functioning

After each ATN transition, the agent suspends its activity to scan the state changes of the perception, reasoning and communication modules. Depending on the nature of change, the agent may suspend its current reasoning process to deal with the new perceived data or new received messages.

Suppose our *SignalProcessor* is scanning its sensors with period 8 seconds. It detects an alarming symptom at 12:07:31 pm. Then it sends an alarm signal (urgent message) to *VentilationAnalysis*. The latter suspends its reasoning process, sends a message to *SignalProcessor* to increase its sample frequency and then reactivates its reasoning. *SignalProcessor* increases its frequency, but the alarm is still present. After 4 seconds, i.e. at 12:07:35 pm, it sends another signal to *VentilationAnalysis*. When receiving this second signal, *VentilationAnalysis* starts an analysis, diagnoses a persistent apnea at: 12:07:35 pm and informs *TherapeuticActions*. This diagnosis takes some milliseconds. *TherapeuticActions* starts its actions at 12:07:36 and ends at 12:07:37 pm.

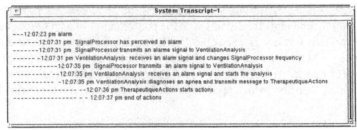

Fig. 9. Example of alarm processing (simulation data).

The total response time is the sum of transmission time, reaction time, parsing time and action time (see Fig. 10). The transmission time belongs to the interval [0, 8 sec] (8 sec is the period of *SignalProcessor*). The reaction time is the elapsed time between the perception of the alarm signal by *SignalProcessor* and the date at which the signal is taken into account by *VentilationAnalysis*. It corresponds to the run time of an ATN transition. The parsing time is the elapsed time between the date at which the message has been received by *VentilationAnalysis* and the date at which the signal has been parsed by its reasoning module. It corresponds to the run time of an ATN transition to deal with the urgent message sent by *SignalProcessor* and the firing of 4 metarules to activate the rules which parse the alarm signal. The action time is the elapsed time between the date at which the message has been received by *TherapeuticActions* and the end of the action on the ventilator. It corresponds to the run time of an ATN transition to deal with the urgent message sent by *VentilationAnalysis*, the activation of 2 metarules and one rule to act on the ventilator to change the therapy.

The total response time is about 14 seconds which is an excellent response time.

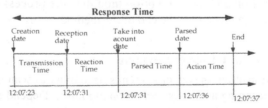

Fig. 10. Important dates in the life of an event

6 Discussion

As we saw earlier, realistic agent models require the combination of reactive and cognitive abilities. Using such hybrid models for real-time application needs to allow interactions between cognitive modules and reactive modules which have different time scales. The solution we propose has two main characteristics. First, we introduce a supervision module based on an ATN to control the interactions between modules that can be reactive or cognitive and to impose a global temporal sequencing. Second, the parallelism granularity of the time scale is based on the firing of a rule.

We have chosen an environment which combines actor, objects, production rules and processes. We benefit from the well known mechanisms of objects-oriented programming. Thus, by using the inheritance mechanism, the model can be easily extended. For example, to study communication between agents, we may integrate a specific module based on speech acts (such as [Bouron 1992]). Our system may be seen as a "framework" in the sense of object-oriented software engineering [Johnson 1994].

The experimental application describes here reuses the whole of the operational NéoGanesh system. We plan to run it in the same medical environment as NéoGanesh, and thus to obtain real-life performance measurements. Note that recent works (which rely, for the most part, on blackboards [Hayes-Roth et al. 1992; Quaglini et al. 1992; Sukuvaara et al. 1993]), so far lacks in clinical experiments.

Beside the medical application, we are using our platform to develop a manufacturing process simulator [Guessoum 1995] and an economic modeling [Guessoum and Durand 1995]. Other applications are currently under development.

Finally, our model uses well known distributed paradigms such as "access to resources" and "mail box messages communication". To avoid inconsistencies and conflicts, it uses dependency and anti-interference mechanisms. It would be interesting to explore other approaches such as organization, exchanging meta-level information and local planning.

Acknowledgment

The authors would like to thank **J-F Perrot** for his many useful criticisms and suggestions. His detailed comments have greatly improved the quality of this paper.

References

[Agha 1986]   G. Agha. *Actors: a model of concurrent computation in distributed systems.* Cambridge MA (USA), MIT Press 1986.

[Barachini and Granec 1993]   F. Barachini and R. Granec. *Productions systems for process control: advances and experiences.* Applied Artificial Intelligence 7: 301-316, 1993.

[Bouron 1992] T. Bouron. *What architecture for communication among computational agents?* Report LAFORIA 92/35, November 1992.

[Briot 1989]   J-P. Briot. *Actalk: a testbed for classifying and designing actor languages in the Smalltalk-80 environment.* Proc. of ECOOP'89, Cook, p. 109-130, 1989.

[Briot 1995]   J-P. Briot. *Modélisation et classification de langages de programmation concurrente à objets : l'expérience Actalk.* Proc. of LMO'95, Grenoble, 1995.

[Bussmann and Demazeau 1994]   S. Bussmann and Y. Demazeau. *An agent model combining reactive and cognitive capabilities.* Proc. of IEEE International Conference on Intelligent Robots and Systems - IROS' 94, München, 1994.

[Charpillet and Boyer 1994]   F. Charpillet and A. Boyer . *Incorporating AI techniques into predictable real-time systems: Reakt outcome.* Proc. of 14ème journées internationales Avignon'94, Avignon, p. 121-135, 1994.

[Charpillet and Théret 1994]   F. Charpillet and P. Théret. *I.A. et temps réel.* Bulletin de l'AFIA 17: 19-42, 1994.

[Dojat and Pachet 1992]   M. Dojat and F. Pachet. *NéoGanesh: an extensible Knowledge-Based System for the Control of Mechanical Ventilation.* 14th IEEE-EMBS, Paris, p. 920-921, 1992.

[Dojat et al. 1995]   M. Dojat M. Harf, D. Touchard M. Laforest, H. Lemaire and L. Brochard. *Clinical evaluation of a knowledge-based system providing ventilatory management and decision for extubation during weaning from mechanical ventilation.* American Journal of Respiratory and Critical Care Medicine : to appear, 1995.

[Dojat and Sayettat 1996]   M. Dojat and C. Sayettat. *A realistic model for temporal reasoning in real-time patient monitoring.* Applied Artificial Intelligence : to appear in vol. 10 n°2, 1996.

[Durfee et al. 1987]   E. H. Durfee, V. Lesser, D. D. Corkill. *Coherent Cooperation Among Communicating Problem Solvers.* IEEE Transactions on Computers 36(11): 1275-1291, 1987.

[Erman et al. 1980]   L. D. Erman, F. Hayes-Roth, V. Lesser. *The Hearsay II speech understanding system: integrating knowledge to resolve uncertainty.* ACM Computing Surveys 12 (2), 1980.

[Ferber 1995]   J. Ferber. *Les systèmes multi-agents, vers une intelligence collective.* InterEditions, Paris, 1995.

[Ferber and Briot 1988]   J. Ferber and J-P. Briot. *Design of concurrent language for distributed artificial intelligence.* Proc. of International Conference on Fifth Generation Computer Systems, Tokyo, Icot, p. 755-762, 1988.

[Ferguson 1992]   I. A. Ferguson. *TouringMachines: An Architecture for Dynamic, Rational, Mobile Agents.* PhD thesis, Clare Hall, University of Cambridge, UK.

[Gasser 1992]   L. Gasser. *An Overview of DAI.* In Distributed Artificial Intelligence. N. M. Avouris and L. Gasser (eds.), Klewer Academic Publisher, Boston, 1992.

[Garvey and Lesser 1994]   A. Garvey and V. Lesser. A survey of research in deliberative real-time artificial intelligence. Journal of Real-Time Systems 6 (3): 313-347, 1994.

[Guessoum 1994]   Z. Guessoum. *Systèmes asynchrones de production.* Proc. of 2ème Journées IADSMA'94, Voiron, p. 169-180, 9-11 may, 1994.

[Guessoum 1995]   Z. Guessoum. *A framework integrating an object-oriented multi-agent system and discrete event simulation.* Proc. of First LAAS ICCS'95, Beirut, p. 165-173, 1995.

[Guessoum and Durand 1995]   Z. Guessoum and R. Durand. *Un système multi-agents pour modéliser l'évolution économique.* Report LAFORIA, to appear, 1995.

[Hayes-Roth 1985]   B. Hayes-Roth. *Blackboard architecture for control.* A rtificial Intelligence 26: 251-321, 1985.

203

[Hayes-Roth et al. 1992]   B. Hayes-Roth, R. Washington, D. Ash, R. Hewett, A. Collinot, A. Vina and A. Seiveur. *Guardian: a prototype intelligent agent for intensive-care monitoring.* Artificial Intelligence in Medicine 4: 165-185, 1992.

[Hewitt 1977]   C. Hewitt. *Viewing control structures as patterns of passing messages.* Artificial Intelligence 8 (3): 323-364, 1977.

[Ishida 1990]   T. Ishida. *Methods and effectiveness of parallel rule firing.* IEEE Conf. on Artificial Intelligence Applications, Washington, p. 116-122, 1990.

[Johnson 1994]   Johnson R. *How to Develop Frameworks*, Tutorial notes (10), 8th ECOOP'94, Bologna, 1994.

[Müller and Pischel 1994]   J.P. Müller and M. Pischel. *Modelling reactive behaviour in vertically layered agent architectures.* Proc. of ECAI'94, p. 709-713, Amsterdam, (NL), 1994.

[Musliner et al. 1995]   D. J. Musliner, J. A. Hendler, A. K. Agrawala, E. H. Durfee, J.K. Strosnider and C.J. Paul.. *The Challenge of Real-Time AI.* Computer (January): 58-66, 1995.

[Nii et al. 1989]   H. P. Nii, N. Aiello, J. Rice. *Experiments on Cage and Poligon: measuring the performance of parallel blackboard systems.* Distributed Artificial Intelligence. L. Gasser and M. N. Huhns. San Mateo (Ca), Morgan Kaufmann. 2: 319-383, 1989.

[Pachet 1992]   F. Pachet. *Représentation de connaissances par objets et règles : le système NéOpus.* PhD thesis, LAFORIA, Paris 6, 1992.

[Pachet and Perrot 1994]   F. Pachet and J-F. Perrot. *Rule Firing with MetaRules.* Proc. of SEKE'94, Jurmala, Latvia, p. 322-329, 1994.

[Pachet 1995]   F. Pachet. *On the Embeddability of Production Rules in Object-Oriented Languages.* Journal of Object-Oriented Programming 8(4): 19-24, 1995.

[Quaglini et al. 1992] S. Quaglini, R. Bellazi, C. Brzuini, M. Stefanelli and G. Barosi. *Hybrid Knowledge-Based Systems for Therapy Planning.* Artificial Intelligence in Medicine 4: 207-226, 1992.

[Shoham 1993] Y. Shoham. *Agent-Oriented Programming.* Artificial Intelligence 60: 139-159, 1993.

[Sukuvaara et al. 1993]   T. I. Sukuvaara, M. E. Sydänmaa, H.O. Nieminen, A. Heikelä and E. M. Koski. *Object-Oriented Implementation of an Architecture for Patient Monitoring.* IEEE Transactions in Biology Engineering 12 (4): 69-81, 1993.

[Wolinski 1994]   F. Wolinski. *RPC-Talk : une librairie RPC pour Smalltalk, Introduction à RPC et utilisations de RPC-Talk.* Report LAFORIA 94/26, November, 1994;

[Woods 1970]   W. Woods. *Transition Network Grammar for Natural Language Analysis.* Communication of Association of Computing Machinery 13 (10): 591-606, 1970.

[Yokote and Tokoro 1987]   Y. Yokote and M. Tokoro. *Experience and Evolution of Concurrent Smalltalk.* Proc. of OOPSLA'87, Orlando (USA), Special issue of SIGPLAN notices, ACM, p. 406-415, 1987.

[Yonezawa et al. 1986]   A. Yonezawa, J-P. Briot, E. Shibayama. *Object-Oriented Concurrent Programming in ABCL/1.* Proc. of OOPSLA'86, Portland (USA), Special issue of SIGPLAN notices, ACM, p. 258-268, 1986.

Coalition Formation Among Rational Information Agents

Matthias Klusch[1] and Onn Shehory[2]

[1] Institut für Informatik,
Christian-Albrechts-University Kiel,
24118 Kiel, Germany
e-mail: *mkl@informatik.uni-kiel.d400.de*
[2] Department of Mathematic & Computer Science,
Bar Ilan University,
Ramat Gan, 52900 Israel
e-mail: *shechory@bimacs.cs.biu.ac.il*

Abstract. Information agents can be an important tool for information-gathering and query-answering for the expanding WWW service as well as the large number of existing autonomous databases. Such agents behave like active intelligent front-ends of the stand-alone information systems. Information agents may work as individuals trying to satisfy thier own query-answering, i.e., a set of given information search tasks. However, they must cooperate efficiently with one another in order to gather information in non-local domains. In this paper we present an approach for cooperation and coalition formation among information agents for heterogeneous databases. In order to deal with the required association autonomy of these agents, we have developed a special decentralized coalition formation mechanism. It allows individually rational cooperation among the agents for information search. The semi-automatic creation of a local terminological information model enables each agent to hide local schema data as well as allowing for automated search-task processing. Knowledge-based productions from information search-tasks are sets of terminological interdatabase dependencies. These productions are obtained by classifying the search term of the task according to the local information model. An underlying cooperation convention in this federative agent system is that only members of a fixed coalition are mutually committed to provide the availability of all of the local information that they have used for building this particular coalition.

1 Introduction

Since the last decade there is a growing interest in coupling a set of already existing, heterogeneous and autonomous database systems. Active interoperability of databases in the sense of task-oriented cooperation between respectively attached intelligent front-ends has led to the paradigm of cooperative information systems introduced in [25]. Dependencies between data in different databases are called interdatabase dependencies (IDD). Any declarative specification of IDDs like in [32], [11] or [10] presumes somehow gained knowledge about where to find which kind of semantically related data. The recognition of such relations is needed e.g. for being able to specify queries which span several heterogeneous, autonomous databases or just discover the available distributed non-local information space as it is the case in a multidatabase environment. Most works towards the interoperability of databases, like the well-known approach of federated databases[31], or recent efforts in cooperative information gathering, presumes that this recognition problem is already solved or ignore the required strict autonomy of each database. The first approach for recognizing such interdatabase dependencies in a decentralized and autonomous environment by rationally cooperating information agents was introduced in [17],[18] and [19]. It utilizes methods from both research areas, distributed artificial intelligence (DAI) and terminological knowledge representation and reasoning. No centralized global or partial schema integration takes place. A federative agent system FCSI[3] is constituted by a set of autonomous information agents which behave like intelligent front-ends for the database each of them is uniquely associated with. In order to be able to search for relevant non-local schema-data while protecting the own local schema structure each of them builds a local terminological information model LIM on top of its conceptual database schema. Mutual terminological classification of parts of their information models enables them for an automated search as well as local processing of requested search terms. There is no need for a central mediator or information broker agent. The cooperative information search and selective data sharing is driven by an utilitarian coalition formation process.

The remainder of this paper is organized as follows. Section 2 contains an introductory overview of the related research areas of federated databases and terminological knowledge representation. Section 3 briefly describes the FCSI approach for cooperative information search. A short overview of utilitarian coalition formation in DAI is in Section 4, while the special coalition types and a new decentralized formation algorithm for the FCSI is described in section 5.

2 A Brief Introduction to Some Related Research Areas

2.1 Federated Database Systems

The following short introduction bases on the work of [31].

A *federated database system* (FDBS) is a collection of cooperating but autonomous component databases. In contrast to a distributed database system a FDBS is created in a bottom-up fashion, i.e., by a partial integration of already pre-existing databases while respecting particularly their association autonomy and solving the semantic heterogeneity between them. Semantic heterogeneity occurs when there is a disagreement about the meaning or intended use of the same or related data, like homonyms, synonyms, value or domain conflicts as presented e.g. in [10]. Association autonomy implies that each component database decides itself which kind of its private schema-data in the local conceptual schema it is willing to share. There is no centralized control for data sharing in a federated architecture.

The development of a FDBS includes the equivalent translation of the given local schemas into homogeneous *component schemas* using a canonical data model, the definition of the available parts of these component schemas as *export schemas* and finally their integration into a *federated schema* of a federation leading to a five-level schema architecture. An *external schema* defines a schema or view customized for each user. The *federal data dictionary or directory* is for auxiliary purposes. It includes e.g. information about the translations, mappings and the addresses of the federation participants. Federated databases can be further classified with respect to who creates and manages the federation and how the component databases are integrated. A *tightly coupled* FDBS provides location, replication, and distribution transparency. This is accomplished by developing a federated schema that integrates multiple export schemas. The transparencies are provided by the mappings between the federated and the export schemas such that the user can pose a query against one single or multiple federation schemas without knowing where the requested data is

---

[3] FCSI is a shortcut for 'Federative Cell System for discovery of Interdatabase dependencies'.

located. A central federation administrator defines and manages the federated schema and the external schemas related to it. There may exist a single or multiple federated schemas within one tightly-coupled FDBS.

In contrast, in *loosely coupled* systems no global or partial static schema integration takes place and no transparency is provided. Instead of a central federation administrator, the user himself must find the appropriate export schemas that can provide the required data, and then to define the respective mapping operations. Systems which base on dynamic integration of export schemas by the use of an extended query language (e.g. MSQL[22]), are also called Multidatabase-Language Systems [8].

Following [11], interdependent data are data which are related by an integrity constraint specifying their mutual dependency. Kinds of semantic heterogeneity determine respective interdatabase dependencies. Examples of interdependent data include replicated data, partially replicated data or summary data. Approaches for a declarative or functional specification of such dependencies can be found e.g. in [32], [11] and [10]. The approach of [32] denotes directed data dependencies by a logical predicate using relational algebra while in [10] a SQL-based language is used for this purpose. We omit the description of other approaches here.

To enable the specification of interdatabase dependencies, the locations of various related data must be known. That is, it is necessary to know how to acquire this relevance knowledge and how to automate the underlying decentralized search for such intensional relationships. Some criticism on federated database systems as in [25] state in particular their lack of support with respect to the recognition and maintenance of interdatabase dependencies. In loosely coupled federated databases no global integrity constraints can be expressed across sites, because no mechanism exists to detect the underlying data relationships and then to enforce them. In tightly coupled FDBS, where the local export schemas are integrated into a fixed federated schema by the central administrator, some descriptive information about the local semantics of the available schema-data must be provided in advance. The IDD recognition process shall be performed without any efforts at static schema integration, or necessity for the user to browse through known export schemas, as required in tightly coupled and loosely coupled FDBS, respectively. One main drawback of browsing through export schemas is that the local interpretation of importable, non-local schema structures is heavily burden to the potential importer and relies on the unique mutual understanding of the semantic descriptions attached to these schema-data by the exporter. Besides, all parts of one export schema are visible in the same degree for all participants in the federation as well as for others.

The FCSI provides an approach for cooperatively discovering intensionally related data in a decentralized and autonomous environment by utilizing techniques from terminological knowledge representation and reasoning.

2.2 Terminological Knowledge Representation

Terminological knowledge representation and reasoning deal with investigations of *description logics*. Most of them are decidable fragments of first-order predicate logic and much more expressive than propositional logic. They are based on the work of Brachman and Schmolze, the KL-ONE System[7]. Such terminological or concept languages provide a structured formalism to axiomatically describe the relevant *concepts* of an application domain and the interactions between these concepts using *roles*. Concepts and roles can be seen as unary and binary predicates, respectively. Complex concepts will be inductively build from primitive components or atomic concepts and roles by given *term-forming operators*. A *terminology* (Tbox) is a set of such complete or partial definitions, i.e. *terminological axioms*, of named concepts and roles. Unlike in other conceptual or semantic data models it is possible to describe concepts and roles using intensional descriptions phrased only in terms of necessary but not sufficient properties that must be satisfied by their instances. Common term-forming operators are, among others, conjunction and complement for concepts, and number and value restrictions for roles. In addition, concrete domain objects can be explicitly asserted as concept instances and related to other objects via roles by a set of *assertional axioms* (Abox). This is similar to the classical distinction between the schema and state level in the database area. The terminological and the assertional formalism together constitute a *hybrid knowledge representation language*. *Classification* of some concept into a given terminology bases on the notion of *subsumption*. One concept subsumes another if, in all possible worlds, its set of instances is contained in that of the other. It is possible to determine subsumption between concepts as well as roles only by considering their given terminological definitions and a structural comparison of respective terms. This leads to a *subsumption hierarchy* of named terms, the concept and the role taxonomy.

Although for almost all expressive description logics term-subsumption is decidable (it is decidable for $\mathcal{ALC}$[34], but not for KL-ONE [27]), its computation is inherently intractable [24]. Thus, for pragmatic reasons most terminological systems use an incomplete but polynomial subsumption algorithm (e.g. CLASSIC[6] or KRIS[1]). For a more details on hybrid terminological knowledge representation and reasoning we refer the reader to [23].

3 FCSI Information Agents

The FCSI approach for recognizing interdatabase dependencies in a decentralized and autonomous environment works without any effort in centralized global or partial schema integration. There is also no need to browse through other export schemas like in loosely-coupled federated databases in order to find some available and possibly intensional relevant schema-data. An agent will be provided only with the necessary descriptions for semantical interpretation of imported schema parts for local processing, but it will not have access to the local schema-data which is linked to this description. The federative agent system FCSI is constituted by a set of autonomous information agents which are each the front-end of the database with which it is uniquely associated (cf. Fig. 1).

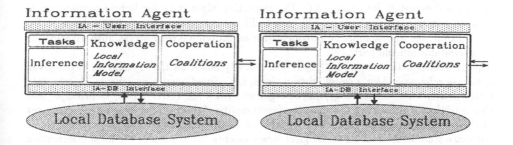

Fig. 1. FCSI Information Agents

To enable automatic search for relevant non-local schema-data, yet protect the own local schema structure, each agent builds a local terminological information model LIM on top of its conceptual database schema. A mutual terminological classification of parts of their information-models enables the agents for an automated search as well as local processing of requested search terms. No central mediator or information broker agent is necessary. There are several possibilities for an agent to construct its LIM, all rely on terminological knowledge representation methods.

The search for relevant data is achieved by a rational cooperation among the FCSI information agents which is performed via a decentralized, utilitarian coalition formation (cf. Sects. 4, 5). Based on the discovery of some interdatabase dependencies, each agent can then pose directed, intensional data requests to the respective members of the same coalition.

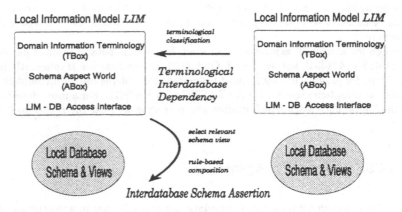

Fig. 2. Recognition of Interdatabase Dependencies

Essentially, a local information model LIM entails a more linguistic based, i.e., a terminological description of a given set of views or aspects of database schema-objects. It has the following three components: a local **Domain Information Terminology DIT** (TBox), the **Schema Aspect World W** (ABox) as its instantiation and the internal **LIM-DB Interface** as an DB Access Interface. For construction purposes an *information terminological formalism* ITF as well as a *schema aspect assertional formalism* SAF as its conservative extension[23] is available. ITF provides some most usual term-forming operators such as conjunction of concepts, number, value and existential restriction for roles as well as atomic concept negation and attribute sets. Both formalisms constitute together the hybrid terminological description language $\mathcal{ITL}$. The respective algorithms for hybrid terminological reasoning in this language are used by each FCSI agent to create its own LIM automatically. In addition, the agents must be provided with an individual read-access authorization for each available schema part.

The LIM construction-methods ([16, 18]) are mostly based on the translation of the given database schema and/or a set of schema-views, i.e. named queries on schema-objects, into a (schema or view) terminology, maybe together with a respective ABox. In principle, the choice of the $\mathcal{ITL}$ does not influence the functionality of the FCSI agents. However, the set of their term-forming operators restricts the set of schema-views which are compilable to database state-equivalent terminological view concepts [4]. Creation of the local information model and linking of available schema data into this terminological knowledge base is done semi-automatically by the information agent. Each local schema-view has a twofold description: first at intensional (i.e., terminological) level, it is described by a compiled *aspect*

---

[4] Obviously, there exist several alternatives for hybrid terminological reasoning within each agent like the more expressive $\mathcal{ALCNR}$ [34].

term and second, at database schema and state level, by the respective view qualification constraint.

Thus, each FCSI information agent is able to detect two different kinds of interdatabase dependencies: first, a *terminological interdatabase dependency (i-IDD)* by a mutual terminological classification of terminological view descriptions into the LIM of another information agent and then, projecting down to the local schema; second, an *interdatabase schema assertion (IDSA)* by rule-based composition of both of the underlying view-qualification constraints, formulated in the local DML into a global integrity constraint. This is comparable e.g. to the boolean-valued data dependency predicate in [32].

For example, the terminological interdatabase dependency $p - intsub(o_1, o_2, M, N)$ means that schema-object o_1 is partially, intensionally subsumed by the schema-object o_2. This bases on the detected term-subsumptions concerning some of the aspect terms of o_1 as given in the set M by those aspect terms of o_2 in the set N. The complete definitions and processes can be found in [16, 18, 20]. A simple example is provided below.

Example 1:

Let FCSI agent a_2 have the following representations of its schema-view 'female person' (vid_2) of the schema-object 'Person' (wrt. its own LIM): (and Mensch$_p$ Frau$_p$ (not Mann$_p$)) and the linked view qualification constraint $(p.WM =' W')$, and let FCSI agent a_1 have the following aspect term for its schema-view 'female student' (vid_1) of the schema-object 'Student' (wrt. its own LIM):
(and Human$_p$ Woman$_p$ Student$_p$ (not Man$_p$) (all has $-$ child$_p$ Child$_p$)
(atleast has $-$ child$_p$ 1)(atmost has $-$ child$_p$ 3)).
Then 'female persons' of agent a_2 terminologically subsumes 'female Student' of agent a_1.

- **cooperative recognition of terminological interdatabase dependencies:**

FCSI Agent a_1:   **FCSI Agent a_2:**

FIND-Task: FIND-Task:
- aspect term for 'female student'   - aspect term for 'female person'
- $p - intsub(Student, ?, \{vid_1\}, \{?\})$ - $p - intsub(?, Person, \{?\}, \{vid_2\})$

exchange and process tasks: produce task satisfying terminological interdatabase dependencies;
try to rationally coalesce with other information agent:
   determine utilities and coalition offers (cf. Sect. 5)

Information Availability within a Coalition (IAC Convention):
All members of a coalition are mutually committed to provide
the availability of their local schema information they used for
building exactly this coalition.

- **Intensional Data Request:**

FCSI Agent a_1:   **FCSI Agent a_2:**

'Names of Persons related to female Students'
request-for *Name* **from** *Person* **wrt** vid_2 check $(Person, vid_2)$:
                                              get view vid_2 qualification constraint ;
                                              compile into local EER-DML query:
                                                 retrieve $p.Name$ from $Person$
                                                 where $p.WM =' W'$

A search task (FIND-task) is satisfied iff the result of the included PROLOG-query is not empty, means any terminological interdatabase dependency of the requested type satisfies this task. The required coalition information availability (IAC) has several impacts. One is that an agent has to send an aspect term included in a FIND-task to other agents only if it is a description of an own local schema-view, which will be available for them in cases of cooperation. Other impacts of the IAC assumption on coalition formation will be described in Sect. 5.

4 Coalition Formation in DAI

Distributed artificial intelligence (DAI) is concerned with problem solving in which several agents interact in order to achieve goals. During the past few years, several solutions to the coalition formation problem have been presented by researchers in the field of DAI [28, 30, 26, 15, 38]. These solutions are appropriate for a variety of environments (TOD's, superadditive and general environments). Some are appropriate for individually rational agents while others are designed for cases of bounded rationality. There are models that were designed for Distributed Problem Solvers (DPS) systems while others were developed for Multi-Agent systems (MAS). While some of these solutions are based on concepts from game theory, others are based on operations research, graph theory and algorithmic aspects of combinatorics.

Cooperation among autonomous agents may be mutually beneficial even if the agents are selfish and try to maximize their own expected payoffs [21, 35, 37]. Mutual benefit may arise from resource sharing and task redistribution. Coalition formation is an important method for cooperation in multi-agent environments. Agent membership in a coalition may increase the agent's ability to satisfy goals and maximize either the personal or the system's outcome. This may lead designers of computational agent-systems to adopt such methods. Facing the variety of coalition formation methods, designers of distributed computational agent-systems may be puzzled when trying to incorporate such a mechanism into their system. Game theory, which is most commonly employed by DAI researchers, usually answers the question of what coalition will form, and what reasons and processes will lead the agents to form a particular coalition among all possible coalitions. The designers of agent-systems are mostly interested in the question of which procedure should their agents use to coordinate their actions, cooperate and, if necessary, form a coalition. They must take into consideration the constraints of a multi-agent environment, such as communication costs and limited computation time. This was done by the DAI researchers that have provided coalition formation models. However, when a specific agent-system is been dealt with, the coalition formation methods shall be thoroughly examined before adopted, and well adapted to fit the special properties of the specific system. Otherwise, even the best coalition formation algorithm may lead to a poor performance of the system.

In this paper we adjust a DAI coalition formation method to a set of cooperating, autonomous database systems in which each database is represented by an autonomous information agent. As described in the previous section, these agents are autonomous individually rational agents. That is, they try to increase their own personal benefits, and not necessarily the outcome of the system as a whole. The tasks of the agents are query-answering tasks (cf. Sect.3, Example 1). We assume that the agents (or their owners) receive some kind of payment for the answers to these queries, and that there is an agreed-upon method to assess the monetary or abstract utility value of each query before it was answered. Upon these properties, we seek a coalition formation method for rational agents in a MAS, that will not be limited to superadditive environments. However, we must adjust the method we adopt to the information agents case. In particular, the privacy of information as well as the coalition information availability convention (IAC) mentioned in Sect.3 has to be taken into consideration. Following the IAC assumption, members of a newly-formed coalition have to reveal some of their private information to others in the same coalition. Such a requirement constrains the coalition formation, because it may affect the advisability of the coalition for its members. The details of the adjusted coalition formation procedure are in the next section.

5 Coalitions of FCSI Agents

The main aim of utilitarian coalition building is to increase the ability of the FCSI agents to satisfy their search tasks via cooperation, thus increasing their benefits. The coalition formation in this case requires to find partitions of the agents with respect to their utilities. These utilities are calculated and result from the execution of either the agents' own search tasks or tasks that they receive from other FCSI agents. If the agents are rational, then such partitions, or coalitions, will form iff each member of a coalition will gain more if it joins the coalition than it could gain by itself previously. However, in the special case of FCSI information agents this requirement is not sufficient. The need to respect the association autonomy of the databases, each represented by a FCSI agent, implies that the coalition formation procedure should not allow coalitions in which there are information-agents that do not explicitly cooperate. This is because the formation of a coalition causes that the members of the potential coalition reveal some of their information to one another (in particular the aspect term and desired type of terminological interdatabase dependency as included in a search task). Thus, they already lose some of their privacy during the coalition formation. In cases of no cooperation, the agents prevent the access to the respective schema information that they would have allowed the committed coalition members. Therefore, an agent that decides to avoid the membership in a potential coalition during the formation process, will have access only to the information that will tell it what do the other agents search for, in terms of the terminological descriptions that it received from them. It will not get their respectively associated local schema-data. Hence, only coalitions in which all of the members have to cooperate are allowed in the FCSI environment.

The IAC convention that all of the FCSI coalitions must respect differentiates them from both the common game theoretic coalitions types and the existing DAI approaches to coalitions. For coalition formation within the FCSI we adapted the production-oriented approach of Shehory and Kraus[28]. The agents' utility functions are calculated with respect to the agents' utility from their own knowledge-based productions, obtained by execution of received or own FIND-tasks (cf. Table 1). The utility that an agent obtains when it sat-

Table 1. Let $\mathcal{A}$ set of n FCSI agents, $a_i, a_k, a_j \in \mathcal{A}, C \subseteq \mathcal{A}, p(t^{a_k}_{tid_x, a_j})$ knowledge-based production of agent a_k for search task t_{tid_x} it received from agent a_j, $Prod_{a_k, C}$ set of agent a_k's productions for search tasks received from agents of potential coalition $C \subseteq \mathcal{A}$, C_i coalition without a_i, C_i^π set of agents without agent a_i according to the permutation π on $\mathcal{A}$ before a_i ($\mid S_n \mid= n!$).

Agent Utility Function	$U^{type}_{agent_{id}}(p(t^{a_k}_{tid_x, a_j}))$, with production $p(t^{a_k}_{tid_x, a_j})$
Coalition Value	$v(C)$: $\mathcal{P}(\mathcal{A}) \mapsto \mathbb{R}^+,$
	$v(C) := \sum_{a_k \in C, \, p \in Prod_{a_k}, C} U_k(p)$
Marginal Contribution of Agent a_i	
to Coalition C_i	$v(C_i \cup \{a_i\}) - v(C_i)$
Self-Value of Agent a_i	$v(\{a_i\})$
Shapley-Value of agent a_i	$sv_C(a_i) := \frac{1}{n!} \sum_\pi (v(C_i^\pi \cup \{a_i\}) - v(C_i^\pi))$
bilateral Shapley-Value for 2-agent entities	$sv_{\{a_i, a_j\}}(a_i) = \frac{1}{2}v(\{a_i\}) + \frac{1}{2}(v(\{a_j, a_i\}) - v(\{a_i\}))$
Individual Rationality	$sv_C(a_i) \geq v(\{a_i\})$

Different types of agent utility functions lead to respectively different coalition types.

isfies its own tasks exclusively by itself is denoted as the agent's self-value. The coalition value is the sum of these utilities of all its potential coalition members. Considering the marginal contributions of agents to all possible coalitions and computing their averaged sum leads to a fair division of the coalition value to all members using the agents' Shapley values [13]. For bilateral coalition negotiation we obtain a more simple term for its calculation. We assume that the agents know of the coalition value function and agree on the utility division method. The currently used coalition negotiation algorithm for building fair coalition configurations bases on [14] (cf. section 5.2).

5.1 FCSI Coalition Types

One FCSI coalition type, the so-called *task interaction coalition type* (C_{ti}) bases on the notion of FIND-task *interaction*. This means that one terminological dependency, which satisfies the goal of the received as well as an own FIND-task, was found. The amount of such task interactions determines the agent's utility on its task-oriented productions, i.e. the terminological dependencies, for this special type of coalition (cf. Table 2).

Table 2. Task Interaction Coalition Type C_{ti}

$$\text{FIND-}task\ interaction \quad t^{a_i}_{tid_1,a_j} \xrightarrow{<intrel>(o_k,o_j,M,N)} t^{a_i}_{tid_2} :\Leftrightarrow$$

$$\text{i-IDD} < intrel > \text{satisfies \underline{both} FIND-Tasks}$$

$$C_{ti}\text{-}utility\ function\ U^{ti}_k \quad U^{ti}_k(p(t^{a_k}_{tid_x,a_j})) := | \{t^{a_k}_{tid_x,a_j} \xrightarrow{<ir>(o_k,o_j,M,N)} t^{a_k}_{tid_y}\} | \in \mathbb{N}_0$$

$$C_{ti}\text{-}coalition\ value \quad v_{ti}(\mathcal{C}) = \sum\nolimits_{a_k \in C, p \in Prod_{a_k,C}} U^{ti}_k(p)$$

Each rational FCSI agent tries to coalesce with other FCSI agents which would maximize its own utility in satisfying its FIND-tasks as much as possible. The detailed algorithm for local determination of task interactions between two FCSI-agents can be found in [16].

Example 2:

Consider the FCSI agents $\{a_1, a_2\} = \mathcal{A}$ as in the examples above, and suppose both aspect terms as part of mutually exchanged FIND-tasks $t^{a_1}_{y,a_2}, t^{a_2}_{x,a_1}$. According to their respective local knowledge about each other, both agents are able to determine FIND-task interactions, e.g. $t^{a_1}_{y,a_2} \xrightarrow{p-intsub(Student,Person,\{vid_1\},\{vid_2\})} t^{a_1}_{x}$ by agent a_1. Further, let their self-values be $v_{ti}(\{a_1\}) = 0$ and $v_{ti}(\{a_2\}) = 3$, i.e. only agent a_2 can satisfy 3 of its own FIND-tasks exclusively by itself through considering all reflexive task-interactions induced by dependencies relating local objects.

This yields $v_{ti}(\{a_1, a_2\}) = v_{ti}(\{a_1\}) + v_{ti}(\{a_2\}) + U^{ti}_1(\{p - intsub(Student, Person, \{vid_1\}, \{vid_2\})\})$ $+ U^{ti}_2(\{p - intsub(Student, Person, \{vid_1\}, \{vid_2\})\}) = 0 + 3 + 1 + 1 = 5$, thus for the marginal contribution of a_1 to $\{a_2\}$: $5 - 3 = 2$ and in turn for a_2: 5 - 0 = 5, which leads to the agents' bilateral Shapley-values $sv_{\{a_1,a_2\}}(a_1) = 1$, $sv_{\{a_1,a_2\}}(a_2) = 4$. Since their fair individual rationality is fulfilled and since no better offer from other agents exists, both agents try to coalesce with each other. They are then mutually committed to get access to all respective schema-views by some now mutually allowed intensional data requests. □

There exist other coalition types within the FCSI which do not restrict the productions utility to such mutual task satisfaction. E.g. the C_{atsat} coalition type relies exclusively on the amount of satisfied own and submitted FIND-tasks, wherein the agent utility for the C_{otsat} type considers the amount of all satisfied own FIND-tasks independent from the fact that they were submitted to the satisfying agent. The 'benevolent' agent utility function for C_{tserv} coalitions considers only the satisfaction of the received tasks of an agent as a server. In addition, we currently investigate agent utility functions which take in addition the *quality of search task satisfactions* into consideration. Such utility bases heavily on uncertain terminological interdatabase dependencies, thus leading to uncertain FIND-task satisfaction. At the physical level one could imagine utility functions which base, for example, on transportation costs, including the amount of visited nodes as well as probable sizes of potentially requested relevant schema-data, and so on.

5.2 Decentralized Coalition Formation Between FCSI Agents

The method for coalition formation between FCSI agents is a modification of the decentralized, bilateral coalition formation algorithm in [14] adapted for the cooperative recognition process within the FCSI [16]. A brief summary of the main steps in the FCSI coalition process is given as follows.

1. communication

   for each agent:
   - ▶ if in the first round:
     send to each agent a set of aspect terms. The local own schema-data which are associated to these terms have to be available for the receiving agent;
   - ▶ if not in the first round: send to each negotiation entity the own self-value.

2. local calculation of utilities on coalition participation

   for each agent:
   - ▶ produce for each received FIND-task all possible i-IDDs (cf. section 3.2)

   for each coalition type:
   - ▶ compute the own utility on these productions and respective coalition values
   - ▶ determine an individually rational *preference list of agents*:
     ordered list of local agent's 'bilateral Shapley-Values' for particular two-entity coalitions

3. bilateral negotiation about coalition offer

   for each agent:
   - ▶ consider head of the preference list, means the agent who provides the maximum utility
   - ▶ lookup for an alternative coalition from the tail of the list as follows:
     calculate an alternative coalition value by successively adding the values from the tail of the preference list until the sum is greater than the particular value of the head[5].

For the alternative coalition it is required that there are no interdatabase dependencies detected between the head and at least one member of it. Moreover, each pair of members of the alternative coalition should have recognized at least one mutual dependency[6].

   - ▶ request the members of the alternative coalition for the existence of interrelation between them: an interrelation is constituted by the mutual recognition of at least one i-IDD;

---

[5] This calculation is limited by 2, at most the local agent's preference value for the head plus 1.
[6] These conditions must hold in order to enable the agents to satisfy the information availability within a coalition (IAC) as mentioned in section 3.

Note that this requires just the current value of a boolean flag and not any further information concerning which schema-data the respective interdatabase dependency relates. Each flag reflects the existence of an interrelation between the requested agent and the rest of the candidates of the alternative coalition. It will be false if at least one interrelation does not exist.

▶ Upon this information choose between the head and the alternative coalition: having received all the flags from the requested agents of the alternative coalition if all of them are true choose the alternative coalition, otherwise choose the head.

▶ Send coalition offers: if the head was chosen then send its 'Shapley-Value' for the mutual two-entity coalition as a coalition offer, otherwise send the respective values to all the candidates of the alternative coalition.

4. coalition commitment

for each agent:
for each coalition type:
▶ receive offers for coalition formation
▶ select the maximum value of these offers
▶ if and only if the agent who sends this maximum is also preferred by the (receiving) agent they commit to coalesce with each other in a proto-coalition.
▶ if all of the candidates of the alternative coalition or atleast one of them have rejected the respective offer, means that this coalition proposal is not valid for the agent anymore: Get the information about the other proto-coalitions formed by these candidates and then erase all the members of these announced proto-coalitions from the preference list[7].
▶ consider such a proto-coalition as one negotiation entity; repeat the process until no new proto-coalition is formed and then fix them.

The most calculation consuming step of this algorithm is the local calculation one. There, each agent a_i performs $o(s_i \cdot m_i)$ computational operations [8]. All other steps require less than this amount of computations. There are $o(n^2)$ bilateral inter-agent communications. The number of rounds is limited by $n - 1$. Therefore the overall communication complexity is cubic, the computational complexity in terms of classification operations is $o((\sum_{a_i \in \mathcal{A}} s_i \cdot m_i) \cdot n - 1)$.
Each agent can participate at several coalitions of different types by concurrent coalition negotiations for each different type of a FCSI coalition utility. This enables a fine-grained mutual utilitarian assessment between the information agents. Since proto-coalitions are treated as an negotiation entity in the following round during the coalition formation, as an impact of the above mentioned information availability assumption (IAC) all values have to be recomputed. In particular, any coalition entity has to compute its self-value with respect to the agents currently staying outside their coalition and vice versa. This means that only the so-called *contributable amount* of the self-value of an 1- or n-agent coalition

---

[7] Note that this deletion prevents considering the possible number of partitions which would result in an overall exponential complexity of coalition formation. The same is valid in [14].

[8] Note that $| \mathcal{A} |= n$, let $s_i := \sum_{a_j \in \mathcal{A} \setminus \{a_i\}} | RecT_{a_j}^{a_i} | \cdot m$, with m_i number of local aspect terms from a_i's LIM which have to be classified against search (aspect) terms (included in the set of search tasks of a_i from a_j: $RecT_{a_j}^{a_i} := \{t_{tid_x, a_i}^{a_i}\}$) received from other agents in $\mathcal{A} \setminus \{a_i\}$.

entity will be brought in the next calculation step[9]. We can distinguish between two kinds agent's rational behaviour: being fairly rational in the sense that it compares the received coalition offers, means the bilateral Shapley-values as expected participation utilities, with the respectively contributable amounts of its self-value; being selfish rational if these comparisons are done with respect to its whole self-value which is not necessarily known by the other agents. Since the second type may lead to coalitions of deceiving information agents, hence violate the IAC assumption, FCSI agents are committed to the first type of individually rational behaviour.

6 Conclusion

The shortly proposed FCSI realizes a cooperative, decentralized search for semantically related data in heterogeneous and autonomous databases by the use of:

- *Local, Terminological Information Models*
  on top of local conceptual database schema;

- Recognition of *terminological dependencies* (i-IDD) and
  respectively induced *interdatabase schema assertions* (IDSA);

- *Utilitarian Coalition Formation* between FCSI Agents;

- *Directed Intensional Requests* for semantically related data.

Thus it enables the user to discover some intensionally relevant data without the need to browse through all available schema structures first without any help. In particular it is even not possible to get access to the local schema or state level before any utilitarian coalition commitment with other rational agents is fixed. Data Dependency recognition is exclusively done by the FCSI agents at information type level, i.e. by formal terminological classification of some considered aspect term independent from its actually attached and sofar protected data structures. This is similar to the idea of incrementally building and using some shared ontology for contextual interchange[4] respecting association autonomy[31]. Thus, possible data sharing as well as proposing global integrity constraints (IDSAs) is determined by the necessarily prior success and kind of such mutual aspect term classification and restricted on the respective aspect valuations specified by user. There has been only little related research on using formal terminological classification for the object discovery problem like in [9]. Recent works on system approaches which have influenced the FCSI approach are in particular [4] and [12]. Other partially related works are [2] and [3]. In contrast to our work, [33] aims for schema integration. Since cooperation as well as the acquisition and propagation of knowledge about data relevance between autonomous FCSI agents rely on decentralized, utilitarian coalition building there exists no global information agent [3] or central mediator agent [4]. Terminological representation and corresponding classification enables in particular an automated, local processing.

The main benefit of the proposed algorithm for coalition formation is that in the case of non-superadditive environments it prevents building a coalition which after its formation needs an internal, complex commitment agreement about data sharing among its mem-

---

[9] Based on the recomputation of contributable amounts of coalition values it is possible that such a value for a potential coalition is *less* than the sum of both entities self-values like in a non-superadditive environment.

[10] This material also bases on work supported in part by the NSF under grant No. IRI-9123967 and the Israeli Science Ministry grant No. 6288.

bers. This is because in contrast to the original application of the coalition algorithm of [14] as it is presented in [18] each agent receives more information about existing interrelations among its preferred agents. Exchange of this additional information is done without violating the demanded autonomy of the respective agents. Towards an implementation of FCSI agents an *Interactive Development Environment for the specification and simulation of Agent Systems* IDEAS [20] has been recently implemented on a network of SUN-workstations. Ongoing research on the FCSI includes the formal description of an FCSI agent, its possible implementation in IDEAS and further investigations on coalition formation in the FCSI for cooperative information search.

Acknowledgements:
We would like to thank Prof. Dieter Klusch, Prof. Peter Kandzia and Prof. Sarit Kraus for supporting this work by giving many helpfully hints and advices[10].

References

1. Baader,F., Hollunder,B., 1991, "A Terminological Knowledge Representation System with complete inference algorithms", LNAI 567, Springer
2. Beck, H.W., et al., 1989,"Classification as a query processing technique in the CANDIDE SDM",IEEE Computer
3. Barbuceanu,M., Fox,M.S., 1994,"The information agent: an infrastructure for collaboration in the integrated enterprise", Proc. CKBS-94, Keele(UK)
4. Behrendt,W., et al., 1993,"Using an intelligent agent to mediate multibase information access",Proc. CKBS-93, Keele(UK)
5. Blanco,J.M. et al., 1994, "Building a federated relational database systems: an approach using a knowledge-based system", Intern. Journal on Intelligent Coop. Inform. Syst. 3(4)
6. Borgida, A. et al., 1989,"CLASSIC: a structural data model for objects",ACM SIGMOD
7. Brachman,R.J., Schmolze,J.G., 1985, "An overview of the KL-ONE knowledge representation system", Cognitive Science
8. Bright,M.W., Hurson,A.R., 1991, "Multidatabasesystems: an advanced concept in handling distributed data", Advances in Computers
9. Catarci,T., Lenzerini,M., 1993,"Representing and using interschema knowledge in cooperative Information Systems", in IJICIS 2(4)
10. Ceri, S., Widom, J., 1992,"Managing semantic heterogeneity with production rules and persistent queues", Politecnico Milano TR 92-078
11. Elmagarmid, E., Zhang, A., 1992,"Enforceable interdatabase constraints in combining multiple autonomous databases", Purdue Tech. Rep. CSD-TR-92-008
12. Hammer,J., et al., 1993,"Object discovery and unification in FDBS",IEEE RIDE-93,Wien
13. Kahan/Rapoport, 1984, *Theories of coalition formation*, Lawrence Erlbaum, London
14. Ketchpel, S., 1993,"Coalition formation among autonomous agents", Proc. MAAMAW-93
15. Ketchpel, S., 1994, "Forming coalitions in the face of uncertain rewards", Proc. AAAI-94, Seattle, Washington
16. Klusch, M., 1996, *Rational kooperative Erkennung von Interdatenbankabhängigkeiten*, Dissertation, Computer Science Dept., University of Kiel, (in preparation)
17. Klusch, M., 1994,"Using a cooperative agent system for a context-based recognition of interdatabase dependencies", Proc. CIKM-94 Workshop on 'Intelligent Information Agents', Gaithersburg (USA)
18. Klusch, M., 1995, "Cooperative Recognition of Interdatabase Dependencies", ACM SIGMOD Proc. 2. Intern. Workshop on Advances in Databases and Information Systems, Moscow
19. Klusch, M., 1995, "Coalition-based cooperation between intelligent agents for a contextual recognition of interdatabase dependencies", Proc. ICMAS-95, San Francisco
20. Klusch, M., 1996, "Utilitarian coalition formation between information agents for a cooperative discovery of interdatabase dependencies", appears in: S. Kirn / G. O'Hare (Eds.), *Cooperative Knowledge Processing*, 1996, Springer Verlag, London

21. Kraus, S., 1993, "Agents contracting tasks in non-collaborative environments", Proc. AAAI-93, Washington D.C.
22. Litwin,W., 1985,"An overview of the Multidatabase System MRDSM",ACM Nation.Conf.
23. Nebel. B., 1990, *Reasoning and revision in hybrid representation systems*, LNAI 422, Springer
24. Nebel. B., 1990, "Terminological reasoning is inherently intractable", AI 43
25. Papazoglou et al.,1992,"An organizational framework for intelligent cooperative IS",IJICIS-1(1)
26. Sandholm,T., Lesser,V., 1995, "Coalition formation among bounded rational agents", Proc.IJCAI-95, Montrèal
27. Schmidt-Schauss,M., 1989, "Subsumption in KL-ONE is undecidable", Proc. 1. Int. Conf. on Principles of Knowledge Repr. & Reason., Toronto
28. Shehory,O., Kraus,S., 1993, "Coalition formation among autonomous agents: Strategies and complexity", Proc. MAAMAW-93,Neuchâtel
29. Shehory,O. Kraus,S., 1994, "Feasible formation of stable coalitions in general environments", Technical Report, Institute for Advanced Computer Studies, University of Maryland
30. Shehory,O. Kraus,S., 1995, "Task allocation via coalition formation among autonomous agents".Proc. IJCAI-95, Montreal
31. Sheth,A.. Larson,J.A.. 1990,"Federated database systems for managing distributed, heterogeneous and autonomous DBS", ACM CS 22(3)
32. Sheth, A.. et al., 1991,"Specifying interdatabase dependencies in a MDB environment", IEEE Computer (see also Bellcore TM-STS-018609/1)
33. Sheth,A. et al., 1993,"On automatic reasoning for schema integration",Int.Journ.ICIS,2(1)
34. Smolka/Schmidt-Schauß,1991,"Attributive concept description with complements",AI-48
35. Sycara,K.. 1990, "Persuasive argumentation in negotiation", Theory and Decision, 28:203–242
36. Wooldridge.M., Jennings,N., 1995, "Intelligent Agents: Theory and Practice", Knowledge Engin. Review
37. Zlotkin,G., Rosenschein,J.S., 1991, "Cooperation and conflict resolution via negotiation among autonomous agents in noncooperative domains". IEEE Transactions SMC, 21(6):1317–1324
38. Zlotkin.G.. Rosenschein,J.S., 1994, "Coalition, cryptography, and stability: Mechanisms for coalition formation in task oriented domains", Proc. of AAAI-94. Seattle, Washington

Cooperating Agents

Implementing Distributed Patient Management

Giordano Lanzola, Sabina Falasconi and Mario Stefanelli
University of Pavia, Dept. of Informatics and Systems Science
Medical Informatics Laboratory
Via Abbiategrasso 209 - 27100 Pavia - Italy
{giordano,sabina,mario@ipvstefa.unipv.it}

Abstract. Managing patients is a knowledge intensive activity requiring a high interoperability among the health care professionals involved. To support cooperative work in medical care, computer technology should therefore either augment the capabilities of individual specialists and enhance their ability of interacting with each other and with computational resources. However, despite the efforts spent in the Artificial Intelligence research field in the past years for developing innovative tools, there are still very few cases of systems which are proficiently used on a routine basis for providing health care related services. One way to overcome those limitations is to redesign the set of software tools in order that they be more appropriated for an interoperable environment, and perhaps the most promising approach nowadays is based on the so called distributed computing paradigm applied to Artificial Intelligence. In this paper we describe a methodology for implementing a network of cooperating software agents aimed at improving the health care delivery process. Moreover, we will also illustrate some examples from a set of tools we are developing for evaluating that methodology.

1 Introduction

The management of a patient in a shared-care context is a knowledge intensive activity also requiring a high interoperability level among the several health care providers involved, who must be able to exchange information and share a common understanding of the patient's clinical evolution. Moreover, providing health care services requires the expertise of highly qualified medical, technical and administrative personnel, often appointed to use specialized technical resources and very expensive equipment. Such distinctive features of medicine have led to the development of several sites, each one trained on a particular medical specialty. As a result the patient lifelong medical record is often highly fragmented because of the many clinical settings he/she has been visiting in his/her past, and the information needed to assess his/her clinical status turns out to be often incomplete, incorrect or unavailable. So, new organizational infrastructures should be pursued for exploiting an advanced integration of physical and knowledgeable resources in an effort of helping professionals in promptly assessing the patient's clinical state and reducing the overall cost-efficiency ratio of the health care delivery process.

Yet, despite the efforts spent in AI research during the past years for developing advanced methodologies and implementing innovative tools helping health care providers, so far there has been very few cases of systems tackling real-world problems which are proficiently employed on a routine basis. Van Bemmel [21] carried out a comprehensive analysis aimed at pointing out the main reasons which have hindered so far a widespread distribution of decision support systems (DSS) in the real clinical practice. By far the first alleged motivation is concerned with the failure of integrating DSSs with the rest of the knowledge/data sources already in use at a clinical setting such as patient databases, medical record systems, standardizations of terminologies and coding schemes. The author also points out that a comprehensive analysis of the cooperation model controlling the interoperability among the health care providers involved as well as the identification of how the infomation/data flow develops among them have never been performed.

In order to overcome the aforementioned limitations software implementations are increasingly seen as collections of autonomous agents, each one addressing a different task and cooperating towards the achievement of a common goal. This approach, which is referred to as the Distributed Artificial Intelligence paradigm [24], seems to be the most appropriate to pursue as it combines most of the techniques usually adopted in software engineering. In fact, the efforts needed to implement a viable computer system and the ensuing complexity of any all-inclusive software implementation have called since long for a solution based on its decomposition in terms of smaller submodules. Besides simplifying the computational tractability, the multi agent paradigm also fits the finiteness of the human expertise which requires the cooperation of different specialists, each one contributing with different skills, for identifying the solution of a given problem.

However, adopting a similar approach in a computational environment raises some additional problems mainly concerning the agent social interaction. Some of the open issues require the identification of suitable communication protocols, languages for transferring knowledge, paradigms for achieving a factual cooperation among the agents as well as a clear identification of the functionality each agent is able to provide. Obviously some of the issues concerning interoperability among human beings are implicitly solved by their communication capabilities and don't need to be overly formalized except for the major aspects addressing the professional cooperation model.

In this paper we discuss a methodology for implementing a network of cooperating software agents aimed at improving the health care delivery process, and we also illustrate some examples from a set of tools we developed based on the proposed methodology. The underlying idea entails the incremental construction and maintenance of a consistent *patient model* shared by each cooperating agent. That model allows either storage and retrieval of patient information as well as generating a suitable interpretation based on that information and formulating the proper advice for helping professionals in accomplishing their daily tasks (e.g. medical, legal, insurance or financial assessments, population studies, etc...).

2 Agents and Agent Construction Tools

Computer-based systems and human operators can be seen as agents in that, while sharing physical resources, they encapsulate specialistic information, information processing capabilities and procedures determining their external behavior.

Activities and services explicated by agents take place in a common environment, which in principle can be as large as the area covered by worldwide telecommunication

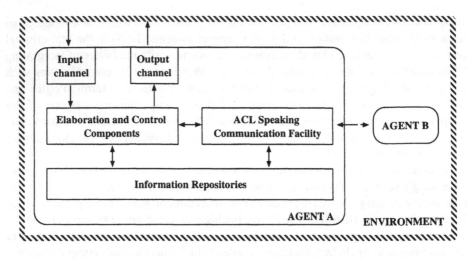

Fig. 1. A general software agent model.

networks. A realistic vision involves a number of relatively small communities of networked agents including humans. Taking inspiration from the seminal Minsky's ideas [13] we named *agencies* those communities of highly interoperating agents, in that an external observer may consider the community as a sort of "structured" agent offering multiple services.

With regards to computer-based agency components, we focus on the emerging notion of *software agent*, defined as an at least semi-autonomous process able to interoperate with other processes (running on the same or on a separate machine) through a suitable Agent Communication Language (ACL) [6]. That is, we assume an intuitive general software agent model shown in Figure 1, loosely based on the more formal one described by Burmeister and Sundermeyer [2]. In our model each "isolated" entity possesses one or more conveniently represented information repositories. Using that information the agent may perform processing activities by means of opportune elaboration and control components, without any coordination with other agents. The information flows along the agent I/O channels facing the environment (e.g. sensors and actuators) adopting a representation which is specific to the agent itself. Cooperation with other agents is achieved by extending the representation mechanisms of this isolated entity with ACL communication primitives. An essential feature of such primitives is that they must allow agent integration at the knowledge level, that is, in a manner independent of implementation related aspects. For the sake of simplicity, the inter-agent communication facility is shown as a self-contained module in the figure.

Various agent types can be discerned according to the main role they play within the agents community. *Library/Server* agents provide other agents with information elements from their own repositories, structured as bodies of sharable and reusable components, that can be employed as building blocks for agent construction or expansion. Instances of this category can be terminology servers, ontology servers, problem solvers servers, data servers and so on, each server being named after the kind of information chunks it's able to offer. *Application agents* are endowed with specialistic competence (e.g. Knowledge Based Systems); thus they can reply to queries pertaining to their expertise field. *Personal agents* are tools, usually combined with adaptive user interfaces, tailored to meet single user's wishes and requirements.

To allow knowledge level integration of heterogeneous systems the definitions are to be specified of the technical terms and of the conceptual entities involved in inter-agent information transactions. Among the existing research approaches coping with such problems of semantic foundation, we took the Darpa Knowledge Sharing Effort (KSE) project [14] as a source of material and inspiration for the design and implementation of our agencies. Within the AIM project GAMES-II we used the KSE ontology specification language Ontolingua [7] to implement a preliminary library of medical ontologies described in [4, 23] in order to state the ontological commitments for our envisioned medical agency: that is, a set of knowledge-level common definitions on which all the agents agree and base their interactions.

We also took into consideration other knowledge and software engineering methodologies such as the KADS modelling approach [25], and the HELIOS [3] environment devoted to the development and maintenance of multimedia distributed medical applications. Finally, current attempts to provide medical terminological aids were examined, such as those resulting from the GALEN [19] and UMLS [12] efforts, that aim at making it possible to compare, map or refer one's terminological choices to extensive, uniform and controlled vocabularies and classification schemes.

3 A Networked Agents Community

There are several issues which need to be tackled when applying the distributed computation paradigm to AI, all aimed at achieving a functional community of interoperating agents [8]. First an analysis must be carried out concerning the different minimal services required in a networked environment. All those services must be provided from within the community itself in order that it be self-sufficient. Such a problem translates into a careful planning of the informational / knowledgeable support each agent has to fullfill. Then a suitable protocol for exchanging knowledge and expressing communication directives among the agents must be devised. This is aimed at identifying the nature of all the possible transactions which may occur among them. Finally, one of the most interesting and challenging problems associated with the multi-agent paradigm concerns their ability to actively cooperate in the process of finding a solution for a given problem. This is usually referred to as *the control problem* and is concerned with endowing each agent at least with the following capabilities:

- Grasping the nature of the problem to be solved,
- Understanding when it is able to provide some kind of support which is deemed useful by the whole community, or when it requires the intervention of an another agent,
- Deciding how to contact which other agent to provide or request some service.

In the rest of this paper we shall illustrate a possible solution for solving the aforementioned problems which is presently being used in our laboratory for implementing a community of cooperating software agents. More precisely, in the past

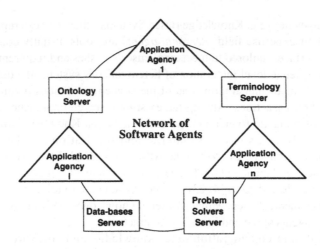

Fig. 2. A diagram illustrating the Network of Software Agents.

few years a set of standalone prototypes have been developed addressing several aspects of knowledge representation and problem solving in medicine [1, 9, 23]. The undergoing effort involves the *agentification* of many of the prototypes developed so far in order to implement a distributed framework exploiting and integrating multiple formalisms and methods for helping the different health care operators, namely physicians, nurses, technicians and hospital administrators, in accomplishing their daily work. This is also useful for defining the nature of the transactions occurring among the different agents.

3.1 The Agents Functionality

A possible classification of the different agent types required for building up a distributed community, based on the functionality provided by each one of them, is shown in Figure 2.

Ontology repositories are mandatory in a distributed environment, and every other agent in the network must be linked at least to one of those. Those agents have the burden of defining a common semantics which once adopted by two or more agents can be used as the basis for successfully exchanging and interpreting either data or knowledge chunks. Of course, in a distributed environment several ontology servers may be present, thus defining different and possibly incompatible ontologies. However, if two or more agents intend to exchange some information among themselves it is required that either they share the same ontology or the adopted ontologies overlap so that they actually share the same semantics for that particular subset of their application domains encompassing the information to be exchanged.

The definition of an ontology is only possible if we agree upon a standard terminology for expressing the concepts of interest. Defining entities, features and attributes as well as the relationships occurring among those in a given domain may only be accomplished starting from a basic set of well understood terms. Moreover in medicine, just as in many other experimental sciences, a generally adopted standard is lacking, so it is quite usual that the same term is used by members of different communities with a slightly different meaning. This is a potential cause of misunderstanding which is quite easily overcome by human agents by accurately referring each term to the context of the discourse through different means, such as stress, intonation, gestures, etc. While such a behavior is suitable for humans, it is quite impossible to be adopted by software agents, and a mean for clearly and uniquely expressing the adopted terminology is therefore mandatory. This task is accomplished by specialized agents acting as *terminology suppliers*, and their use is required in order to be able to construct a suitable ontology.

Both terminology and ontology servers may be considered as the fundamental agents on top of which all the remaining ones are constructed. *Data base servers*, for example, play the role of distributed data repositories exploiting either a relational or an object oriented model.

Within our architecture a problem solver may be defined as a specialized chunk of application knowledge represented through a specific formalism and combined with a method for exploiting it. So, while all the agents introduced so far may be considered as ones acting as supporters for task execution, problem solvers are in fact able to accomplish some task given either the knowledge they have been provided with and that made available by some other agents. A cooperating network of agents for implementing patient management should not commit itself to any specific problem solver, allowing instead to choose among a wide set of those.

To this aim we foresee the existence of several *Problem Solver Servers* where different representation formalisms and methods are made available for solving problems in a distributed environment. In fact there are several reasons supporting the use of different problem solvers in medical reasoning. It is well known that medical knowledge is often ill-shaped and incomplete. This accounts for adopting, even within the same medical task, the representation formalism which is best applicable given the context at hand and the goal to be solved. Moreover, distinct reasoning techniques may also have very different computational requirements and explanation capabilities, so that even when coping with a very specific application domain it is almost impossible to identify a single criterion for ranking them. Finally, each reasoning technique is strongly dependent on the particular ontology adopted so that in many cases some of them may turn out to be definitely inappropriate.

3.2 The Medical Workstation

All the agents discussed so far are able to provide a generic functionality to the whole network, which is not biased towards any specific user class. Hence, another useful criterium for ranking agents may distinguish between those providing *basic services* and agents biased towards more *user oriented services*. Basic service agents feature a high level of generality which justifies their exploitation in different applications thus enforcing knowledge reusability. Agents providing user oriented services are built instead to satisfy the specific needs of a particular professional, and in doing so they will heavily exploit some of the services provided by the former ones. Their goal is to shape a particular view on the agents community which is best suited given the nature of the task to be solved by the professional.

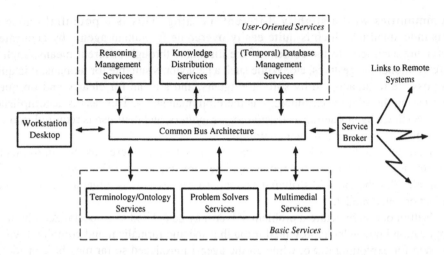

Fig. 3. The generic medical workstation hosting different agents.

All those agents may reside on several hardware platforms connected through the network, as shown in Figure 3, allowing the dynamic assembly of multiple virtual application agencies. Implementing a viable application will therefore need the contributions of at least one agent for each of the three types shown in the lower box of Figure 3, which roughly correspond to those illustrated in the previous paragraph. Obviously, the components of an agency do not have to be located on the same hardware platform but may be spread on several hosts possibly very far away from each other. Users performing different tasks will then access the very same agents available on the net, so sharing knowledge and data among themselves.

However, despite the fact that different users share the same knowledge and data, they definitely need distinct views on those to properly exploit the distributed architecture in their daily work. On one side, this means that they might need to look at the same data in different ways. For example, the local data base of an hospital where all the patient records are stored may be accessed both by the physician and the hospital manager. The application agency used by the former will have to access the patient full medical record for helping the professional in assessing the patient clinical state, planning the therapy and monitoring the course of his/her disease. Hospital administrators however, because of their different duties, will be interested at the expenditures beared by the institution such as hospitalization periods, surgical interventions, tests and examinations performed over patients, in order that they be able to assess the financial status of the institution and plan its future development. So, even if they might be using the very same agent responsible of upkeeping the patient records, they should access separate parts of it and in different ways.

On the other side providing different views is a way of taking into account that tasks to be carried out by distinct professional might substantially differ in their schedules and prioritizations. For example, even if knowledge in a given medical specialty is well established, its exploitation strictly depends on the context. If a patient has been just admitted into the first-aid emergency room, and he is in a life-threatening condition, the set of tasks scheduled for assessing his state and plannning a treatment will be different from those scheduled if the patient was merely an ordinary in-patient.

This aspect concerning the customization of a user access to the network is accomplished through the existence of some other agents, shown in the upper box of Figure 3, namely *reasoning management services, knowledge distribution services*, and *data management services*. All those services are plugged in on a common bus which also hosts a *workstation desktop* and a *service broker*. This is in line with the current research efforts which see a medical workstation as a graphical desktop tailored to the needs of each particular user, and allowing him to access a network-wide set of facilities accomplishing different tasks [20].

4 The Agent Architecture

The desktop agent mainly consists of a set of graphical procedures and acts as an operational interface towards the other user-oriented agents. Any data management and reasoning management service must be connected with a suitable set of ontology providers. This has the purpose of defining a common domain model for the application itself. So when the desktop agent is subsequently connected to the data management service, the data-base servers available on the network will no longer play the role of repositories of unstructured information, but the data available will be organized, interpreted and used according to that model. The data management agent, for example, may successfully exploit the ontology to make sure that any new data acquired fits into the context defined by the already existing information. In case of a discrepancy between the value supplied and the expected one, the data management agent may send out a message to the agent requesting the storage of the new datum, asking for a further confirmation. In the same way a reasoning management agent must be configured by selecting and integrating into the application a suitable set of problem solvers exploiting the most appropriate reasoning techniques for interpreting the available data and assessing the current situation.

Given the aforementioned situation it turns out that the key issue to be solved when defining and representing an ontology involves finding a suitable formalism which be easily understandable by other agents. We first performed a preliminary conceptualization aimed at identifying all the entities and the relationships existing in a given domain, as well as the roles played by them with respect to each task [18]. Each one of those is then modeled in terms of more formal concepts such as *class, instance, relation* and *function*, which are quite similar to the most essential ones proposed by Ontolingua [7], within the Knowledge Sharing Effort [14]. As a very simple example illustrating this point, Figure 4 shows the modeling of findings, abstractions as well as the relationships existing among them. The boxes in regular typeface represent classes, solid links are relationships among classes, and dashed links point to instances of classes which are indicated in italic typeface. Finally dotted lines represent instantiations of relationships defined among classes, thereby linking their instances. Actually, to avoid overly cluttering the diagram the only links of this kind which have been shown are those stemming from *Age, Sex Anemia* and *Hemoglobin* instances.

From that representation it transpires that findings are arranged into groups (R3) as well as abstractions are (R4), and both kinds of groups are structured into a taxonomical

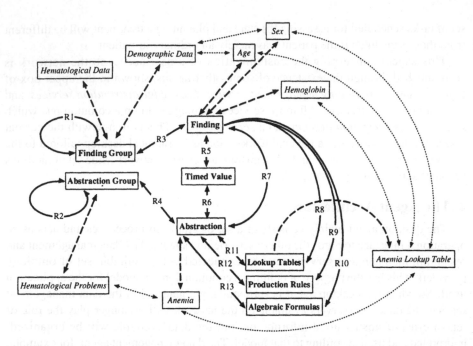

Fig. 4. Representing an ontology as a semantic network. Regular typeface is used for labeling classes, while instances are shown in italic. Solid lines represent relationships among classes, while dashed ones are class-instance links. Finally dotted lines represent instantiations of relationships defined among classes, thereby linking their instances.

arrangement (R1 and R2). Abstractions may have timed values (R6), depend on some findings (R7), and are connected with the knowledge chunks useful for deriving their value (R11, R12 and R13). Having adopted a representation of an ontology modeled in terms of a very small set of primitives greatly simplifies the query-and-reply process for exchanging it among multiple agents. Suppose that agent A is in the need of finding out a value for *Anemia* which is an entity in a medical domain. It may then contact a medical ontology provider asking for the definition of *Anemia*. Once it discovers that *Anemia* is an abstraction, by using very few primitives it may traverse the semantic network and see that *Anemia* depends on the values of three findings, namely *Age*, *Sex* and *Hemoglobin*. If all their values are known, then the agent may also ask the ontology provider for the knowledge needed to infer the value of *Anemia*, pass it to a problem solver able to handle it, which in this case turns out to be a lookup table interpreter, and finally collect the result.

As several researchers point out [16, 22, 25], problem solving is an intense reasoning activity involving each time either the dynamic selection of a goal to pursue and the subsequent choice of a particular method which is best applicable given the context at hand. We therefore identify two different knowledge types involved with the construction of an agent implementing the problem solving process. One type complements the application ontology, and is aimed at defining all the relationships allowing to hypothesize the solutions of a problem given its features as well as at

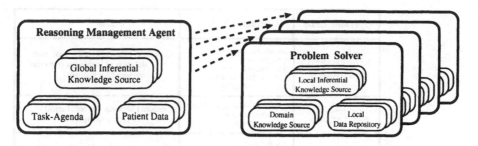

Fig. 5. The internal architecture of a reasoning management agent.

deriving the expected consequences from each hypothesis. This is usually referred to as the application knowledge. The other type concerns instead the procedures able to manage the available application knowledge in order to solve problems, and is referred to as inferential knowledge. The inner structuring of a reasoning management agent actually reflects this two-layered organization, as indicated in Figure 5. The leftmost box representing the inferential knowledge is built as a separate module whose goal is to bring about the overall control regime of the agent itself. This entails selecting a suitable strategy to reach a solution for a given problem in sight of the capabilities available within the agent. Each time the agent is invoked, the control is passed to its inferential knowledge which is activated. As a consequence a sequence of tasks will be dynamically planned, each one involving the invocation of some specialized problem solvers, which are shown in the right part of the figure. The inferential knowledge also has the duty of stopping the process either when a satisfactory solution is achieved, or when it realizes that no problem solver is applicable nor able to provide new useful solution elements.

Although the selection of a reasoning strategy is accomplished by the inferential knowledge, problem solvers do not include only domain specific knowledge, but they also encompass a small inferential knowledge submodule. This is required for providing all the specialized control features needed to cope with the formalisms implemented by the problem solver and it is referred to as a method. In fact such an inferential knowledge deals with modeling of specific strategies too closely tied with the representational formalisms implemented by the problem solver itself which therefore cannot be included as part of the inferential knowledge of the whole agent.

Nevertheless, in a multi-agent environment the most interesting element of the whole architecture is represented by the agent control component. In fact it is this single module which has the burden of representing all the control knowledge required to shape the agent social behavior. For representing that knowledge we decided to adopt the metarule formalism, since it proved to be the most appropriate for associating control situations with actions to perform [10]. Using metarules the actions themselves may be represented in a declarative and therefore most intuitive way, and each control situation may be stated in terms of logical expressions over classes, instances, relationships and their attributes, checking either the patient data in the agent's working memory or the task list. As a result the process of acquiring knowledge is simplified and sped up since the operational semantics of a single rule is neither affected by the clause

	Operator Class	Available Choices	Use

Simple-clause
 	
Operators
	Blackboard
	Mediators
		`Is_BB_Instance`
		`Del_BB_Instance`
		`Put_BB_Instance`
		`Create_BB_Instance`
		`Is_Instance_Field`
			Creation, retrieval, addition and deletion of instances from the system Blackboard.

	Ontology
	Mediators
		`Is_Ontological_Instance`
		`Is_Subclass_of`
		`Is_Feature_of`
			Clauses checking for ontological relationships.

	Testers	`Is_Equal_To`
		`Is_Greater/Less_Than`
		`Is_in_Set`
		`Is_in_Range`
		`Happens_Before/After`
			Clauses checking for relationships between values without any ontological commitment.

	Variable
	Handlers
		`Set/Get_Variable_Value`
		`Count_Variable_Elements`
		`Group_Variables`
			Instantiation of variables, grouping of several items into a new variable.

	Inference Mediators	`Invoke_Problem_Solver` `Perform_Task`	Invocation of problem solvers and tasks.

	Controllers	`Print`
		`Notice`
		`Ask_User`
			Implementation of miscellaneaous control operations

Complex-clause
 	
Operators
	Connectors	`And`
		`Or`
		`Not`
		`For Always`
		`Collect`
		`Repeat`
			Linking clauses into complex clauses

Fig. 6. The operator classes available for building metarule clauses.

ordering within the same rule nor by clauses mentioned in other rules. This accounts for acquiring knowledge in little modular chunks, and makes it possible to analyze how the agent behavior is affected by each separate directive. Finally, this formalism proved to successfully satisfy also the last requirement we decided to fulfill, by showing a semantics which can be directly made operational within the system. By means of a special parser each clause entered by the user is translated into the matching piece of code executable by the system without any change in its meaning, so that the agent behavior will be fully qualified by the set of clauses as they have been entered by the user.

For parsing rule clauses, a set of operators has been devised, each one able to interpret the syntax of a different statement. Operators are grouped into classes according to their operational semantics, as shown in Figure 6. The seven main classes are shown in the left column of the figure, while in the central one is indicated the list of operators available for each class. Each operator is identified by a keyword chosen to be reminder for the statement the operator itself is able to express. The first class, namely *Blackboard Mediators,* may be used for accessing or modifying values in the agent working memory, which is structured according to the blackboard architecture paradigm [15]. *Ontology Mediators* are used for sending requests to the ontology services, looking for information concerning classes, instances or relationships, while *Testers* and *Variable Handlers* are suited for implementing all the conditions required for controlling the activation of the remotely located problem solvers, invoked by the operators falling in the *Inference Mediator* class. Finally *Connectors* are used for joining clauses together into more complex ones, while *Controllers* allow users to set up some traces for monitoring the agent's behavior.

By appropriately assembling clauses the user is able to model knowledge chunks concerning either the planning of suitable actions and the interaction among agents implementing different problem solvers. As an example, let's consider a metarule referenced in one of the reasoning management agents we are current implementing as a testbed for controlling the cooperation of a small agent community. The goal in that case is to identify a suitable therapeutic conditioning regimen for patients affected by Acute Myeloid Leukemia who will undergo a Bone Marrow Transplantation. Usually the therapy is assessed by physicians using a small set of heuristic rules but, as a recent study points out [17], when time, reliability and costs required for acquiring clinical information are also taken into account the problem becomes more complex and may be best represented by an Influence Diagram (ID). More specifically, when several alternate therapies are applicable, the ID checks first if their expected utilities are comparable in terms of their outcomes. If they are, it goes on taking into account also any other parameter defining the specific therapeutic problem. If on the contrary the expected utilities of any two therapies aren't comparable inasmuch their outcomes are of concern, then using the ID will be rejected. Here is how such a cooperation may be represented in terms of a metarule.

```
IF
and     focus-to-pursue has_value ?var1
        fails invoke_problem_solver production_rules for
                                eliminative_induction on ?var1
        or      cant_find is_ontological_instance abductive_props
                                for ?var1 has_value infl-diag
                and     is_ontological_instance abductive_props
                                for ?var1 has_value infl-diag
                fails invoke_problem_solver infl-diag for
                                abduction on ?var1
THEN
invoke_problem_solver production_rules for abduction on ?var1
```

The first clause instantiates ?var1 with the focus to pursue, which has been instantiated during the accomplishment of previous subtask. Then a request to production rules problem solver is issued looking if there is one able to eliminate that focus. If there is no problem solver able to do that (i.e. the request fails) then an "or" check is made on one of the following:

• a request is sent out to the ontology provider looking if the *abductive_props* attribute of the focus to pursue has no associaed ID (infl-diag);

- the previous request is able to come up with an associated ID, but once a problem solver is invoked on that ID it fails.

Taken as a whole the "or" check means that an ID is unapplicable (either there is no ID or the invocation of an agent processing that ID doesn't succeed), in which case a request is issued to the production rules problem solver in order to assess the therapy.

5 Discussion

As we have anticipated in the previous chapters, the work described in this paper is still heavily in progress, and mainly originates from an *agentification* process involving several other previously implemented tools which used to run as standalone ones thus far. By now we have developed a set of protoypical agent communities serving three different classes of users, namely physicians, nurses and administrators, which we are using as a testbed for the proposed methodology. Although able to accomplish different tasks, all those communities use virtually the same set of agents therefore enforcing knowledge and data sharing and reuse among themselves, and demonstrating the potential of an approach based on multiple cooperating agents. Nevertheless what seems to be an outstanding success also conceals a momentary limitation. In fact, since the availability of agents implementing basic services is extremely limited thus far, it turns out that each agent implementing a user oriented service knows in advance which are going to be its counterparts in solving which task. Therefore in some sense there is no real resource or task negotiation right now. However, for enabling all the different agents to communicate with each other we have already developed a communication protocol similar to KQML [5] and fully supporting also the possibility of sending broadcast messages. Thus, as soon as we will have more than a single agent implementing the same service each query will be anticipated by a transaction request whose aim will be that of contacting a suitable peer agent willing to provide the service. That's exactly where the box labeled *Service Broker* shown in Figure 3 will come into play. We also didn't tackle in our first experiments any security related problem, so that there is no possibility of authenticating requests in sight of a possible denial of a service.

Notwithstanding that, a major breakthrough of this paper is to propose a methodology integrating into a single framework several already existing techniques. In fact, we heavily borrowed both from the technologies of databases and distributed computing and we merged those with work on object oriented programming and artificial intelligence. The blackboard model for problem solving [15], which has been just hinted when discussing the control module of the reasoning management agent, is recognized as one of the most promising approaches to the implementation of multi-agent reasoning, and has widely been used for implementing several applications in AI. Our approach further extends the blackboard notion, considering it as a shared communication mean among all the agents available on the network. This gives rise to the D-CBA (Distributed Control Blackboard Architecture), which is described in [11].

Finally, the possibility of representing ontologies in a computational way should be investigated to a greater extent. This also involves the possibility of implementing bidirectional translators between the possibly different ontological representations adopted by single agents and a standard ontology specification language, so that a wide set of agents may be used interchangeably for the same purposes while adopting different domain models.

Acknowledgments. This work is part of the project T-IDDM supported by the European Commission within the Health Care Telematics Applications. It is also supported by a MURST grant.

References

1. Bellazzi, R., Quaglini, S., Berzuini, C. and Stefanelli M. (1991). GAMEES: a probabilistic environment for expert systems. *Computer Methods and Programs in Biomedicine*, 35:177-191.

2. Burmeister, W. and Sundermeyer, K. (1992). Cooperative problem-solving guided by intention and perception. In *Proceedings of the Third European Workshop on Modelling Autonomous Agents in a Multi-Agent World*, pp. 77-92, (Werner and Demazeau Eds.), Kaiserlautern, Germany.

3. Engelmann, U., Jean, F.C., and Degoulet, P. (1994). The HELIOS Software Engineering Environment. *Computer Methods and Programs in Biomedicine*, 45 S1-S152.

4. Falasconi, S., Stefanelli, M. (1994). A library of medical ontologies. In Mars, N. J. I., editor, *Proceedings of the ECAI94 Workshop Comparison of Implemented Ontologies*, pages 81-91, Amsterdam.

5. Finin, T., Weber, J., Wiederhold, G., Genesereth, M. R., Fritzson, R., McKay, D., McGuire, J., Pelavin, P., Shapiro, S. and Beck, C. (1993). Specification of the KQML Agent Communication Language. Technical Report EIT 92-04, Enterprise Integration Technologies, Palo Alto, CA.

6. Genesereth, M. R., Ketchpel, S. P. (1994). Software agents. *Communications of the ACM*, 7(37):48-53.

7. Gruber, T. R. (1993). A translation approach to portable ontology specifications. *Knowledge Acquisition*, 5:199-220.

8. Jennings, N.R. (1995). Controlling cooperative problem solving in industrial multi-agent systems using joint intentions. *Artificial Intelligence*, 75:195-240.

9. Lanzola, G. and Stefanelli, M. (1992). A Specialized Framework for Medical Diagnostic Knowledge-Based Systems. *Computers and Biomedical Research*, 25:351-365.

10. Lanzola, G. and Stefanelli, M. (1993). Inferential knowledge acquisition. *Artificial Intelligence in Medicine*, 5:253-268.

11. Lanzola, G. and Stefanelli, M. (1993). Computational Model 3.0. Technical Report GAMES-II Deliverable 25, Laboratory of Medical Informatics, University of Pavia, Italy.

12. Lindberg, D., Humphreys, B. and McCray, A. (1993). The Unified Medical Language System. In van Bemmel, J., editor, *1993 Yearbook of Medical Informatics*, pages 41-53, International Medical Informatics Association, Amsterdam.

13. Minski, M. (1985). *The society of mind*, Simon and Schuster, New York.

14. Neches, R., Fikes, R. E., Finin, T., Gruber, T. R., Patil, R., Senator, T. and Swartout, W. (1991). Enabling technology for knowledge sharing. *AI Magazine*, 12:36-56.

15. Nii, H. P. (1986). Blackboard Systems: The blackboard model of problem solving and the evolution of blackboard architectures (part i). *AI Magazine*, 38-53.

16. Puerta, A. R., Tu, S. W. and Musen, M. A. (1992) Modeling Tasks with Mechanisms, *International Journal of Intelligent Systems*.

17. Quaglini, S., Bellazzi, R., Locatelli, F., Stefanelli, M. and Salvaneschi C. (1994). An influence diagram for assessing GVHD prophylaxis after bone marrow transplantation in children. *Medical Decision Making*, 14:223-235.

18. Ramoni, M., Stefanelli, M., Magnani, L., and Barosi, G. (1992). An Epistemological Framework for Medical Knowledge-Based Systems. *IEEE Transactions on Systems, Man, and Cybernetics*, 6(22):1361-1375.

19. Rector, A. L., Solomon, W. D., Nowlan, W. A. and Rush, T. W. (1994). A terminology server for medical language and medical information systems. Technical Report, Department of Computer Science, University of Manchester.

20. Tang, P. C., Annevelink, J., Suermondt, H.J and Young, C.Y. (1994). Semantic Integration of Information in a Physician Workstation. *International Journal of Biomedical Computing*, 35:47-60.

21. van Bemmel, J.H. (1993). Criteria for the acceptance of decision-support systems by clinicians; lessons from ECG interpretation system. *Proceedings of the Artificial Intelligence in Medicine Conference AIME-93* (IOS Press), 7-10.

22. van Heijst, G., Lanzola, G., Schreiber, G. and Stefanelli, M. (1994). Foundations for a Methodology for Medical KBS Development. *Knowledge Acquisition*, 6:395-434.

23. van Heijst, G., Falasconi, S., Abu-Hanna, A., Schreiber, G. and Stefanelli, M. (1995). A case study in ontology library construction. *Artificial Intelligence in Medicine*, 7:227-255.

24. Werner, E., (1992). The design of multi-agent systems. In *Proceedings of the Third European Workshop on Modelling Autonomous Agents in a Multi-Agent World*, pp. 3-28, (Werner and Demazeau Eds.), Kaiserlautern, Germany.

24. Wielinga, B. J., Schreiber, A., Th. and Breuker, J., A. (1992). KADS: a modelling approach to knowledge engineering. *Knowledge Acquisition*, 4:5-53.

Lecture Notes in Artificial Intelligence (LNAI)

Vol. 847: A. Ralescu (Ed.) Fuzzy Logic in Artificial Intelligence. Proceedings, 1993. VII, 128 pages. 1994.

Vol: 861: B. Nebel, L. Dreschler-Fischer (Eds.), KI-94: Advances in Artificial Intelligence. Proceedings, 1994. IX, 401 pages. 1994.

Vol. 862: R. C. Carrasco, J. Oncina (Eds.), Grammatical Inference and Applications. Proceedings, 1994. VIII, 290 pages. 1994.

Vol 867: L. Steels, G. Schreiber, W. Van de Velde (Eds.), A Future for Knowledge Acquisition. Proceedings, 1994. XII, 414 pages. 1994.

Vol. 869: Z. W. Raś, M. Zemankova (Eds.), Methodologies for Intelligent Systems. Proceedings, 1994. X, 613 pages. 1994.

Vol. 872: S Arikawa, K. P. Jantke (Eds.), Algorithmic Learning Theory. Proceedings, 1994. XIV, 575 pages. 1994.

Vol. 878: T. Ishida, Parallel, Distributed and Multiagent Production Systems. XVII, 166 pages. 1994.

Vol. 886: M. M. Veloso, Planning and Learning by Analogical Reasoning. XIII, 181 pages. 1994.

Vol. 890: M. J. Wooldridge, N. R. Jennings (Eds.), Intelligent Agents. Proceedings, 1994. VIII, 407 pages. 1995.

Vol. 897: M. Fisher, R. Owens (Eds.), Executable Modal and Temporal Logics. Proceedings, 1993. VII, 180 pages. 1995.

Vol. 898: P. Steffens (Ed.), Machine Translation and the Lexicon. Proceedings, 1993. X, 251 pages. 1995.

Vol. 904: P. Vitányi (Ed.), Computational Learning Theory. EuroCOLT'95. Proceedings, 1995. XVII, 415 pages. 1995.

Vol. 912: N. Lavrač S. Wrobel (Eds.), Machine Learning: ECML – 95. Proceedings, 1995. XI, 370 pages. 1995.

Vol. 918: P. Baumgartner, R. Hähnle, J. Posegga (Eds.), Theorem Proving with Analytic Tableaux and Related Methods. Proceedings, 1995. X, 352 pages. 1995.

Vol. 927: J. Dix, L. Moniz Pereira, T.C. Przymusinski (Eds.), Non-Monotonic Extensions of Logic Programming. Proceedings, 1994. IX, 229 pages. 1995.

Vol. 928: V.W. Marek, A. Nerode, M. Truszczynski (Eds.), Logic Programming and Nonmonotonic Reasoning. Proceedings, 1995. VIII, 417 pages. 1995.

Vol. 929: F. Morán, A. Moreno, J.J. Merelo, P.Chacón (Eds.), Advances in Artificial Life. Proceedings, 1995. XIII, 960 pages. 1995.

Vol. 934: P. Barahona, M. Stefanelli, J. Wyatt (Eds.), Artificial Intelligence in Medicine. Proceedings, 1995. XI, 449 pages. 1995.

Vol. 941: M. Cadoli, Tractable Reasoning in Artificial Intelligence. XVII, 247 pages. 1995.

Vol. 946: C. Froidevaux, J. Kohlas (Eds.), Symbolic Quantitative and Approaches to Reasoning under Uncertainty. Proceedings, 1995. X, 430 pages. 1995.

Vol. 954: G. Ellis, R. Levinson, W. Rich. J.F. Sowa (Eds.), Conceptual Structures: Applications, Implementation and Theory. Proceedings, 1995. IX, 353 pages. 1995.

Vol. 956: X. Yao (Ed.), Progress in Evolutionary Computation. Proceedings, 1993, 1994. VIII, 314 pages. 1995.

Vol. 957: C. Castelfranchi, J.-P. Müller (Eds.), From Reaction to Cognition. Proceedings, 1993. VI, 252 pages. 1995.

Vol. 961: K.P. Jantke. S. Lange (Eds.), Algorithmic Learning for Knowledge-Based Systems. X, 511 pages. 1995.

Vol. 981: I. Wachsmuth, C.-R. Rollinger, W. Brauer (Eds.), KI-95: Advances in Artificial Intelligence. Proceedings, 1995. XII, 269 pages. 1995.

Vol. 984: J.-M. Haton, M. Keane, M. Manago (Eds.), Advances in Case-Based Reasoning. Proceedings, 1994. VIII, 307 pages. 1995.

Vol. 990: C. Pinto-Ferreira, N.J. Mamede (Eds.), Progress in Artificial Intelligence. Proceedings, 1995. XIV, 487 pages. 1995.

Vol. 991: J. Wainer, A. Carvalho (Eds.), Advances in Artificial Intelligence. Proceedings, 1995. XII, 342 pages. 1995.

Vol. 992: M. Gori, G. Soda (Eds.), Topics in Artificial Intelligence. Proceedings, 1995. XII, 451 pages. 1995.

Vol. 997: K. P. Jantke, T. Shinohara, T. Zeugmann (Eds.), Algorithmic Learning Theory. Proceedings, 1995. XV, 319 pages. 1995.

Vol. 1003: P. Pandurang Nayak, Automated Modeling of Physical Systems. XXI, 232 pages. 1995.

Vol. 1010: M. Veloso, A. Aamodt (Eds.), Case-Based Reasoning Research and Development. Proceedings, 1995. X, 576 pages. 1995.

Vol. 1011: T. Furuhashi (Ed.), Advances in Fuzzy Logic, Neural Networks and Genetic Algorithms. Proceedings, 1994. VIII, 223 pages. 1995.

Vol. 1020: I. D. Watson (Ed.), Progress in Case-Based Reasoning. Proceedings, 1995. VIII, 209 pages. 1995.

Vol. 1037: M. Wooldridge, J.P. Müller, M. Tambe (Eds.), Intelligent Agents II. Proceedings, 1995. XVI, 437 pages, 1996.

Vol. 1038: W. Van de Velde, J.W. Perram (Eds.), Agents Breaking Away. Proceedings, 1996. XIV, 232 pages, 1996.

Lecture Notes in Computer Science